Success Is An Exaggeration

Success Is An Exaggeration

Deb Dutta

Library of Congress Control Number: 2013920978

ISBN:	Hardcover	978-1-4931-2973-7
	Softcover	978-1-4931-2972-0
	eBook	978-1-4931-2974-4

Cover Design: Prashant Patel/Infologi Pte. Ltd.
Photograph: Sumeet Singla

Rev. date: 02/28/2014

To order additional copies of this book, contact:
Xlibris LLC
1-800-455-039
www.xlibris.com.au
Orders@xlibris.com.au
513691

Contents

Acknowledgments 11

Foreword 13

Getting Started 17

Why Put in Any Effort When You Do Not Know the *Why*? 23

Greed Is Good: The Parable from *Wall Street* 26

Solving the Wrong Problem 31

First Among Equals: Effort or Attainment 35

Networking—Getting it Right 40

The Making of the Independent Professional 46

The Anatomy of the Leader 52

Leadership Models—What Is Relevant Today? 55

Criticism Is for the Fortunate: Use it Wisely 61

Let Me Give You the Bad News First 65

Sunshine and Service—An Exceptional Combo 68

Personal Branding: Express Yourself, but Be Truthful 73

Strategy and Tactics: Jekyll and Hyde 80

Standing Tall While Cold Calling 84

Driving Organizational Vision 89

Goals Setting—Does Stakeholder Participation Make Sense? 95

F1 Singapore, 2008—Super Show, but What Does it Take? 99

WYSIWYG—The Art of Perfect Execution....104
The Art of Tequila at Work and Play: Lick—Slam—Suck....110
Hiring "Great" and Hiring "Right"....117
Leadership When the Chips Are Down....123
Who Bombed My Company? Preparing for the Inevitable....129
Is Changing a Habit Even Worth It?....135
Asking for that Raise Is Fantastic, but Do You Deserve It?....140
You Read the Driver's Manual—Now Take the Keys and Drive the Car...145
Loyalty—Is it Only about Dogs?....151
How Come it Didn't Happen? How Come it Did?....155
Go, David, Go! 10 Bullets for Winning Professional Combats....158
Where Have All the Salesmen Gone?....163
The V-Word Unleashed....168
Energize a Teen, Transform the World....172
Personal Branding: A Primer on Workplace Readiness....177
In Need of an Inspiration....180
Visualization Is Power . . . But Are You Competent to Use It?....185
Looking Out for Greatness....191
Life Lessons from the Super Bowl....197
Plan, Execute, and Reflect....202
Step by Step: The Nails in the Coffin of the Financial System....210
Internships—A Step Above the Rest....214
Getting into the Groove: The Year Ahead....219
Smarter, Stronger, Wiser . . . Now!....223
Will You Own the End Game of Leadership?....226
It Is Not *All* about Work....230
New Year—Harsh Starts....233

Leading Inside Chaos and Disruption 237
A Mixed Bag of Beans 245
When Work Seems Too Much Like Play 250
Moving Up and Moving Out 253
Multinational Leaders Who "Win" 260
Think Like a Champ—Tune Your Engines 265
Reach for the Sky . . . There's a Carrot in the Right Corner 271
Interviews: Tricks to Gatecrash the Party 275
Farmers and Hunters 280
Where Is *Your* Strategy Headed? 283
Life's Little Chances 286
What Is Your Leverage? 291
Guts and Glory: The Success Recipe 299
Innovation and Disruption Need Chaos and Darkness 304
Heralding the New Normal 308
Understanding the Flow of Cash 317

Afterword 329
Index 337
About the Author 341

To my mothers . . . Lila and Supriya

Thanks for everything!

We can't solve problems by using the same kind of thinking we used when we created them.

—Albert Einstein

Acknowledgments

I did not rush myself while writing this book. The extended time enabled me to capture a broader canvas of life at work and away from it. I attribute this live canvas that helped construct the script to the educational institutions, the organizations, and every environment that I lived and worked in. They all helped me shape my life, my professional career, and my destiny. I wish to thank the incredible colleagues and friends that I am fortunate to be professionally and socially involved with and countless others whom I have not met and do not know but who have inspired me nevertheless and have provided the anecdotes that I have documented in this book to exemplify my beliefs.

I thank John Harten for his patience and skill in bearing with my demanding schedules, for diligently reviewing the text that I was throwing at him, and for skillfully shaping the narrative to give the book the form it now possesses. To Don Trinidad, Joy Daniels, and the rest of the team at Xlibris Publishing and its distribution channel, without whose support, this book would not have reached you. I am thankful to Jennifer Victorian for managing my blog site (www.debdutta.com) that supported the preview of the book, continually providing addendums, and making the book available to a global audience. Finally, to my friend Daniel Soh for being kind enough to write the foreword for the book despite his demanding schedule.

I cannot complete this section without gratitude for my family in bearing with me, encouraging me, and providing fodder for the manuscript. Healthy, sometimes animated debates with my wife Mousumi, my daughter Airashi and sister Bulbul were valuable in lending substance to the script and the flow. My brother in law, Robin was meticulous in going through the final manuscript with the thoroughness that characterises him. Their valuable insights and perspectives helped construct, shape, and reshape many of my thoughts as they appear in the book. They played their roles ably to make my writing experience rewarding.

Finally, to all of you who are reading this book: thank you! How you respond and benefit from the pages that follow will be the final testament of my effort.

Foreword

Over the last several years, the world experienced one of its worst financial and economic downturns. The Asia and Pacific region where I have been doing most of my work has changed rapidly and seen shifts in its fortunes. Every country in the region has its uniqueness and cultural differences. An acceptable practice in one country may not be so in another. Given the speed with which the Asian markets have developed, the trend is clear. Asia will, over time, equal and challenge the United States and Europe in terms of economic influence. Having said that, the formula to attain success in these very diverse environments anywhere in the world remains the same—identifying certain simple but unique behaviors and repeating them over and over again, like Deb Dutta articulates in this book.

There always seems to be an undercurrent of optimism and energy in the air wherever I travel in the region. Whether I am in business meetings or just having a meal with colleagues or clients, I always get the sense that everyone is hungry for success and curious to explore the unknown in the quest for success. Ultimately, I believe this is a positive catalyst for innovation and new ideas, propelling people, organizations, and nations to regional and global success. But what does this mean for you?

I have the best job in the world—partnering chief executives and independent board directors to identify, recruit, and onboard their senior management teams. Through the course of my work, I have been introduced to and interviewed successful individuals and observed their habits in and outside of their workspaces. Of course, Deb Dutta is one of them. I have watched Deb build his businesses over many years and successfully put into practice many of the elements that he has discussed in the book.

Often, people will ask me, "What does it take to succeed?"

Possessing the hard science of industry and product knowledge, competitive analysis, and excellent reputation in personal integrity and corporate governance is a given. The successful modern-day leader also needs soft skills, adaptability, and agility to respond quickly and leverage changing business environments. A leader (or anyone) who is authentic, is consistently efficient, and embodies integrity, conviction, and passion will naturally draw loyal followers.

What does success mean to you?

Specific industries, job functions, and roles have their metrics of success. Even you have every right to define your own benchmark of success as long as you are prepared to live with its consequences.

In the complex and interconnected world that we are all faced with, we will need to maintain a delicate balance of economic interests, environmental and societal risks, and boundless opportunities. It is very important to work hard without being blindly ambitious. Hard and smart work coupled with the repeatable good habits discussed plentifully in this book will lead to predictable performance, which will be recognized eventually and will create the path to success. Regardless of your definition of achievements, this book debunks the myths of success and puts it within your reach in anything that you choose to do.

Personally, I am motivated by working to make things at least a little better every day. I also aim to blend emotional and spiritual stability, which makes life meaningful. Despite the change and complexities of our times, to me, the founding principles of accomplishment and success remain the same: clarity, commitment, and a consistent display of accountability.

I am certain that the rich and diverse personal experiences, situational examples, and data shared by Deb in this book will not only be insightful to you (as they have been for me) but also provide practical wisdom and advice for you to succeed in your own way wherever you live in this beautiful world!

Daniel Soh, Managing Partner—Asia,
Leadership Advisory Inc.

Getting Started

Thanks for turning the first pages of this book, a book that will take you and me down a path of understanding ourselves, the exciting world that surrounds us, and the endless possibilities that we are faced with.

I feel fortunate and am content with what life has served me so far. Not that I do not strive for anything more. What meaning would life hold without goals to reach out to, to accomplish and finally rejoice with the sense of fulfillment? But my goals are of a different sort now—different from the past years! Like writing this book, reaching out to people like you and making this engagement with you a worthwhile experience. There are other goals I am seeking to accomplish—daunting, challenging ones. It is a lot of fun.

I am a technology executive with a track record of building more than one successful multinational business. I am also a part of a wonderful family. The thought of trading off parts of my life with an alternate outcome has never occurred to me. That does not mean that I always had the silver spoon thrust between my teeth. Life has not always been kind, leave alone fair—it is not meant to be that way for anyone. There are phases in my life that I absolutely cruised through. Everything worked like a charm. Then there were the pitfalls where I got muddied, dusted myself off, and learnt life lessons that no Ivy League school could teach me.

So here I stand today, content thus far. Quite a contrarian thought, is it not? In a world where "success" is all about not being satisfied, about asking for more, taking on more, and reaching for the stars till you are able to pierce nothingness and collect everything in between, being content rates rather low on the scale. I'm taking quite a contrarian position here as I go about writing a book on success. I consider myself fairly successful based on the metrics that businesses and societies use to measure success. That said, my drive, going forward, is now based on seeking accomplishments, which would not have been material in my past state. I am seeking a different form of success that seems less definitive and definitely more abstract, while being substantially more rewarding in every way than conventional success. More about that later.

I had a privileged childhood, cocooned in the comfort of love and affection. My parents and family goaded me to learn freely and do whatever pleased me (save breaking rules, which was strictly detested at home); I generally enjoyed my childhood to the extent of being spoiled rotten.

My teen and young adult years were spent in the company of friends with whom I satiated my inquisitiveness, tasted adventures, played sports, soaked in all the knowledge I could gather, and had a great time. I loved to read and would mentally and visually gobble whatever I could lay my hands on: fiction, facts, journals, you name it—anything that could give me a respite from traditional academics and the methodology of rote learning that came along with it. In my freshman year at college, I took a break from Crichton, Ludlum, Archer, Flint, Galman, Hawkins, and Clark when I chanced upon Ayn Rand and her epic, *The Fountainhead.* I reveled soaking in the characters of Howard Roark, Dominique Francon, and Peter Keating, the three protagonists, as they waded through the world of architectural genius and human egos. It was memorable! I can recall when Rand philosophized about "greatness being an exaggeration, and like all exaggerations of dimension, it connoted the basic axiom of emptiness" as she dissects Roark's mindset on the conventional definition of greatness and success. I did not realize then, but the seeds of the book that you are holding were sowed then and there as I read the lines Rand wrote.

Then followed adulthood and work life. I was fortunate to woo and marry one of the smartest girls in my class, who helped me build a loving family as our two daughters were born. I then had the opportunity to work with some of the smartest professionals that you could round up in the technology industry in some of the most scalable business circumstances you could find. Again, not that there were no pitfalls, but I am "the glass is half full" kind of a guy. This company of exceptional humans, coupled with the confidence, drive, and my out-of-the-box knowledge, helped create a rocket fuel that propelled my personal, professional, financial, and social orbits beyond where I had ever thought I was capable of—a long way from my humble beginnings. Every time I thanked the force field out there for catapulting me into the zone where I felt privileged, part of my gratitude had me to start to think about accomplishment, success and legacy.

If greatness could be "an exaggeration," could success not be an exaggeration as well? Are the effort and application every individual puts into the process of attaining success an exaggeration? Is everything that we have learnt or felt about what it takes to be successful all made up?

Of course, it is not. I respect every individual, workgroup, department, fraternity, institution, or organization in the history of mankind that have attained success. Most (bar a few upon whom success has been thrust) have worked hard on a proven formula to attain the status of being successful. Most of them have demonstrated consistent qualities that have led them to the high ground, where they stand tall throughout history and into the future.

That said, look around, and you will see large-scale exaggeration in what success is made out to be from what it truly is. It happens so, after "n" degrees of separation between the narrator and the documenter. It also stems from the creative genius of the "successful" narrator who wishes to elevate his accomplishments beyond where they really stand. We all have the desire to play to the galleries, and even if we do not, our egos certainly do! No surprises then, that success has become complex mechanics that is seemingly unattainable for the mere mortal. Success is an accomplishment that we are mostly programmed to admire and applaud when someone stands on a pedestal but not a target for most to aspire for.

Nature has programmed humans for mediocrity. Humans seek comfort in the situations and circumstances they subject themselves habitually to, and that fact makes it okay to be mediocre. You see people doing the same thing over and over, making the same mistake over and over in schools, at the work place, in social settings, at home, and in sports. They do not get any better at what they do because they comfort themselves thinking that changing their habit is difficult and that it's okay to be the way they are—even if this means they perform below what they are capable of. Frankly, this does not bother me because these individuals make the choice of what they want to be. In the process, they join the ranks that nature has allocated for mediocrity.

On the flip side, I am saddened when I see a hint of a quality or attitude that demonstrates the "constellation of talents" that spells success in an individual like a flash in the pan. Then it simply disappears, never to be seen again. There are two reasons this happens: one, the individual is probably unaware of the talent. They are not aware that if these behaviour patterns i.e. talent or attitude, are honed into habits, some form of success is inevitable. Two, most people stay comfortable in nature's induced 'programmed state of mediocrity'. Even awareness of a talent they possess is unable to light up their rocket fuel, that could have propelled them forward. Ahead of the mediocrity that surround them.

The human race has progressed because of ordinary people who chose to attain extraordinary outcomes. From my vantage point, I see small but piercingly wonderful instances of this every day in every sphere of life. As I started writing this book, I became more acutely aware of my surroundings and the people in them. These observations were borrowed from the parts of the canvas of life that I admire the most—the workplace, sports, and movies—and all have lent inspiration and ideas to this book.

This is not a self-help book for workplace success. This is not a book only for people who trudge to work every day to earn a living, trying to figure out a way to make their life work. This is a book about human beings and human nature, irrespective of whoever you are and whatever you do: student, housewife, educator, social worker, professional sportsperson, employee, self-employed, deejay, or surfer. The stories and examples in the book are intended to nudge and wake you up to things that you probably already know. It is a book that debunks the myths of success and puts it within your reach in anything that you choose to do. In the next pages, I share my observations on the nuances of the human character that can propel common people to greater heights and allow them to attain better results by doing little things that make a difference, if done regularly and consistently. Extraordinary outcomes come about when we transform these random actions into consistent habits—habits that ultimately build the character that is capable of scaling the pedestal of success.

I have seen some incredible instances of what a timely nudge does to people. I hope that, with this book, I can provide you the nudge you need to succeed in your own way, in your own space.

If I can nudge even one among you to success, my goal would be met . . .

Deb Dutta
December 2013

Why Put in Any Effort When You Do Not Know the *Why*?

Teenagers are smart these days. I cannot make my daughters do *anything* unless they know *why* they need to do it and *what* they will gain if they do so. I do not blame them because there is a perfectly good reason why they ask these questions. No task or initiative that consumes time and energy should really be done unless the people involved know the "why" (the reason to spend time doing the task) and the "what" (the foreseeable outcome of the task).

Sounds like a no-brainer, right? If you have any doubts, check with the first teen you meet out there. However skeptical you are, there is always a 'why' and a 'what' to everything that is said or done. What matters is this: do we dwell on these long enough?

Walk into a workplace teeming with intellectual capital, and see how many 'whys' and 'whats' are traded across the work floor. You won't find many. Most employees go about doing their tasks because they are told to do so. Naturally, this leads to (at best) mediocre passion, energy, creativity and innovation, which finally lead to (you guessed it) mediocre results . . .

The individuals toiling away all day usually have no clue regarding the impact of their efforts on the final result. They have no interest in recommending improvements or suggesting new ideas and often, no avenue to taking pride in the final result that crown their effort. All this, because they do not bother to ask the 'why' and the 'what'.

It's difficult to imagine a player competing in the National Football League in the United States, executing a play without knowing the 'why' and the 'what' involved. Sometimes, it's time to pass along and other times to call for a handoff that blasts through the defensive line. Either way, the context and how the play links to the larger strategy is key to proper execution. It is also critical to getting the most out of the individual player. Running a pattern without knowing the why is a dangerous form of ignorance. The conditions on the field are so fluid that the end goal (achieving the first down or scoring) must be kept in mind if the play is to be successful. A team that runs the play without knowing the "why" will be threatened by opposing players whose responses conform to the pattern in the playbook. Any player or team who is not interested in the "why" does not belong in professional athletics. The same goes with any other arena of life.

I have tried asking the cause of this apparent lack of inquisitiveness. Fear, lack of preparedness, embarrassment, workload, and even stress are some candid responses. Map these attributes with those linked to non-performance within individuals and teams and you make a startling discovery: they match!

I take pride in encouraging my direct and extended teams to *not* do anything unless they understand *why* they are doing it and *what* outcomes they should expect to accomplish. Once they do, they are on a natural high to achieve the desired outcome. I see many of them adopting this attribute and actually practicing it on me. Not that I mind at all; leadership skills in an individual or a group environment always requires the ability to seek and explain the 'why' and the 'what' in every situation, whether it is demanded or not.

I do wish my daughters were more forgiving though . . .

Next, let's take a look at a specific "why" that, while perhaps not viewed in a very positive light, does create far-reaching consequences and provides some valuable learning in our path to success. I am talking about . . . greed.

Greed Is Good: The Parable from *Wall Street*

I have always been a movie buff. My growing-up years were often laced with two or sometimes three movies a week. These hours spent inside a dark theater was my window to the colorful world that was beyond my horizon—my visualization of my future.

In my freshman undergraduate year, I watched Oliver Stone's *Wall Street.* Within two hours, I was thoroughly immersed in the style of the Street, not to mention Michael Douglas's Gordon Gekko character that personified the summary and celebration of free market capitalism. Gordon Gekko stayed with me as I grew through the haze of young adulthood with stars in my eyes, dreaming of professional and financial success. Gekko's rhetoric kept ringing in my ears: "I am not talking about the regular Wall Street stiff, flying first class and being comfortable. I am talking liquid—rich enough to own your own jet, rich enough not to waste time. Fifty . . . a hundred million a year . . . a player." Discount inflation and fifty or a hundred million was a lot of money back then and and is a lot of money, even today.

The movie closes with Gekko ending up in prison but not before very successfully hammering in greed as a virtue for the continued innovation and evolution of mankind and the human spirit. The sequel showed up some years ago with Gekko (now a free man) with a daughter who hates him and an ambitious prospective son-in-law in tow, prophesying against everything he had stood for a few decades before and announcing doomsday for financial and free market capitalism, as we know it today. (Life has also taken its toll on Michael Douglas; he announced in 2010 that he had been diagnosed with throat cancer. Two years later, it was great to hear that the grueling doses of chemotherapy had done their job, and Douglas was declared cancer free. I wish him a long, healthy life.)

Now, let's leave Gekko alone and ponder on greed for a bit. I want to do this because of the potentially negative label the word carries, stemming from its inclusion in the seven deadly sins. I somewhat agree with Gordon Gekko's summation. The manifestation of greed emerges from your own perspective of the word. Most achievements of any proportion arise out of greed of some sort: greed drives desire, desire leads to focused actions, and actions lead to results. I do believe that greed of some form (not necessarily the in-your-face look of it that most of you will associate in people you call greedy) is the catalyst to above-average results. Whether it benefits an individual, a group, a community, a nation, or mankind or causes it harm is another matter!

The scale of the benefit that greed led action drives, defines the power of greed and is possibly what Gordon Gekko was alluding to when he labeled it as "good". Among Aristotle, Archimedes, Mozart, Picasso, Gandhi, Luther King, Edison, Carnegie, Gates, Jobs to even Mr. Buffet, there is an incredible internal motivation to build innovative models in arts, science, technology, human rights, government, politics, and finance that catapulted mankind to new heights. This is inevitably followed by very focused execution that has provided incremental value to hundreds of millions of people around the world for years. All these individuals experienced a form of greed (very often not directed toward immediate personal gratification) that drove these innovations and, in the end, provided value to people.

So what is that internal motivation that led these individuals to do what they did? It was greed, undoubtedly. "An intense desire to accomplish unperceivable and previously unaccomplished outcomes that serves humanity and helps fulfill an internal need of the individual." The continuing "internal need" does not need to be for monetary gain, for many of the individuals I cite were wealthy anyway. In most instances, the accomplishments of these individuals gave meaning to their lives and built their legacies. In the process, they positively affected the lives of whole generations around the world. This greed (whilst not totally selfless) should sound good to most of us.

On the other hand, as the world today reels after the largest financial catastrophe of our lifetime, I question where greed sits in the equation. The treatment of subprime mortgages, the collateralized debt obligations, credit default swaps, and the leveraged positions that are breaking not just the largest financial institutions but also pension funds and personal savings of the common man and the most powerful nation in the world were not meant to be what they finally evolved into. Who and what led that evolution? It is the other form of greed: the kind that put Gekko himself behind bars.

So how is this form of greed different? Well, it still drives massive benefits but specifically to an individual or a small group of individuals at the expense of a much larger majority. For example, "while Richard Fuld of Lehman was pleading with Secretary Paulson for federal rescue, Lehman was recommending to its compensation committee four days before its bankruptcy filing that three departing execs should receive more than twenty million in 'special payments'" (*Straits Times*, 8 October 2008). This is one of many examples of how this industry prioritized executive compensation at the expense of the hapless shareholders and the average taxpayer, who had to contribute to the 700 billion bailout package to save the US economy.

I hope that we will see collaboration between the government, regulators, and the industry worldwide to tidy over this mess with not too severe a global impact. (I am the eternal optimist.) I am also quite certain that in the aftermath of this debacle, more stringent governance measures will be implemented as the pendulum shifts to the other extreme. Massive changes in work processes will be implemented, and workflow will get more complicated and drawn out, but learning from our mistakes is laudable.

The ultimate test, however, will be time and human nature . . . so we are back to greed. Greed will drive humanity again into taking little chances; it will spur small shifts from the dictum in the name of innovation and value creation to drive the economy and industry. Government, regulators, and industry will all be drawn into the party till we are hit by another tidal wave, and the same cycle will run again.

For better or for worse, greed will live on, and we will have to learn to deal with the inevitable Gordon Gekkos as we navigate through our times.

As a human being, greed for receiving a payback from my actions often seduces me like it does most of you. The one step that I force myself to take is to visualize the end state that my greed fuels. If it betters a situation or adds value to people other than myself without causing harm to anyone, then by all means I steer myself to go ahead with the actions that will deliver the projected results and give me my reward.

Anything that is to the contrary requires some serious thinking and/or advice from people I trust and respect.

Greed can, as Gordon Gekko says, “be good”. But it also spells problems. When a problem presents itself, the first order of business is to make sure you’ve identified exactly what the problem is: the size, dependencies, and consequences.

A lack in preparation in addressing the problem often leads to situations that are more challenging than the problem itself.

Solving the Wrong Problem

We have become very used to living in a world filled with instant gratification in which almost every external stimulus receives an immediate response. Just look around and see people with their cell phones, tablets, and opinions, participating in team discussion sessions. They are eager to speak and quick to respond. Consider times when you left someone a voice mail or sent him or her an e-mail on a matter of urgency, and they took their time to respond. How frustrating was that? You were disappointed and unimpressed about the other person's professionalism, almost felt slighted, and, in some cases, were even determined to pay back in the same coin. Note your own expectation of immediate gratification so that when others approach you for a response, you can respond most effectively. However, is it not right that your response speed be based on the nature and complexity of the request and not only on your own personal expectations of quick gratification?

I have worked hard on honing this specific skill, and I often ask people around me, to "listen between the lines and understand others' perspectives before responding." It's amazing to observe how people, instead of "listening," are actually mentally rehearsing their own lines of response while someone else is talking, just waiting for the other person to finish before they commence their own rhetoric. Some of the North Asian cultures encourage reflection, even deliberation, followed by a consensus-based response involving more than one person. The twenty-first century business cultures are unfortunately erasing these great habits. A consensus-based response is not only better because it takes into account more than one point of view, it also has the benefit of encouraging individuals to see their input in the context of others' opinions and makes us less focused on simply having our say.

I have come across situations where talented, result-oriented individuals and groups get together to study a situation and define the underlying problem. However, the individual members, being a product of the instant gratification culture and faced with tight deadlines, often define the problem incorrectly in the rush of getting things done quickly. The urge to hurriedly move on to the "solution" phase (the part where their opinions take center stage) can create a situation in which the problem is cemented long before it is fully understood.

Even though the stage has been wrongly set up, the group then sets forth at full steam to solve the "wrong" problem. All the while, there is a lot of visible activity. The reporting hierarchies are happy with the development, and in some instances, the individuals are also rewarded or publicly recognized. But none of this matter if the true problem has not been correctly studied defined and addressed. When the initial euphoria settles, and the desired results are not visible, some of the participants own up that they expected better results, while some try and sweep the result under the carpet and violently defend their action. Rework becomes inevitable, leading to overruns in time, cost, and delayed impact.

The crux here is the value of the "thinking exercise", be it an individual or a workgroup, the sharpening of the axe before beginning to chop down the tree. On a small and personal scale, we've all experienced this in the form of buyer's remorse. How many of us have purchased a new car, only to find that it doesn't meet our needs? It doesn't drive as well as the old one, and its racy look blinded us to the fact that it doesn't get the mileage we expected nor does its taut suspension provide a comforting ride when we have to drive interstate to meet Grandma in Albuquerque. The aerodynamic chassis accommodates a small boot not big enough to hold the weekly groceries that now spills into the already compact interior of the car. You get the drift. Rushing to the desired conclusion—the rush to put our input into action—can often encourage us to leap over the true situation we are trying to address.

An imperfect situation that needs to be fixed absolutely demands the time for thinking and analyzing to determine what is causing the imperfection—the problem itself. Often, what meets the eye and seems like the obvious cause is not the right one. Matrix organizations and the formation of cross-functional groups present opportunities for gathering varied perspectives on the same set of circumstances and data. This approach allows an adequate focus on defining the true problem rather than getting distracted too soon and focusing on a solution that might or might not address what needs to be solved.

If you are a team member, leverage these varied views, contribute yours, and encourage the team to reach a balanced conclusion based on the consolidated set of opinions. If you are a leader and do not necessarily want to make a consensus-based decision, ask questions, challenge individual views, and take a holistic view of the surrounding circumstances or data to define the problem before commencing the "fix".

While it is mostly a drag to dwell long on the problem instead of setting out at light speed to solve it, you will serve yourself, your team, and your organization or community well in terms of time, effort, and investment by choosing to define the problem better. Once the problem is truly defined, better and long-lasting solutions come quickly, and you can be assured that they are addressing the *actual* or *close to actual problem* instead of the incorrectly *perceived* problem. This is important in a business context, but it is as important in other realms. The problem-first approach leads us to a better solution whether you are growing your business, expanding your home, planning a move to another city, or just organizing a shopping spree during Christmas.

Solving problems definitely requires effort. On the other hand, a problem is not considered resolved if the desired outcome of the resolution is not attained. So let us examine Effort and Attainment next.

First Among Equals: Effort or Attainment

I never cease to be impressed by teens and adolescents. They are intuitive, direct, and downright smart.

My teenage daughter and I were out hiking one weekend some years ago. Singapore's equatorial sun was beating down on us, but fortunately, the sea breeze was holding. Before she could get into one of her teen tantrums on "how the weather sucks" and that it makes a lot more sense to stay indoors rather than hike in the blazing sun, I decided to engage her in conversation. She loves a spirited chat, and I reckoned it was the best way to keep her mind off the heat and the exercise.

We spoke for a little while, and then, she abruptly asked, "What is more important—effort or attainment?" She went on to explain that her projects in school were being graded on those two parameters. I asked her what *she* thought was more important, and she said, "Effort, definitely. If the effort is in place, attainment will follow." She felt effort could be controlled, but not attainment, which obviously depends on the quirks of whoever happens to be the teacher grading the paper. What better way to set expectations with the term results due just round the corner!

In December 2011, the Department of Economics at Oxford University presented a paper on Student Effort and Educational

Attainment, using the English football team to identify the Education Production Function. (*http://www.economics.ox.ac.uk/Research/wp/pdf/paper586.pdf*)

The abstract states that the paper uses a sharp, exogenous, and repeated change in the value of leisure to identify the impact of student effort on educational achievement. The research reviews the partial overlap of the world's major international football tournaments with the exam period in England. Performance is measured using the high-stakes tests that all students take at the end of compulsory schooling. The finding states that the average impact of a fall in effort is 0.12 standard deviations of student performance, significantly larger for male and disadvantaged students, often as high as many educational policy changes.

Though I believe in this correlation between Effort and Attainment, I could argue that football today touches a broader community than the sample that was examined. I would love to see the results on a broader sample not limited to males or disadvantaged demographic groups. My daughters follow the English Premier League ardently and root for Chelsea as if they are vested in the team. Second, the category of the demographic sample being studied must have other sports and non-sports distractions during the non-FIFA World Cup and UEFA years, so why do these distractions not impact their attainment in those years? The kids from the Indian sub-continent are in a category that is strangely not impacted. This sports crazy lot might not be very much into football but are die-hard followers of cricket, which is bound to be played during the summer months somewhere in the world involving England or their home countries and telecast into England. Why does this distraction not impact their attainment?

Many questions but regardless, a fascinating study.

I reasoned with my daughter for a bit but finally conceded that in a learning environment, I would rate effort higher than the immediate attainment, at least in the very short term. Very often, institutions of learning are too focused on grades rather than the actual learning process. This makes the learning process very mechanical. It also promotes that behavior I absolutely dread in the workplace: doing things without understanding "why they are doing what they are doing." (See the chapter, "Why Put in Any Effort When You Do Not Know the *Why*"). Consequently, I also agree that with the right level of effort, intellect, guidance, and discipline, attainment is bound to follow.

At work, I have faced similar dilemmas while judging employee productivity, performance, and development. I have seen ways in which performance of the employee is mapped and measured in the appraisal process. While the usual ratings—Top, Strong, Solid, Needs Development, and Manage Out (or derivatives of these)—are quite common, I have used a broader framework in judging employees within these categories, i.e. the "what" and the "how." This would mean that for every performance measurement criterion, taking ownership, setting expectations, working with cross-functional teams, and so on, I have an index for what the individual does and how he does it in addition to the regular grading—Top, Strong, Solid and so on.

The "what" actually alludes to the attainment, while the "how" alludes to the effort that my daughter was talking about. Usually, the Top and the Manage Out categories are absolute categories, while the other three intermediate categories have a "what" and "how" flavor, that is, we rate the individual's performance with an emphasis on what results were achieved and how these results were achieved.

In any typical organization setting, what and how are crucial. However, considering that the primary goal of the business is to generate shareholder value, the "what" (attainment) shows up as the first among equals.

Before we get too ahead of ourselves with the "what", the "how" (the right kind of effort) is not far behind in value. Attaining results at any cost often leads to defying the prevailing strictures and governance. It is not a recommended form of action. Any behavior that is forced, bent, and against the grain of standard practices will have long-term ramifications for the individual or the group. We have all seen plenty of these instances in the midst of the current financial crisis and in all instances of crisis of any scale around the world.

So my daughter and I rounded off our conversation, agreeing that school might be an appropriate place for learning and experimentation, one in which effort deserves a tad more advantage than attainment. The workplace, on the contrary, is far more exacting and demanding, and the results have far-reaching consequences. Experimentation is often welcomed, even encouraged, but needs to be professionally managed so that it is not at the expense of attainment of overall expected financial or operational results.

As my daughter flirted with another topic, I just wanted to have a last word on school before she could forcibly move me away from the current topic. I said, "Just ensure that your grades show up good. Effort wins when you are in a class session, but come exam day, attainment comes top." I am learning fast on how to set my expectations clearly with this smart kid walking beside me. She gave me a quizzical look and a shrug that characterizes almost everyone in her age group, but I bet she knows what I meant: two seemingly isolated concepts that need to be intertwined in a complex network of actions and results that deliver the goals and objectives that individuals, communities, and organizations seek.

Networks—a fascinating concept that has many connotations. Let's move on and look into what they stand for.

Networking—Getting it Right

Metcalf's Law fascinates me. It states that the value of a telecommunication network is proportional to the square of the number of connected users of the system (n^2). Attributed to Robert Metcalf, in regard to the Ethernet (the collective network that connects all the electronic devices we see and share data between), Metcalfe's law characterizes many of the effects of communication technologies and networks. All these attributes have revolutionized the world in terms of how we consume information, interact, live, work, and entertain ourselves via the Internet, social networks and the World Wide Web.

The concept, expectation, and impact of networking have changed as dramatically as the world. The means to "network" and the modes of networking have evolved. From an individual engagement involving two people to serve mutual needs, the networking scope has scaled to involve communities that can easily collaborate over vast distances, jurisdictions, cultures, and practices while seeking common goals and beliefs. These ubiquitous networks deliver different levels of efficiency and are being used to extract varied levels of objectives and value by those who use them. The evolution of enabling, easy-to-use technology, and distributing the technology-enabled mobile devices in the hands of people has played a big role in making this happen.

None of us today associate networking with business and financial gains alone. I have seen friends closely associated with the church, healthcare, and other humanitarian pursuits where networking (both electronic and social) get people with similar psychological and physical challenges or the desire to serve others to bond, share, and support. These are also demonstrations of incredible effort that underlines the selflessness of the people who organize these groups and invest their time to help others. Their effort, enthusiasm, and involvement are sustained because of the powerful networks that such like-minded people create that guide them through all adversity and their personal highs and lows.

With networking becoming a core skill in every individual's social, profit, and non-profit go-to-action model, and with many people tired of the network of people they already know, differentiation in how you network is crucial.

So here are ten tips that I have picked up from my time at work. I am not the oracle from the mountains doling out sermons; these are behavior patterns that have either helped me triumph when I followed them or have led me to take a beating when I did not.

1. I understand who I am. I analyze my strengths and weaknesses and **I represent myself honestly** with no pretensions. No one is perfect, so forcing a face of "perfection" is neither important for me, nor does it put any pressure on me. Then I place my best foot forward.
2. **I treat people with respect and grace**, irrespective of the level of my familiarity. An unassuming exterior often conceals very capable personalities within. The reverse is true as well.

Who uses social networking sites

% of internet users within each group who use social networking sites

	All internet users (n=1,895)	72%
a	Men (n=874)	70
b	Women (n=1,021)	74
	Race/ethnicity	
a	White, Non-Hispanic (n=1,331)	70
b	Black, Non-Hispanic (n=207)	75
c	Hispanic (n=196)	80^{a}
	Age	
a	18-29 (n=395)	89^{bcd}
b	30-49 (n=542)	78^{cd}
c	50-64 (n=553)	60^{d}
d	65+ (n=356)	43
	Education level	
a	No high school diploma (n=99)	67
b	High school grad (n=473)	72
c	Some College (n=517)	73
d	College + (n=790)	72
	Annual household income	
a	Less than $30,000/yr (n=417)	75
b	$30,000-$49,999 (n=320)	72
c	$50,000-$74,999 (n=279)	74
d	$75,000+ (n=559)	71
	Urbanity	
a	Urban (n=649)	74
b	Suburban (n=893)	71
c	Rural (n=351)	69

Source: Pew Research Center's Internet & American Life Project Spring Tracking Survey, April 17 – May 19, 2013. N=1,895 adult internet users ages 18+. Interviews were conducted in English and Spanish and on landline and cell phones. The margin of error for results based on all internet users is +/- 2.5 percentage points.
Note: Percentages marked with a superscript letter (e.g., [a]) indicate a statistically significant difference between that row and the row designated by that superscript letter, among categories of each demographic characteristic (e.g. age).

3. **I take a long-term view of all my relationships**. I do not focus on instant gratification. I let the engagement evolve rather than force it. In certain cultures, mutual trust (not professional capability) is the primary catalyst for a relationship to bloom—in business or in life generally.
4. **I keep every relationship "alive"** even after an immediate objective that gave rise to the relationship has been served. Many a great opportunity for a larger mutual leverage is lost because the people involved took a short-term perspective of the relationship, after the initial need to relate was met.
5. **I make a positive impact on people** when I meet them, especially for the first time. I give them a reason to remember me in a positive light after they have moved on. Appropriate compliments, graciousness, eye contact, desire to unearth common interests, willingness to listen with genuine interest and intent, humor, or even a warm smile (when not overdone) are easily appreciated . . . I have heard of qualities like charisma, charm, and personal magnetism that supposedly attract people; to me, these qualities are quite abstract and hard to master, even if you want to. The list above seems to me like an easier bet, and it works.
6. **I make people comfortable** in my presence (refer to #5 above). A shifting gaze, a nervous laugh, short binary answers, unwillingness to start a new conversation, extended silence from the other person are telltale signs of wanting to go away from you.
7. **I try to be a fabulous listener**. There is a reason why we have two ears and one mouth (boy, do most of us struggle with this!). A great listener gathers far more from a conversation than someone with an over eagerness to speak. Besides, good listening skill adds balance to a conversation and draws out other

discussion points that prolongs and spices the conversation. Willingness to listen to others will draw them to you and make them want to listen to what you have to say. Just being a listener with zero desire to speak and share also douses the interest of the other party quite rapidly. The right balance is key.

8. **I find a way to intrigue** the other person while serving snippets of my positive attributes. Ask intelligent questions, make intuitive observations, and use humor during your interaction, be it in person or electronically (e-mails, social networking sites, etc.). Many people talk just because they want to be heard. Their words neither have substance nor show them in a favorable light.
9. **I refer people I know to other people** I know. Find ways to grow their network if you want them to grow yours. Again, some empathy and maturity is needed here. Keep compatibility and common interests in mind while facilitating these introductions. Put genuine effort in getting people together—do not walk away after a bland introduction and think that you have done your part.
10. I try and come out of each engagement, making the **other person feeling generally optimistic, more informed, and definitely better off than before they met me**. I also generously show my appreciation for what I received from the person in course of the engagement.

Like Metcalf's findings, your personal networks (if properly nurtured) will open up new vistas, expose you to new realities, enable you to expand your wisdom, and potentially add dramatic value to your life just like you possibly will do to those you network with. The possibilities, as they say, are endless.

I wish you all the very best in the quest for building valuable, fulfilling, engaging, and incredibly rewarding networks in every sphere of your lives. Should you be in a stage in your professional career where you wish to work independently outside of the corporate workplace, your current personal network and your ability to rapidly extend it will help determine whether you succeed or fail.

The Making of the Independent Professional

With the expansion and diversification of business, especially the service industry, the world of opportunities for the independent professional has dramatically exploded, especially in financial services, tourism, education, media, technology, and other niche verticals where knowledge is a key differentiator for preferential end results. People with certain specialized skills have rapidly become conscious of the fact that it makes sense to serve more organizations and individuals rather than being tied to a single one. In addition to the independence and flexibility that such an arrangement provides, the individual is able to expand his "knowledge and execution capability" by being exposed to diverse cross-functional circumstances within the various organizations he serves. This ability leads to bigger bucks while ensuring freedom with multiple income streams. The choice is clear!

CNN Money states that independent freelance professionals now make up more than 25% of the US working population. The Aberdeen Report (2010) says that nearly 60% of organizations across the globe expect the contingent labor market shift to include more Statement of Work, independent contractor, and project-based work over the next two years.

Elance, the large independent professional network, published data that shows Mobile app developers have seen a 98% increase in job demand in 2010 over the previous year. Most other specialized skills are seeing similar trends.

While being independent has its benefits, it is never easy to leave a familiar and comfortable professional career in an organization with a monthly paycheck and sail into the unknown world of going solo. Change and uncertainty are painful and frightening, and human nature will always resist them. What matters most is what the heart desires. If we have a dream of professional independence, the capability and discipline that needs to go along with it, and a plan to make it happen, then why not follow your heart and go for it. Don't begin unless you know what you are doing and are wholly committed to success. "I want to start something on my own and be my own boss" has been the famous last words of many an entrepreneur. However, if you are properly set, begin immediately, and don't waver from your course.

Once we know what you most want to do—what will make work seem more like play and leave us feeling satisfied and accomplished at the end of each day—we are ready. First, research your chosen field inside and out. Understand potential pitfalls and the skills needed for success. Skills that you need are not just the core skills but day-to-day business-running skills like basic bookkeeping and basic operations that you will have to do on your own when you are self-employed. You could outsource these services, but this will increase your expenses; even if you can afford to outsource, you still need to know how money flows. Jumping into any trade without understanding finance is foolhardiness (see the last chapter).

Source: Quora—http://www.quora.com/What-is-the-market-size-for-independent-professionals-in-the-US

Armed with that information, let's honestly assess our skills and potential to discover whether we have what it takes to succeed. Don't be concerned if you don't have all the talents needed in your chosen field; successful entrepreneurs leverage their skills and bring in other talented people to make up for abilities they lack. However, I would always ensure I have the core skills before I embark. For instance, I would never start tutoring if I did not have any inclination to academics, or pursue a career in insurance sales if I disliked meeting unknown people and build rapport with them while discussing illness and death.

The most successful independent professionals are disciplined, financially savvy, self-motivated, extremely organized, great communicators, and relationship magnets. Let's lead with these strengths if we have them and are not deterred by our weaknesses. We will have opportunities to improve areas of weakness, but let that not hold us back and kill time. However, if we absolutely lack these baseline skills, then let's reassess our options. There are a lot of other things that we love to do that need skills, which match our personal attributes and capabilities—let's pursue those options.

Once we have a professional goal in place, let's not commit until we have tested the waters. A great idea is to just talk about our plan with trusted friends and family until they also think it is great plan. New Coke is a good example of this. Coca Cola was determined that the time was ripe for a new recipe for their iconic product, but their customers disagreed. Coca Cola would have known this ahead of its launch if they had done their homework and merely asked their customers.

Due diligence often saves time, money, and lost opportunities. Accepting that your product or service isn't right for the current market does not mean that the sky is falling on our heads: commonly, the right analysis will allow you to make the tweaks necessary to turn it into something the market will embrace. It's best to do this research with other people's money. I believe that working for an organization in the same space before striking out on your own is a brilliant way to learn with other people's money. There is no dearth of examples where I have seen people try out something and then decide that it was not their cup of tea anyway! Imagine if they had gone in with their own money!

The independent professional's success depends solely on their commitment to the business and the work they put into it. There is no organizational support: the individual *is* the organization. Being an independent professional is about being independent—independence in terms of time, effort, and earnings. Professional discipline is therefore key! Countless talented independent professionals have gone down because they lacked sufficient work ethic and discipline.

Assuming that the individual is disciplined or diligent, clients and human networks from the past will contribute a great part of that success. This is the prospect base for the new independent professional, one that can be leveraged, milked, and converted into long-term association and value. The most common barrier to entry or a very visible pitfall in the profession is not having a client base to turn to for support in the early days of the independent life. While old networks can help jump-start the journey, cold calling (however painful) is a MUST. No one likes to do it, but what every successful professional will tell you is about the need to grind on and spend time cold calling and filling in your Rolodex with entries of new contacts you have met and are developing. This is a priceless habit needed throughout one's professional life, and I have devoted an entire chapter to it later in this book. Your addressable market of relationships needs to continually grow to enable you to scale your results. Smart usage of the web, social networking platforms, and messaging technologies in moderation can help in accomplishing this.

Ultimately, business is about sales. Once you have a business you believe in, you have to make the clients believe in it too and have them part with their money. Push for the sale: the ones that can't be convinced will say no, and you move on. Sales is as much about rejection as it is about acceptance. The dejection and the pain of rejection are infinitesimally more detrimental than the euphoria of success. Success requires hardening oneself to the feelings that accompany rejection with a sense of detachment. On the flip side, let's celebrate the success of a sale wildly, to drown any remnants of failure while goading ourselves to strive for similar wins. We often make the mistake of seeking instant gratification. When we do not get it, we feel hurt. The most loyal customers you will make are often those who take the longest time to buy from you. They stay part convinced, part undecided for a long time . . . they hurt you. Then they step into your world and stay forever. Patience is powerful!

Once we have a client, the challenge will be to keep the client forever. Empathy, sensitivity, knowledge, trust, and quality of service are often the primary factors here. Very often, providers are more intent on selling what they have in their bags rather than what the customer wants to buy. Understanding customer needs and providing a suitable solution that addresses them is a no-brainer. It sounds like a Sales 101 cliché but is often ignored even by experienced pros and has been the end of many formerly successful businesses. Your clients and the financial and operational benefits you deliver to them through your offerings are more important than any other aspect of your business.

Once we have wowed the customer, we will begin to generate a revenue flow that will become more predictable and will require less effort, provided we do not stamp out our customer-retention skills. The time has then arrived for us to work *on* our business rather than *in* our business. We will still need to continue to cold call though: growing our customer portfolio is like providing lifeblood to our initiative. As we start to build the right skills and begin to see success, even cold calling can become fun. We get better at it because knowing we have many satisfied customers will energize us and enable us to convey that enthusiasm to new prospects. We should not miss the opportunity of allowing our existing customers to sell for us. Strong customer references are often more effective in getting new customers than the most enthusiastic salesperson.

Being an independent professional is about you and your vision. Confucius said, "Do something you love and you'll never work a day in your life." The days will be long and the work challenging, but after your first sale, you'll be sure you never want to work for anyone else ever again.

This kind of professional independence is heady stuff, and it puts us in a position to lead ourselves first before we lead others. It makes us understand the Anatomy of Leadership in a very unique way.

The Anatomy of the Leader

It is my belief that everyone has a leader within and that it is the individual's prerogative to demonstrate that leadership in everyday life. Leadership does not mean having to lead a group of people. Leadership starts from within an individual as he starts to lead himself methodically toward desirable outcomes; its manifestation then cascades rapidly onto others and, subsequently, has the ability to touch thousands, millions, or more.

Many people are moved to formal and informal leadership positions every year. I am very happy for them, especially if they grow and rise through the ranks. Their rise exemplifies their accomplishments and the organization's trust and people philosophy. I enjoy personally communicating with these newly minted leaders, congratulating them and spending a moment sharing their happiness and celebrating their success. I also communicate to them with all honesty that the expectations of them from there on are very different from the past. The qualities that have brought them this far are not necessarily the ones that will take them to the next level.

I like the sound of the word "leader" more than "manager"; to me, the connotations are very different. A leader is a superset of a manager. A leader demonstrates all the characteristics of a manager—time management, ability to resolve conflicts, ensuring near-term performance, objectivity, and accountability. However, the archetypal manager need not be a leader and very often is not.

Through my readings and by observing people's behaviors, I see leaders painting the vision, energizing and inspiring the team, challenging them with extended goals, and providing support to help them achieve the goals. Leaders do not just chart and deliver near-term and mid-term performance of the team. They are driven to grow each team member personally and professionally while generally inspiring everyone with a positive outlook of life and the future. A manager who manages the team toward metrics, focused more on the "what" than the "why," is largely tactical in approach and mostly uses positional power, discipline, and, in some instances, even coercion to get the work done. Most disciplined managers play based on someone else's playbook—most likely their supervisor's.

A leader might need to behave like a manager in certain situations. Having the credibility and trust within the team and taking time to clearly explain the "why" to the team often cushions the more "manager like" behaviors. Visualize this . . . the manager leads from the rear with the stick; the leader is out front with the carrot. In many instances, this could just be situational.

Being a leader is about playing many roles—expert guide, coach, friend, enabler, and critic. While playing these roles, the leader takes difficult but fair decisions, demonstrates tenderness and firmness, and leads by example where needed. He allows the spotlight to be on the people in the trenches rather than on himself. He acts in the interest of the organization, team, and the individual, in that order. He basks in reflected glory when his team does well and is recognized.

Managers are relatively easier to develop. With the prescription of the organization behind them, managers wield their influence and skills to ensure execution. Managers commonly experience success, but mostly that success is due to the push factor—top managers instill the sense of accountability within their teams that eliminates the need to micro manage. Their teams perform because they want to. Employees under a manager achieve for short-term or mid-term reasons: pleasing superiors, keeping their job, earning the compensation. Leaders wield the same authority but choose to inspire rather than coerce. A leader *pulls* his or her team toward success by ensuring that all share the same long-term goals. A team with a true leader performs better than one under a manager because their focus is on group rather than on individual achievement—they focus on a long-term vision rather than a short-term goal. This allows for better collaboration and for the synergy of collective effort that individual effort does not have access to.

Having shared my views on the attributes of leaders and managers, I fervently hope to see every manager who has done a great job in climbing the stairway to success, to now move toward the carriageway of leadership. I hope they do so without losing the key managerial skill of tactical execution. As we move further into leadership, let me share the various models of leadership that I have seen come to play.

Leadership Models—What Is Relevant Today?

The year 2009 was a busy one for my organization and me. After stamping our leadership in a specific technology space for most part of twelve years, we needed to expand our total addressable market beyond our core domain into the broader Ethernet LAN/WAN networking space. Toward the end of 2009, we completed a multi billion dollar acquisition, a staggering sum in the difficult money market of the day. Having made such a big bet, it was critical for us to ensure that the integration between the two organizations concluded swiftly and satisfactorily while communicating comfort and confidence to the customers and partners that would enable us to bring our end goals (revenue and non-revenue) of the acquisition to fruition. The task demanded the capabilities of both the leader and the manager. As things turned out, I was pleased that most of the things we needed to do stayed on track, and I am happy as a leader with the progress we made as a team during the period.

Starting in June 2009, I was a judge on the *MBA Challenge*—Asia's first online reality show. It aired exclusively over the web where two teams had to sequentially present and defend a business methodology (from a Business Case that was provided earlier) to each other. The judges would note each participant's performance based on multiple criteria, and one participant would be eliminated at the end of each episode. Two MBA seats worth $25,000 were up for grabs. This was the first season of *MBA Challenge*, and there was a lot of interest from the outset. I wrote this chapter during my tenure as a judge on the show.

Being involved in this reality show gave me the first glimpse of the intensity around the phenomena called social networks and social media. The light speed at which these platforms were emerging as a medium for social interaction, collaboration, and exchange was becoming quite clear. This was the alternative to television and radio. You could draw a critical mass of audience, feed them with content, and even get them to participate by providing much more than just feedback. It is multidirectional and multidimensional information exchange at its best. The Gen Y and Gen Z love it!

As the organizers were putting plans to export the show beyond Singapore, the elimination process had commenced, and we were down to the "last eight." The contestants were all young, energetic, and bubbling with ideas, energy, and perspective—very eager to learn. It was a pleasure and joy to be among these young folks and my interesting co-judges, soaking in everyone's exuberance. I do confess that I come out of each session (definitely not a walk in the park) having learnt more than what I have contributed, while having a lot of fun.

In one of the episodes of the *MBA Challenge*, the judges came down on the contestants hard for not demonstrating "proactive leadership" in a group situation. This is a key attribute of business leaders and an important criterion of an MBA enrollment. Leadership need not just be linked to a position—a person does not need to be a designated team leader to demonstrate leadership qualities. Nothing should stop an individual contributor from demonstrating leadership. Obviously, this trait is enabled because of some specific skills: subject-matter expertise, communication, or just the innate ability of an individual to initiate people to move, collaborate, and contribute toward achieving the end goal. While doing so, a leader demonstrates the ability to guide the effort of all involved to its intended conclusion rather than be a "misguided" part of a pack.

Talking about being "misguided" brings me to the common sight of people hogging airtime and not really communicating meaningful substance. Their belief is in equating visibility to importance. This is hardly so. The audience is intelligent and educated to decipher substance from baloney. In today's connected world, where news travels fast, the results of saying and writing just for the sake of doing so can be quite catastrophic.

In some of the elimination-related discussions and deliberations at the *MBA Challenge* show and the Facebook entries that the show generated, I chanced upon selfless leadership—the "servant-leader" model. This is a model in which the leader is willing to set aside personal needs and wants in seeking the greatest good for others. The leader here is intent on accomplishing through others and serving others rather than seeking personal wins.

James Haskett, a professor from Harvard Business School, has an interesting exemplification of the servant leader in a Forbes magazine blog: (*http://www.forbes.com/sites/hbsworkingknowledge/2013/05/01/why-isnt-servant-leadership-more-prevalent/*). He says, "Servant leadership is an age-old concept, a term loosely used to suggest that a leader's primary role is to serve others, especially employees. I witnessed a practical example of it at a *ServiceMaster* board meeting in the 1990s when CEO

William Pollard spilled a cup of coffee prior to the board meeting. Instead of summoning someone to clean it up, he asked a colleague to get him cleaning compound and a cloth, things easily found in a company that provided cleaning services. Whereupon he proceeded to get down on his hands and knees to clean up the spill himself. The remarkable thing was that board members and employees alike hardly noticed as he did it. It was as if it was expected in a company with self-proclaimed servant leadership."

I have also read about beliefs where the model "super leader" knows intrinsically where he needs to go and how to get there. They are then able to communicate and convince their teams with adequate passion and conviction. Both these concepts could be real, and there may be individuals who successfully live out these roles. However, like in other instances, I will advise reader discretion and will recommend that these concepts be viewed in the right perspective, keeping real world workplaces and circumstances in mind.

The real world has an incredible scarcity of leaders who do not have any personal needs and wants. These needs need not be financial or even material. I just find it hard to imagine a leader being successful in leading a team across the line without any personal skin in the game at all. On the contrary, I would call it a risk in hiring or nominating a leader who has no motivation of a personal monetary or non-monetary gain and is purely serving the team by leading them. To me, the servant leader is a philosophy with a specific place in the leadership doctrine, but not wholly relevant on a practical plane, at least in today's world of dog-eat-dog competition. A world where strong underlying causes and interests are the key reservoirs of motivation and purpose that teams and their leaders reach out to when the chips are down.

Next is the leader who knows where to go and how to get there. This is concept-wise okay, but I question how realistic this is in today's context. At work, I mostly face management challenges that are multidimensional in nature. They are also very dynamic, changing form and shape on a regular basis. Most challenges are also fragmented—I mean that a solution that might work in a specific situation or location where the problem shows up cannot be necessarily be replicated in another situation or location. Solving or even addressing these situations by a generalist leader or one with a single core skill is virtually impossible. Yes, the leader should be able to set directions toward a landing zone in terms of outcome expectations, but he can hardly do anything else to take the team to the desired outcome all by himself. You will see similar situations at home—dealing successfully with one child in a specific way might very well be a recipe for disaster with another child.

Good leaders are "generalists". They surround themselves with great 'specifists' (people with top class specific skills). They have the innate ability to make the human machinery work (regardless of the egos that come with the skills) even when the chips are down. When faced with a situation, they get these smart guys who "get it" and possess intense core competencies and expertise around a table, define the situation and the end goal, and often pretend to be the dumbest person in the room. Almost without exception, the leader asks great questions, solicits involvement and opinions from everyone on the table (the broader the skills mix, the more rounded the discussion and the cumulative opinion), and ensures that the discussion stays on track. These leaders are great at timing their own entry and exit from the group discussion. They do not hog airtime, preferring to be great listeners instead. In almost every instance, they demonstrate immaculate timing in closing the meeting, in following up and bring things to a smooth landing on time.

Once a meeting concludes, these leaders successfully consolidate, summarize, and direct the actions that evolve from the session that will likely address the required end goal. They then keep a hawk-eye watch to ensure that the follow-up actions or any metric that needs to be tracked as an outcome of the meeting is done. They hold their people accountable, hold themselves accountable, and keep working on the actions and outcome till the eventual desired result is accomplished.

So you see, the savvy leader of today purposefully chooses not to exactly know where to go and definitely does not want to know upfront how to get there. He leverages the competency within his team members to determine the possible answers and facilitates crafting a solution that is able to address the end goal.

Leadership is a lifelong path of learning, and in order to open us to its most important lessons, it's necessary to open ourselves to criticism first. Onto the next chapter for more about Criticism.

Criticism Is for the Fortunate: Use it Wisely

Anyone, anywhere normally reacts to criticism with unhappiness, concern, or disdain. Criticism is best done privately. It makes people visibly uncomfortable—not only those who face it, but even those who happen to be around when it is doled out.

I have previously mentioned my role in the *MBA Challenge 2009,* an online reality show in Singapore. Part of my responsibility was to objectively assess a contestant's participation in the course of an episode and set them up for retention or elimination by online viewer voting. In the course of doing so, all the three judges had to be verbally and visibly critical about the contestants with the objective of either showing them the ropes that they need to learn to survive in the show or to make it very clear to the viewers (who control the voting buttons) why some of the contestants need to be eliminated.

In several instances, I felt that we (the judges) were too harsh on these contestants, but then I had second thoughts. I recall my growing-up years. I was the only son, the only brother and the youngest member in a nuclear family, and mostly had my way. It was seldom that anyone at home judged my actions or me critically. It seemed great at the time, and I did not mind one bit nor do I blame my dear ones who lavished the preferential treatment on me. As I grew up and had to start dealing with the outside world with no parental support, I began to see the disadvantage of my privileged childhood. I could not face up and cope with anything even faintly "not-so-good" that was spoken about me, leave alone accept it and benefit from it. It was not that I was too dumb not to realize that I was not right in everything that I said or that I was not perfect at everything I did, but it was very difficult to accept or digest the reality when I was indeed wrong.

As I worked my way through primary and tertiary education and then through my work life, I met, worked with, and learned from incredibly talented individuals who I was fortunate enough to associate with. I learned about work and life and about people and relationships. All this learning has shaped my life, my professional career, and what I have attained over the years. As I progressed and grew in life, I was more willing and agreeable to step outside my comfort zone of personal perfection. I started to open up in seeking feedback from people who saw me from up close and were willing to be constructively critical about personal and work attributes that I needed to work on. Many of their observations were true, and I knew about them even if I did not acknowledge them. These corrections (some, if not all) molded me and made me more adequate in addressing today's challenges at home, work, and social settings. Some other fixes, I am still working on.

Along the way, I learnt that any criticism is a gift, really. Criticism is a seemingly harsh advice or feedback that enables an individual to be aware of a shortcoming that others see. I call this harsh because the cause of the advice might not be immediately visible to the individual. Even if it is visible, he might be in denial about it. Whether this observation is considered valid or what the individual does with the advice is absolutely personal, but at least, it presents a choice. Being aware of and accepting a weakness is halfway to resolving it. On the contrary, if we are not even aware of a shortcoming or violently resist it, how will we eliminate it in the first place? So the next time you are being criticized, view it as a free feedback that you are not compelled to accept but should be open to acknowledge. No one knows you better than yourself. You have the absolute and ultimate authority to determine whether you will accept a criticism or reject it. If you determine that the recommendation is one that improves your current standing, then by all means accept it and take massive action to implement it. Strengthen yourself and thank the outside world and the individual for presenting you with this gift.

I have also seen people who accept criticism in the right spirit and then some who go overboard and often overdo the personal transformation bit. While being closed to acceptance of feedback is not a desirable position, acts of dramatic acceptance are not recommended as well. Look, we all have individual character traits. Depending on age and circumstances, many of these traits are fairly deep-rooted. These traits represent us, make us what we are, and help us to be accepted by our family, friends, and coworkers despite our imperfections. Trying to change these dramatically is not only difficult but also not desirable. When people try to overdo this, the changes that follow might work for a while but will definitely not be sustainable. Such dramatic changes also confuse the people who regularly interact with the individual and sometimes set up wrong expectations.

So here is the balancing act that I will recommend. Let's be self-aware; let's be able judges of our strengths and areas that need fixing. Let's be prepared to actively solicit feedback from people who know us well and who will judge us without bias. While feedback on strengths is welcome and pleasing to the ear, let's lean more on determining areas and traits that need development. Let's find every opportunity to eliminate (to the extent possible) our weaknesses and strengthen our strengths. It does not have to hurt to be open to criticism. Even if some of these are unfairly directed at us, as long as we use them wisely and not emotionally, we will be better for having heard them. Whether we accept or do anything with these is totally up to us. Consequentially, if we choose to do nothing, that is also up to us. Our actions will determine where we go from where we are today.

Our ability to react to both good news and bad news about ourselves is a key part of that journey. Read on.

Let Me Give You the Bad News First

I am liberal and open to providing my opinion about how I view situations, circumstances, opinions, and propositions and how I respond to them to anyone who genuinely seeks it. Life has seen me in different circumstances at work and play—good, bad, memorable, rewarding, and downright ugly. Some I have responded to well, while others have been not much to write home about. Irrespective of the outcome, I have tried hard to learn from them, to reflect upon them, and to promise myself to deal with them better if I were to face them again in the future, especially where I did not fare too well.

We are in a complex world, within complex societies and complex relationships. People I know (me included), fervently believe that by sharing our collective successes and the hard knocks that we have taken will benefit others and save them time, pain, recovery, and missed opportunities. So we venture out and sermonize when solicited.

Look at the flip side, though. Try expressing your views. Everything we say or write is examined and inspected under a microscope. The more visible you are, the deeper the inspection. In a society where bad news and negative outcomes sell more than the good stuff, I am not surprised. Then there is the human ego that internally belittles the individual himself if he agrees to another person's opinion without punching one or more holes in it and then heroically filling that hole with another view that reflects his intellect. The more "knowledgeable" the circle, the more sensitive you need to be with your opinions; else, the arrows will come hurtling down on you.

After debating with myself, I have chosen to stay my course and continue to voice my learning for people to benefit from. There have been a few downsides, even debacles, but the upside where people appreciate, joyfully receive, and at times benefit from this shared learning outweighs the not-so-memorable outcomes. Most importantly, doing this gives me joy, more so if it makes the other person happy as well. I have just learnt to build some caution and tact along the way.

I have also learnt to be absolutely candid: to give a balanced view and to put my point of view purely as my perspective from my experiences—not the absolute truth. But see, when people seek my opinion, it is because they expect me to "know". I am but a mere mortal, far removed from famous seers and psychics like the Pythia from Delphi's temple of Apollo or Nostradamus or Baba Vanga—I neither know it all nor have I seen the future. I candidly say so upfront and sometimes see their faces fall. They thought "I knew." However, it sets me up on the right foot and sets their expectations exactly where they need to be. I also set the tone at the onset that my opinions may not be complete and that they aren't absolute references to the subject. It is for the individuals to take it, rephrase it, reorient it, and use it as they deem fit.

I have learnt to dwell on balance. People who approach me want to hear me say all the bright and positive things about what they want to talk to me about. See, this is how the mind works. Our mind expects to seek out agreement from others and reinforce what it already knows, especially from individuals they have confidence in and categorize as "knowledgeable" in the area where they need advice. I try to be more useful by going exactly against that flow. I try and talk about all the things that I do not expect the individual to have thought about. I give them the bad news first—not exactly what they want to hear, but heck, at least I am giving them an alternate perspective rather than echoing their inner thoughts and just making them happily biased. The good news is already in there; the bad news helps these folks objectively weigh in on the pros and cons before deciding whether the option is worth pursuing. I like the honesty of this approach and also the fact that it indemnifies me from any backlashes about "Deb did not tell me so when he spoke about this . . ." when undesired results occasionally but predictably show up, very contrary to some people's expectations.

Dispensing advice in this balanced way is very applicable in our professional relationship with customers, irrespective of our trade.

Empathy and awareness of the other person's needs will help steer us safely through relationship's rocky shores, similar to the ones I saw in Costa Rica.

Sunshine and Service—An Exceptional Combo

The spring of 2010 saw my wife and I board a flight from Singapore to Costa Rica. We were traveling to attend an annual company event that rewards the best and brightest in the sales organization. Costa Rica is not a very popular destination among Singaporeans or, for that matter, even Asians. To get us there that February, Singapore Airlines had to weave us through the shortest route that takes thirty hours of flying from Singapore to a snow-clad and freezing Moscow, over cold and white Greenland through a wet and unusually chilly Houston, to the tropical Costa Rica.

The white wilderness en route was a sight to behold (it is unfortunately shrinking every year, thanks to the onslaught of global warming). We semi-circumnavigated the world and traveled from one equatorial location, Singapore, to Costa Rica, that also sits on the equator on the other side of the world. All in all, a long trip . . . now you know why Costa Rica is not a popular holiday destination in Singapore despite its amazing landscape.

The unending flying hours notwithstanding, a beautiful island greeted us. On its north Pacific Coast, in the Guanacaste province, lies a body of water called the Gulf of Papagayo. Twelve beaches that extend along the Papagayo land stretch form this Gulf. On the Papagayo peninsula's shores are incredible resorts like the Four Seasons (our host) that combine the outstanding beaches and natural environment with elegant constructions and outstanding recreation facilities both on land and water. Every part of the peninsula offers fantastic views of the Pacific Ocean and the warm waters of the Gulf of Papagayo.

I have been fortunate to experience natural beauty, luxury locales, and gourmet cuisine in some of the most exotic and attractive holiday destinations—Canary Islands, Hayman Island, Bermuda, the islands of Hawaii and so forth. While I have enjoyed each one of them, I have also been suitably spoilt and learnt to take them in my stride. The Four Seasons facility in Costa Rica provided all this as is normally expected from . . . well, the Four Seasons. What really did blow us away was simply the quality of service. Quality, that was definitely so head and shoulders above the rest that you cannot help but notice it. It is no wonder that the resort does roaring business, even in financially hard times. High-quality pampering justifies a premium at all times!

As we reveled in the cocoon of comfort and great service, I started to look out for the telltale signs that together gave the guest such an incredible experience of warmth, efficiency, and hospitality. As the traits began to show up, it was apparent that there are three that are a formula for success for not only this world-class resort but for any service organization or, for that matter, any organization. Let me try to explain these traits.

Being Discreetly Alert

You will often see some organizations trying almost too hard with their customer service routine. How many times have you been in a restaurant where the staff is constantly hovering over and around you watching every morsel on your plate like a hawk? If you happen to idle around with the food on your plate as you chat with your fellow diners, an over attentive attendant offers to whisk your plate away even if you are not done eating. You politely stop him from doing so, and it is not long before another attendant is enthusiastically trying to take away someone else's plate. Great service does not need to be "in your face" . . . on the contrary, it needs to be very discreet. It needs to connect with you and should show up when needed even without being beckoned. Every employee at the Four Seasons was a personification of discreet alertness whether they attended us in our rooms, the buggies that carted us around, in the coffee shop, or in the general areas—they showed up just when you needed them (often without even being beckoned) and simply disappeared when you needed to be by yourselves.

Professionally Competent

No service level can be high enough without knowledge of the service being offered. The Four Seasons' staff wowed us with intimate knowledge about the local cuisine, willingness to modify the recipe to suit our palates and even drop a neat envelope with the recipe in our rooms after we had ordered the same item in the menu a couple of times. They also possessed abundant knowledge of the local landscape, history of the resort, and the surrounding areas. They know the history of the country in specific detail and narrated it with such passion that did not conceal one bit the pride for the roles they played and the country that they belonged to. One of our remarkable experiences was a guided trip through one of the most beautiful golf courses I have seen—lofted tee boxes perched on elevated shelves of greenery on the hillside towering over rolling, closely cropped valleys that made up the fairways with the blue sea as a backdrop for most of the holes. What impressed us besides the natural beauty of the course was the local golf club head-pro—not for his golfing prowess alone but also for the passion and pride with which he educated us about the local flora and fauna in the tropical rain forest that envelops the golf course and Costa Rica in general. So there you have it: professional competence that "wows" is not only about knowledge but also the joy and passion with which the knowledge is dispensed.

Quality Adopted as a Culture

Service does not come out of a playbook, job description, or process. If these are the drivers for service, then the quality of service will at best be artificial, "in your face," unable to scale, and unsustainable. Genuine quality will only emerge when there is absolute commitment and pride to deliver "quality" within every employee at every level of the hierarchy to every customer. There is a deeper purpose and pride in delivering this level of service, which is beyond plain recognition and compensation. Organizations that want to deliver this level of quality and differentiate themselves usually determine this deeper purpose and weave high quality of service across the organization's fabric in the form of organizational culture that prevails over every rank and/or function. The organization's leaders walk the talk and set the tone for the rest of the organization to follow.

While I was proud of successfully lasting the grueling travel that had me spending sixty hours in the clouds, it was a memorable trip, a great experience, and a chance to meet wonderful people and experience their outstanding service.

I look forward to getting back to Costa Rica and to the Four Seasons. I am quite confident that the pristine resort and the "brand" that they have created around their "service quality" will be as resilient as the rocks that border the Gulf of Papagayo.

Next, lets take a closer look at what 'brand' means to you and me.

Personal Branding: Express Yourself, but Be Truthful

Social networks are virtually omnipresent. Unless you have spent the last five years out on the twin orbital moons of Mars or under a rock in the Sub Saharan wilderness, you will likely agree with me. Olivia Barrow at the *Dayton Business Journal* (*http://www.bizjournals.com/dayton/news/2012/12/17/top-15-most-popular-social-media-sites.html*) in December 2012 lists 750 million unique monthly visitors at Facebook, 250 million visitors at Twitter, 110 million at LinkedIn, 65 million at Google Plus, and 15.5 million at Pinterest. Add YouTube to this and you have a full-on social media barrage.

While most people on these platforms are finding joy in talking about the party last night, their latest vacation or how they long to get together with their partners or the newest flick in town or even how their dog is doing (and that's all fine), there is a much smaller community of individuals that is aware of how to utilize this medium for more productive and game-changing purpose of self promotion: enter "personal branding," perhaps the fastest-growing paradigm in today's workplace.

The workplace has grown hypercompetitive. The bastions of loyalty in the employer-employee relationship are faltering everywhere in the face of financial and performance metrics and shareholder expectations. Even in the land of lifelong employment, Japan, Justin Rubio of *The Verge* reported in October 2012 (*http://www.theverge.com/2012/10/20/3530236/sony-layoffs-retirement-minokamo-headquarters*) that "When Kazuo 'Kaz' Hirai, president and CEO of Sony Corporation, announced his 'One Sony' strategy to get the company back on its feet, he explained that the initiative would include a workforce reduction of up to 10,000 employees by the end of 2012, including closure of factories. Additionally, the company implemented an 'early retirement program' that affected approximately 2,000 employees by March 2013. The program is expected to reduce the workforce headcount by 20% at Sony headquarters alone."

This new workplace requires the employee to initiate individual ownership and control on their professional destiny—sounds fair? Instead of focusing on the organization, the division, or the function, how about building individual brand equity that focuses on the individual—a brand that snowballs, grows, and extends beyond the individual's current role or his organization and a brand that defines, projects, or promotes the individual instead? If all this sounds strange to you, or even seems like an act of vanity, it is not. Most, if not all, of the new generation workforce that is showing up for job interviews are very comfortable in doing this, and the people who are interviewing them are okay with this. These candidates are not taking anything (including loyalty rewards) for granted.

In the past months, I found opportunities to discuss the merits and pitfalls of these personal brands in the workplace at a few executive forums. My career has required me to be involved in placements and career mentoring, and I've seen examples of people in the workplace failing at fully attaining their potential because of an inability to properly understand, develop, articulate, and play out their personal brand consistently over time. Be it a young professional who is too overreaching, a company loyalist with more credibility than self-esteem, or even the overbearing and coercive micromanager who somehow believes that he is a charismatic leader—many people have trouble being honest with themselves and the people around them, about who they are. The result is a presentation of the self that is inaccurate and often a misrepresentation.

Developing a real sense of who you are, what you stand for, and what you contribute in a workplace environment is a monumental task. Playing it out consistently for the world to see and trust is even tougher.

Understanding Who You Are and What You Give

When I see an individual who is able to accurately interpret, express, and demonstrate his or her contribution to a situation, I know that I'm looking at someone who has the clarity of mind to succeed. This attribute is all the more important when we introduce ourselves to others, be it online or live.

Making a good impression is essential, but maintaining the honesty of the self with others is a more important asset. As so much engagement, association, and business moves into the virtual realm—as we set up shops, conduct virtual meetings, and perform cross-cultural business interviews via online collaboration platforms like Go to Meeting and Skype—we have to understand that being authentic, credible, and self-aware of our strengths and shortcomings across virtual platforms is critical. More so because the people involved are not in physical proximity.

Authenticity Is the Real Lynchpin

I ask of you, if you're commencing a personal brand campaign, to be honest with yourself and with the communities that you interact and engage with. Be willing to consistently maintain and monitor your contribution, your aspirations, and your value in the community that you are connecting with.

There are two words that I think worth defining here: authenticity and humility.

Most of us understand that accountability and integrity in life are part of how we develop a reputation and a relationship with our family, friends, superiors, peers, subordinates, and customers. As we develop our personal brand (online and in the real world), let's be aware that our ability to deliver what we claim will shape the image others have of us. This external image is "our" real personal brand—not the image that we craft for ourselves. It takes a lot of hard work and time to build and a bad move in a nanosecond to demolish. What should keep us all sober is that any small slip or any undesirable news will get amplified manifold and will move very rapidly in the online world of Social Networks—we are way more exposed than we imagine.

Understanding our contribution, our workplace value, and relating this practically to our aspirations (what makes us tick) is a critical link. This is *huge*. Think about it: if you're being considered by someone who engineers the workplace environment to fit into a function—and you are able to, with clarity and humility, make known your capabilities and your potential and have a fair sense of the value of your contribution—you can make that person's job much easier, assuming that you can accurately deliver what you say you can. The same is true in developing an online personal brand; the virtual world is really no different. Coworkers want capable but humble contributors, supervisors want subordinates who possess "quiet confidence" and clearly understand and deliver the value they bring to the table rather than loudmouths who cannot deliver what they claim, and customers want authenticity. So craft your brand with utmost care—do not go overboard and self-destruct in plain sight of everyone. Beware of the flip side as well—an "overdose" of humility is not warranted either—it represents us incorrectly and "shorts" our opportunities. Let's find the right balance—let's just be what we "really" are.

Putting it Together

Understanding social media platforms and determining ways of using creativity and drive in the development of our personal brand for career success using these platforms is up to us. You really have to take the bull by the horns when it comes to being aggressive about this exercise. Be willing to visualize and strive for achievements over and beyond your past feats (you'd like to be more successful that you are today, right?). Visualize your career roadmap to set your track, but assess and communicate your current position with clarity and honesty.

The implications of the importance of honesty in personal branding go far beyond the workplace. We all lead busy lives, and at times, we have to be very careful about overscheduling. The impulse to help—at our kids' school, at our church, or even in something as simple as helping a friend move—can lead to personal brand problems if we don't follow through on our image as we project ourselves. Showing ourselves as a compulsive do-gooder to people around us and then failing to deliver on that expectation more times than one will be seen as an unreliability of the brand—reputations can be damaged and, depending on the severity of the fallout, be viewed as an outright act of dishonesty.

A relevant and notable example of the implosion of a brilliant personal brand is that of Tiger Woods and his troubles of the past few years. Woods had represented himself in a specific light (a role model, a faithful husband, a champion laser-focused on being the greatest golfer who has ever lived), but part of that image turned out to be quite the contrary. Consequentially, his brand and career took a resounding bashing—very apparent from his tour play ranking, the lost endorsement deals and more importantly the lost admiration of many of his fans.

Now, just a few years later, much of the damage to Tiger's brand has been carefully reconstructed, and he himself has worked phenomenally hard on and off the course to make that happen. In the end, it's not "who Tiger Woods really is" that offended and disappointed people. It's that people object to the misrepresentation of "who he really was and was not" that created the dent in the brand. I have the utmost respect for Tiger's golfing prowess that has taken him to the pinnacle of professional golf and created a vibrant industry and following in the process. The fact that he could elevate his game to the level he did for years despite all the "distractions" off the course makes him an even greater player in my mind purely from that perspective. I am very happy to see how through grit, discipline, and his innate golfing skills, he rebound and led the FedEx Cup leaderboard through the first half of 2013, a summation of all PGA tour outings (as I write this). However, even a sporting genius of his caliber was not spared for not doing justice to his brand!

People will need to be convinced about your past and present to be able to trust your future.

Here are some great resources for picking up ideas and momentum to build your personal brand online:

- Dan Schawbel's Personal Branding Blog
- Seth Godin's LinchPin from DuckTape Marketing
- The Personal Branding segment in my blogsite: www.debdutta.com

Strategy and Tactics: Jekyll and Hyde

Venturing into adjacent markets that are related to the core business is a natural act for most organizations as they grow. These invasions into adjacencies need strategy, preparation, and tact. They also require skill and infrastructure that may be unique to this new market segment.

In 2011, our business expanded into an adjacent market that was lucrative in terms of the potential share we could grab of the TAM (Total Addressable Market). We invested in the product, partnerships, and people. We also hired a leader who would lead our team and set the tone and momentum in this line of business (LOB). He was a precious catch in terms of time and effort spent on headhunting him, so once he agreed to come on board, I decided to invest another hour in talking to him one more time before he signed the paperwork. We discussed the organization, opportunity, role, broad strategy, and the likely pitfalls. I wanted him to sign up with his eyes wide open. He got it, and I was happy.

When he started, I handed him a thirty-day checklist. It is something I have done with all my direct reports ever since I first became a manager. It is a simple check sheet that enables new employees to understand the immediate priorities and people related to their role. It provides them with a baseline to start from, understand core objectives, and navigate through the maze and distractions that most corporations present while building their "own go-forward plan" at the end of the thirty days.

Three days later, our new LOB leader sat in one of my weekly revenue cadence calls. This is a weekly routine where members of the geography leadership team and I speak individually with the regional/country sales leadership to determine the revenue, margin, and profitability forecast by region for the quarter as well as risks, opportunities, competitive dynamics, and assistance needed. The new LOB leader sat quietly through the session. Toward the end of the session, my eyes darted toward him; he seemed shell-shocked. It was clear to me that something was wrong, so I invited him over to my office for a chat as soon as the review calls were done.

He was frank and honest and told me that he was simply blown away by the level of detail that we delved into. He could not imagine that a business approaching half a billion dollars would ever be run this way. He definitely had not seen this in the large organizations that he had been employed by or by the people who ran those organizations. The reviews that he was accustomed to were more "philosophical". I decided right away that he deserved an explanation of why we do the things the way we do.

Business is an interwoven fabric of strategy and tactics. Like Jekyll and Hyde, they are two correlated personas of the same being. A strategy is a broad plan of accomplishing an end goal. Strategy emerged from the Greek word *strategos*, which means the "art of the general." Tactics originated from the Greek word *taktike,* which means, "organizing the army." In modern jargon, the usage of these terms has extended well beyond warfare. Strategy paints the big picture; it makes broad assumptions and draws broad conclusions. It is the 30,000-foot view of the world as it is today and what it needs to be. Tactics, on the contrary, are the short-term responses (many of them quite mundane) that will actually deliver the strategy. They are essential for weeding out the "Devil in the details" of the journey. Regardless of whether you are an individual contributor or a leader, the principles remain the same. To obtain top-class results, individuals and teams will have to rapidly alternate between strategy and tactics to ensure that the desired outcomes for each are being achieved.

Strategy is exciting. It is a theoretical exercise that involves doing new things that will deliver the results that are set out within the strategy. It is often about building something new. It is about disrupting. It is about determining what to do without actually doing it immediately. That's why people feel comfortable with it. Tactics, on the other hand, are all about execution and seeking, collecting and analyzing feedback. You keep looping this sequence till the end goal of the strategy is accomplished. It is the routine, often mundane, activities that must be undertaken in each functional area to provide the results that the strategy assumes or predicts. There is constant measurement—naturally, everyone gets uncomfortable with it.

Our weekly business cadence calls that I explained earlier are downright tactical. They are all about inspecting, judging, and refining execution of the strategies that we collectively build in delivering the goals that the global organization has set for our geography. You see, strategies are built with certain assumptions—some of these are quite broadly set. It is when you actually move to real-life maneuvers that you get to realize the real impact of the strategy. Examining the results closely enables the further refinement of the strategy that often dramatically alters the future outcomes.

To take yet another example from sport, your basketball team's strategy may be to stifle the opposition's offense with a superior man-on-man defense. The tactics applied will have to do with having the right defensive players in the right place at the right time and with the right skills to negate the skills of the opposition once the game is on and the team starts executing. The formulated strategy makes certain assumptions about the skill level of your defense versus the skill level of your rival's offense. If (hopefully early in the game) you find that this assumption is not valid (their offense is running circles around your defense), then it's time to use that tactical feedback to make in-line adjustments to your strategy (possibly by switching to a zone defense).

And there's no doubt—as those of you who are parents have learned—this principle applies at home as well. If your strategy of cajoling your children or promising rewards to do their homework on time is consistently failing during implementation, it's time to accept the tactical feedback and adjust the strategy (many find that taking the Xbox or the iPhone away does wonders). When a specific carrot has not worked, it's time to modify the carrot or even consider a switch to the stick to arrive at the desired outcome. In the old adage, the specific form of the carrot and the stick used is tactics. Approaching the problem with an eye toward persuasion or coercion is strategy.

Do you see the linkages now?

In any sales function, "cold calling" or identifying new customer interest is a key measurable tactic that is crucial to any revenue-linked strategy. Most sales people unfortunately shirk it because it seemingly involves rejection and loss of self-esteem. I have a different take on it that I shall share in the next chapter.

Standing Tall While Cold Calling

I often hear salespeople grudging cold calling. Not just salespeople—ask anyone to step up and engage a stranger in a conversation, let alone give them a proposition of any sort, and they have the jitters. It's human nature. We seek comfort within the known. Venturing out into the unknown with a high probability of being rejected is brave enough. Going further and making a positive impression, getting the attention, then influencing the person to part with money and actually buy something is indeed a tall order.

Cold calling is not easy, and I have not met many who have raved about how much they enjoy it. Meeting new people is probably okay but meeting them and selling them something—not many takers. So let's get the baseline right: cold calling is a must, and every successful salesperson or entrepreneur in any field goes through the grind as they build their turf. In the daily calendar, set aside some time for cold calling and get comfortable with it. Irrespective of how rich your pipeline or account list is, it is wise to protect your targeted customers against tangible and intangible risks. The best way to do it is by *growing* it—and I cannot think of any other better way than constant cold calling.

OK, let's expand this a little further: we shouldn't suppose that cold calling is just the realm of the traditional salesman or the entrepreneur trying to market his gizmo. It's a critical skill for most of us. Are you responsible for raising funds for your child's school? Are you a budding sports pro seeking out an agent or sponsors who will believe and invest? Are you trying to raise capital for your dream business or seeking a loan without collateral or even seeking a job? Most of us will have to become at least competent at cold calling if we are to succeed at getting that donation, sponsorship, project investment, or the coveted job.

Now that I have stated the things that perhaps you will not be happy with, let me also give you some good news. Cold calling actually becomes easier (and even fun, trust me) as we gain in confidence, experience, and have some wins under our belt. The quicker we learn the skills and garner the wins, the quicker the fun begins—so how about we spend some time and learn this game.

Start with the premise that it is okay to be fearful of doing something. Going ahead despite the fear is what bravery is all about. We naturally dislike asking for something from people, especially strangers. Whether they are a stranger or someone we've known for a long time, it often feels like asking for a favor, even a feeling of servitude. It is best avoided if possible. That feeling is the basis for our reluctance. A favor is asking for something without giving back; servitude automatically lowers our self-esteem. Therefore the discomfort. But cold calling isn't a favor. It's an offer of tangible value you are providing against a sum of money. This is a transaction that you are seeking, and the key is to communicate that value during the meeting. A value-for-value proposition (your services for money) is a win-win relationship, not a favor! And, by no means is this servitude.

The basic human fear that comes into play is the fear of rejection. So let's plan our effort in such a way that you stay clear of rejection as much as possible:

- Do your homework—I like to choose my cold calling target prospect based on all available data regarding the "most suitable customer profile" for my product or service. I seek advice and guidance as needed to fine-tune my search and avoid wasting time.
- I prioritize prospects who are introduced by an existing customer, a close friend, or an acquaintance—this makes the interface a little easier.
- I like connecting on the customer's turf (learn and talk about his business) rather than mine. Norb Vonnegut of the *Wall Street Journal* (*http://online.wsj.com/article/SB10001424127887324244304578472734232188750.html*) narrates this fascinating learning from a memorable cold call where he earned the attention and finally the investment account of a loaded ex-office supply business owner who had cashed in. To differentiate himself as a financial broker, he narrated the difference between a UB-120 BK and a UB-120 BLK pen (well known to an office supplier) during a cold call and challenged the prospective client that no Wall Street broker could do so. He says, "I learned the importance of connecting with prospects on their turf—rather than demonstrating my knowledge of Wall Street. Don't get me wrong. There's no need to get divorced in order to call on divorcees. No need to write machine language code or design application specific chip sets in order to sell to Silicon Valley clients. My (education or professional) background was immaterial. Later, I studied optical networking and other sectors to broaden my client reach."

- Know your stuff as well. Once you have the prospect's attention, we should be able to articulate our offering and gain our prospect's attention first and then, his trust and respect. This helps cement a relationship and makes the journey ahead easier. Let's not worry now . . . in most cases, you should know more about your product than the person you are pitching to. So relax!
- I have learnt to make the prospect continually comfortable; engage in a dialogue instead of a monologue. I get to know the person: their likes and dislikes, current challenges, goals, personal wins, concerns/risks, and needs. The more I know, the stronger my position will be. Every prospective customer likes the attention he is getting from me—more so if I make him look smart to himself or, more importantly, to his boss.
- I am sensitive to my prospect's time or the lack of it. He should want to meet me again—not get rid of me in the future.
- Do not spill your entire value proposition in the first meeting—keep some goodies for subsequent encounters. A well-crafted movie trailer is often more impacting than the movie.
- I like working toward building a solution that addresses the prospect's problems rather than trying to sell him a product.
- If through my interaction I determine that the prospect genuinely does not have a need for what I have to offer, I acknowledge it, let him know, and walk away. Stay in touch, and be assured that you will be contacted when the time is right.
- And finally, I never argue or vent negativity during a cold call in a way that shows the customer in a poor light. This is perhaps the easiest way to shoot us in the foot.

These are the cold calling beliefs that shaped my approach. Not that I was ecstatic while doing it, but, I did it; sometimes I got rejected, but in other instances, I built long-term relationships that serve me even today. I learned to brush off the rejections, knowing that they were not rejections of me as a person, but that the person on the other end of the line or on the other side of the table had no need for the benefit I was offering at that time. Knowing how to deal with the unknown and turning virtual strangers into trusting customers and friends slowly grows on you. It gets to the point where it begins to actually tickle you and give you a natural high, all the while helping you build the strong platform of self-confidence on which your successful professional career will stand.

Actions we try to avoid are often not all that bad after all. What informs our experience of potentially uncomfortable tasks is the emotional frame we build around them. If we set out with the knowledge that the benefit we are offering (a new technology, the opportunity to help a good cause, etc.) is defensible, then a rejection is not a criticism of *us.* It's merely a statement that the person we've offered it to hasn't understood the benefit (and you can use that feedback to improve your approach in subsequent calls) or that the offer just isn't right for them at that specific point in time. They aren't saying "no" to who we are but to what we are proposing. And that understanding is most of what's needed to keep going, to improve, and to enjoy the process all along.

Whatever your 'vision' for professional success is, cold calling on people and showing them your skills, value or other propositions will be an important part of making it happen. You may as well have fun while doing it.

Driving Organizational Vision

Organization, department, and even team visions are hugely instrumental in providing guidance, momentum, passion and excitement to operating teams. The same principles apply even for families. A vision can range from a grand organization-wide shift to a focused department initiative for revenue growth, expense optimization or new business development, or a family's desire to determine its core values or plan college funds for the teenage family members. The principle of unfolding the vision will be the same, though the scale and complexity will vary.

If many chefs in a kitchen or surgeons in a surgery concern you, then you get a good feel of what too many visionaries or visions can be for a smaller team or an organization. Visions are not piecemeal constructions, and too much fiddling with them can undermine their value. A pile of sticks does not make a tree, and many good ideas don't necessarily add up to a coherent vision.

The ability to conceive and build a vision is a specific capability, not a general skill. Translating the vision into specific short-term measurable goals and actions and then laying out the implementation path is another competency. Thereafter, leading and participating in the tactical implementation of the vision and delivering predictable results is the third mutually exclusive competency. I have seen these skills demonstrated by three very different profiles of people. However, I have seen exceptional circumstances within small groups where the same individual demonstrates two or even all these three competencies.

I am laying this out up front because for the successful implementation of a vision, all these three roles need to be understood, differentiated, and used. Ownerships and accountabilities need to be set for each of the roles—do this and see the vision unfold into real-world results!

The vision is conceived by the proverbial "visionary" (let's call this individual or group "A"), normally the head of the operating group—this is a very macro view that lays out the broad-based direction the leader(s) wish the group to take based on individual, borrowed, or collective judgment or a mix of all three. The vision at this stage is usually skeletal, possibly oversimplified, and can be usually understood by a selective few who are either closely associated with the working and thinking process of the leader(s) or involved with the core functions of the group (let's call them Team B). Two concrete examples are the genesis of the iPhone and Oakland A's manager Billy Beane's approach to recruitment in Major League Baseball. (This is discussed in greater detail in another chapter of this book, and this was the basis for the book and film *Moneyball.*)

The initial vision of what the iPhone could be and how it would not only transform and dominate the contemporary mobile phone market but also create a new market was the brainchild of Steve Jobs and Apple's design maverick Jonathan Ives. Design details and implementation were then handled by the B and C Teams (Team C is described later in the chapter), but the vision remained intact despite market wisdom that a handheld computer hid inside a mobile phone had no place in the market.

The statistical approach to recruitment that Billy Beane applied to the Oakland A's baseball team was his own, and it experienced resistance from the B and C teams. In the end, the Oakland A reached the playoffs in 2002 and 2003 against teams with much larger budgets for hiring talent.

It is very risky to spill this unbaked vision outside of Team B. The unbaked vision can send wrong signals to the rest of the fraternity; it can de-focus people from their immediate responsibilities or simply confuse them regarding the relationship of the new vision to their current way of doing things. So do ensure that the broader team is insulated from the new direction until the vision has the full support of the organization, is fully baked, and can be communicated safely to Team C.

Having people with competencies in translating the vision into specific tactical short-term measurable objectives and laying out the implementation path come in handy at this time. This is usually contributed by Team B. Team B articulates the "why" behind the vision and provides meat to the initial skeletal structure. They also lay down short-term goals and metrics that will be implemented by usually more than one functional group. While doing this, Team B should explain the rationale of each goal and metric in a manner that the downstream teams will understand and find it easy to adopt. They also prepare plans and methodologies on how these function-specific goals and metrics will be sold to the downstream functional leaders first, who will then communicate this to their teams (Team C).

This stage requires overcommunication between A and B as well as B and C-Team leaders as the vision starts to settle in. New visions also introduce change that Team C members normally resist, and the intensity of resistance grows as you go down the hierarchy. Complement this by reinforced top-down communication, and document and broadcast best practices demonstrated by the early adopters while highlighting and rewarding the early wins or proof points. In parallel, also take in feedback from rank and file, especially on what is *not* working. These often prove more valuable than they apparently seem and ensure that the vision gets further fine-tuned to deal with the real world. The rolling out the vision to Team C plan also includes relating the new activities that emerge out of the implementation of the vision to the current roles, responsibilities, and compensation of those involved. If changes are needed, this is the time to do so rather than leave it till later.

Very often, the vision does not have a bearing on Team C's immediate objectives. This can be a potential melting point that needs diplomacy, communication skills, tact, and most importantly, courage from Team B and Team C leaders to help align. Exceptions regarding compensation (where absolutely needed) should be considered for specific pivotal roles that are critical for the success of the implementation, especially within Team C.

Once Team C has bought into the vision, implementation commences. Team B and Team C leaders need to be very vigilant during this phase and ensure that the goal completion and related metrics are on track. Constant feedback to leadership and the participants is recommended. More importantly, they should continually do the checks and balances to ensure that A's vision or Team B's implementation path is realistic and achievable based on feedback from the trenches. I recommend periodic, methodical communication between teams A, B, and C to accomplish this.

Often, adjustments and modifications early in the implementation process based on fresh internal assessments or even competitive circumstances result in a more impactful realization of the vision. Conversely, I have seen many an implementation turn lackluster because the teams did not consider changing external and internal circumstances while implementing the vision that was originally conceived in a different time and place.

Assuming the implementation is going fine, constant periodic feedback to the team is still recommended till the goals that the vision aspired to start showing. At this time, the leader ought to announce the accomplishment of the immediate goal to everyone involved, lay out the learning, and formally conclude the (shorter-term) exercise. Do not forget to celebrate success thereafter and reward or recognize the high achievers.

For long-term organizational-level visions, short to mid-term goal-setting, performance measurement, feedback, adjustment of the vision, communication of progress, and reinforcement of the vision to all involved are crucial ingredients that keep the vision alive and the teams fired up.

I do not want to conclude this piece without touching on execution of a vision within the family. Setting a vision helps the family bond and come together on a common set of virtues. Unlike an organization, or even a social group, it is conducive they give everyone in the family Team A, B, and C categorization—meaning everyone gets to play all the roles, rather than have the parents typically play the Team A "visionaries" and the children playing Team C. Sharing the roles among the family members improves self-esteem, responsibility, and a sense of equality and collaborative participation among the family members, especially adolescents and teens. They are tomorrow's parents and workplace professionals anyway—give them the responsibility they deserve or need to prepare for. Once the vision is architected, implementation of the family's vision requires as much care, commitment, and diligence as a Fortune 500 corporation seeks.

Once you've mastered your vision, it's time to construct the mechanics of goal setting.

Goals Setting—Does Stakeholder Participation Make Sense?

In my role of business leadership, things begin to really heat up as the year end approaches. The feeling of accomplishment in the past year, the excitement of the coming year, the rum-laden fruitcakes, and the wine and chocolate hampers that go around to be shared with friends and family, the festivities, and the endless parties . . . the year end is a simply wonderful time for all.

Closing the year with business revenue, margin, share, productivity, expenditure, and profit goals accomplished is a fabulous feeling. However, while striving to do so, it is commonplace to be bombarded by the incessant flow of data requests and submission deadlines for setting the goal for the next year. In my early days as a people manager, I would be grossly offended by this "distraction" related to next-year planning when closing the financial year seemed like the most important thing on the planet to me. Over the years, I have wised up as I began to appreciate this other activity.

At year-end, we are typically in quarter four, that is, three quarters would have come and gone, and unfortunately, those results will not change. Even the fourth quarter is mostly done, and depending on the nature of your position and your business, you might have minor influence on the final results at that point.

The following year, on the other hand, lies ahead like the proverbial blank sheet of paper. You can (based on your position) at least partly determine what your individual, team, or organization's footprint will look like on that brand-new surface. Does that not warrant some time, reflection, and attention? The choice is clear, right?

The planning exercise for the following year usually has a quantitative component (revenue, margin, share, capex, opex, etc.) and a qualitative component (initiatives, go-to-market, coverage gaps, partnerships, marketing, resources, skill development, and infrastructure). Make no mistake: both are equally crucial. Most organizations focus unduly on the quantitative element while the smart outfits get the operating teams to focus on the quantitative planning and goals to determine the "what" while the qualitative planning provides the "how."

It is unfortunate and alarming that most organizations spend very little time planning and, more specifically, socializing the next-year goals with the broader set of people who are expected to deliver those goals. That said, it is within every leader's prerogative to socialize quantitative and qualitative objectives for the following year with some relevant people within the team after familiarizing them thoroughly with the overall organizational objectives and the environment that surrounds it.

Socializing goals bottom-up leads to three specific values:

1. It creates a sense of belonging, individual value, and pride within the team, a feeling that their judgment and opinion matters in the organizational context;

2. It brings unique feedback from the trenches, which leads to the creation of potentially new initiatives, strategies, and mindsets to tackle the upcoming annual objectives;
3. Seeking feedback on quantitative goals provides an avenue to do the necessary check and balance to determine whether the quantitative goal is within the practical zone and whether it can be attained.

While setting quantitative goals, I have preached a bottom-up and a top-down approach. A bottom-up approach is fair because it provides the downstream participation and perspective based on several influencing factors that are visible at the field level. A top-down approach sets out the organization's quantitative and qualitative expectations that the shareholders and the board seek. This is without specific bias to a territory or a business line. Both are welcome in determining what goals need to be set. The final rollout needs to be top-down after both the inputs have been considered.

In seeking bottom-up feedback, it is crucial that the right expectations are set with the contributors—think like a shareholder of the company and size up the opportunity you possess correctly. If the final decision on the goals differ significantly from your bottom up outlook, you and your judgment obviously will not look good. Be aware that the quantitative goals that you will be ultimately expected to work on will be determined with the consideration of many data points, including the ones you provide. Doing some preparatory work by engaging with the stakeholders who will contribute the top-down data, empathizing and understand their mindset, and understanding the psychology, goals, and priorities of senior executives are smart ways to plan for bottom-up submission to ensure alignment. Ultimately, the top-down and bottom-up results might differ slightly.

If the deviation is large, then this signals gaps in understanding, assumption, and representation. Fix these quickly, or better still, work in a manner that this does not happen in the first place. The right expectations upfront allow people to go through the exercise with the right mindset and prevent any potential heartburn downstream.

I am preaching for a commitment for involvement here—with reason in lieu of coercion, collaboration in lieu of conflict, and participation in lieu of alienation in every stage of the next-year planning process, whatever the state of quarter four may be.

Good goal setting improves probability of good execution, which then leads to good results. The Formula 1 races in Singapore is a great example of this . . . read on.

F1 Singapore, 2008—Super Show, but What Does it Take?

The 2008 inaugural F1 night race placed Singapore on the map as a world-class destination for high-visibility global events. The practice runs, the qualifying round for the pole position, and the grand finale were executed with the finesse that is associated with any F1 event. The infrastructure and the event execution was equally flawless in supporting the event in its first year in front of a 130,000-strong on-site audience and 500 million television viewers worldwide. Fantastic.

Local outfits did brisk business and enjoyed brand visibility despite a rather gloomy macroeconomic environment. Compliments go out to lead sponsors, Singapore Telecoms, and everybody else associated with hosting the event. Following the kudos, Singapore has to continue to seek excellence by taking pages from city circuit venues like Monaco who have hosted F1 for more than seventy-nine years. Then do some more.

As a spectator at the event, I faced teething problems in transportation, extended roadblocks, seating coordination, and food outlets while the drivers had to contend with bumpy road surfaces and soaring track temperatures. With characteristic execution skills, Singapore has fixed most of these in subsequent years.

Singapore and all of us also have many a lesson to learn from the races: team Ferrari's debacle after taking two out of the three positions from the pole in the finals, then getting knocked out in the final run. Lessons like team coordination and collaboration or the lack of it can ruin the best-laid plans as Ferrari experienced during Filipe Massa's fatal pit stop.

Ferrari's Filipe Massa had established a comfortable lead when Renault's Nelson Piquet Jr. hit a trackside wall. The safety car was let out following a crash per the rules. Seeing that the safety car was out, Massa and the other leading contenders naturally used the opportunity to refuel. What followed was drama. Massa pulled away from the pit while the gasoline rig and hose was still attached to his car. As chaos erupted, a pit crewmember tumbled and fell as he tangled with the fuel hose. Massa was forced to come to a complete stop. By the time his team had untangled their colleague and pulled out the fuel hose from the Ferrari, Massa slid to the 18th spot in the race, from where he never recovered. To make things worse, he was given a further drive-through penalty for unsafe release because he almost collided with another car while leaving the pit with the hose. Such is the harshness of the F1 rulebook, quite similar to the rulebook of life.

This kind of error that relegates the leader from the front of the pack is commonly seen in life outside the rarified circle of F1 and is an excellent cautionary tale for progress and leadership. Massa was so eager to get back into the race that he neglected to assess his position, and it cost him the race. For the technophiles among us, this might be reminiscent of Microsoft's eagerness to jump into the mobile phone and music player markets. Starting from a dominant position in the desktop operating system and productivity space, Microsoft failed to properly assess the new market shifts in device form factors that mobility of the individual and mobile application platforms that Facebook, LinkedIn, and Twitter were bringing about. They raced onto the track, and the Zune and early Microsoft smartphones were similar to the gas hose that trailed behind and forced Masa to stop.

Victory can turn into defeat in a matter of moments; these are the great dramatic moments that we so love in books and in film but that are soul crushing in our personal and business lives. It's important to hold close the lessons that put us within reach of the win in the first place: preparation and situational awareness top among them. When Massa, intoxicated by his early success in the race, abandoned them, he also abandoned the win that he thought himself destined for.

The race also reminded us that opportunism and a positive spirit is a winner's best friend. Fernando Alonso of Renault stood with virtually no chance after the qualifiers but was quick to seize the opportunity as Masa faltered. He eventually won the race on Sunday under the gleaming neon lights, driving with grit and hope. This is a lesson that winning is not necessarily brought about by excelling individually but also by seizing the opportunities created by the opponents' shortcomings as ably demonstrated by Alonso, who was flagged off on Sunday virtually trailing the entire lineup.

All in all, it was an excellent demonstration of speed, discipline, and collaboration, and also the pitfalls and failures that so characterize us as human beings. It was a big win for Singapore and a big win for human innovation and spirit.

There are two lessons that I take away from this glittering event. Whether you are an organization, a society, or an individual, it is wonderful to demonstrate skills to the world, a gallery, or even a small audience—they need to know who you are and what you are capable of doing. However, once we choose to go on stage, the spotlight is on us. Every move that we make will be scrutinized by an extremely critical audience. With the various distractions that prevail today, any performance that borders on the ordinary will be quickly forgotten. So if we do decide to play for the galleries, let's play well with all the preparation that supported our successes up to that point—quite similar to what Singapore has done in hosting the Formula One fare.

Second, the best-laid plans can go wrong despite the planning and the preparation—as what happened with Felipe Massa and the Ferrari team. Despite the collective experience of the Ferrari team and days, months, even years of meticulous practice, Massa was involved in such a horrible mix-up that cost him and the rest of the team dearly. So part of our planning and readiness ought to be centered on recovery. How do we bounce back when the undesirable happens? Life is cruel at times, and it is smart to let go beyond a point, marshal our capabilities, and live to fight another day.

To return to the earlier example of Microsoft, it appears that bouncing back is not an arrow in their quiver. While the Kindle, Nook, Galaxy, and other Android tablets are attempting to steal market share from the iPad, Microsoft's Surface resembles the Zune more than the iPad-killer it was touted as. In July 2013, Microsoft announced that it was taking a $900 million charge on the product by writing off unsold inventory—this, against $853 million in revenue for fiscal year ending June 2013. Their woes continue. However, I admire the company's spirit to persevere. They have recently lowered the price of Surface RT tablets by $150, so they now retail at $350 and that of Surface Pro by $100 for selected markets as they brace themselves. They have also aired a new ad that takes a potshot at the iPad and hinted that upgraded versions of both Surface models are in the pipe.

(*http://venturebeat.com/2013/07/19/following-900m-surface-rt-writeoff-microsoft-launches-new-rt-ad-bashing-the-ipad/#7eOiy56wh DWV2ktS.99*). Microsoft's capability is unquestionable in the desktop software space. Nevertheless, their continual challenges to get a foothold in the mobile markets despite their cash holdings, patents, partnerships, and distribution network reach does make one wonder what they are missing out on.

Consistently perfect 'execution' is a rarity—even among the best organizations and people. However, it sure is a worthy goal to shoot for whether you're organizing an F1 event or managing a company or engineering your own future.

WYSIWYG—The Art of Perfect Execution

Those of you who, like me, saw the early days of the personal computer age will recollect the phrase WYSIWYG ("What You See Is What You Get")—Wikipedia dates the phrase back to 1982 coined by Larry Sinclair, an engineer at Information International, Inc., to express the idea that what the user sees on the computer screen is what the user gets on the printer using a technology called the "page layout system", a pre-press typesetting system. With WYSIWYG, the computer monitor screen started supporting capabilities to display serious graphics. The image on the monitor was close enough to the quality of the printout that the printer spewed out when you hit the print button. WYSIWYG implied the ability to directly manipulate the layout of a document without having to type or remember names of layout commands. Wow! This is still considered a milestone in the history of personal computing.

Technically speaking, WYSIWYG actually symbolizes innovations, inventions, progressions, and discoveries that have radically impacted our world, our civilization, our lives, and everything they hold. It also represents an intrinsic character that every successful individual represents. It is called the power of visualization: i.e. what you *see* is what you most likely *get.*

Rosa Parks boarded a bus for a famous trip on 1 December 1955, where she refused to give up her bus seat to a white person. Martin Luther King said, "I have a dream . . ." as he stood in front of 250,000 civil rights supporters on the steps of the Lincoln Memorial on 28 August 1963. Barack Obama took a five-year journey, which took him from being a civil rights attorney and a teacher of Constitutional Law at the University of Chicago—Law School—to taking up the mantle of the forty-fourth president of the United States of America. These incredible feats were based on rights, equality, freedom, and change. It started with someone visualizing about what the world ought to be rather than accept it as it is, and then the person took a small but historic step. Over the years, the vision broadened, taking into its fold other aspirations and the hopes and dreams of many more people. The vision then rapidly grew in scale and impact, feeding off the millions of people whose lives it touched and finally peaked on an early November day when history was rewritten as America elected its new president, a man of African-American origin.

I enjoy sports and do so because participating or even just watching top-class sportspeople fires me up physically and emotionally. I have read about and observed these greats and seen them focus on the incredible power of visualization. I have seen what their coaches take them through as they help them stay relevant in the highest levels of the game.

Whether it is golf, tennis, or other categories (especially individual sports), watch the intense gaze of these top pros between strokes as they go though their motions or even during a game break. Their eyes are focused, but the gaze seems to be far away, looking at nothing, totally insulated from the crowds and clicking cameras that surround them. They are actually playing out their next moves on a high-res mental video screen over and over. Seeing in the virtual world exactly what they are going to execute next in the physical world, soaking in it, feeling it, and feeling their muscles, bones, and ligaments respond exactly the way they expect them to. Then they step into the physical world, in front of the public glare and flashing cameras, take every conscious thought off their minds, and execute that mental video as accurately as they can. Sure enough, the result is quite close to what they visualized, if not better. I have tried this myself when playing, and depending on my preparedness and the quality of my commitment, I do get the result. The reliability and magnitude of the intended outcome is far more prominent when I test the same principle in my area of true competence—my workplace.

Why do these desired outcomes show up sometimes? Why not always? The key to successful visual results is preparedness. Trust me, I have come across many instances where I have seen trained professionals going out into execution mode without adequate preparedness, and that does not work, regardless of what our caliber and determination level is.

So here is how I see the construct of this philosophy—at the workplace, on the playing field, or in any other aspect of life. I dare to dream big in the area of my interest. I then commit myself by setting some personal goals that are clearly measurable (the more audacious the goal, the better it is. Of course, the goals need to be practical). Next, I make sure that I know the rules and boundaries of playing the game (in organizations, this is also known as operating procedure). Employee handbooks and functional operating guidelines are the normal sources—check these very carefully prior to launching into your drive. Being intimately aware of the rules enables me to take advantage of a specific rule or the lack of it while being fully protected from any form of non-compliance.

Next, I immerse myself in the act of gathering the core skills required to be successful in the function that I am in or to meet or exceed the goals that I have set. Once the baseline skills are met, I will seek out the incremental skills that will differentiate my performance from that of the others. This is where we start to create distance between the rest of the pack and us. While the core skills are usually documented and relatively procedural to build, the incremental skills are not. This is the reason why most people stay mired in mediocrity. An inquisitive mind, seeks out internal and external mentors, builds people networks, understands how adjacent fields work, and fosters a healthy reading habit. It builds a fine platform for incremental skill development. All these qualities are wonderful tools that are available to all of us.

I have noticed that top performers are comfortable in discussing subjects outside of their principal areas of competency. They can, in fact, relate the possible impact of these adjacent subjects to their own function. This broadens their horizon and understanding of their area of competence and makes them stand out in a variety of professional and social settings—a critical step for professional progress. On the contrary, the average individual's knowledge is limited. Even in what supposedly is their subject of competency!

The next step is . . . hard work. There are no shortcuts here, regardless of talent. The lessons learned and skills developed have to be pitched in every conceivable situation till they become a habit. Just like muscles need exercise to get toned, skills need to be practiced to get honed. Judge the results constantly—if the results do not match fair expectations, the exercise routine might need to be retuned. I can literally hear you say, "Easily said, but where is the time or the opportunity?" I totally agree that time is a rare commodity, but how you use it is up to you. You will need to make time for this if you want to win at this game.

The execution of the power of visualization will only work when your inner self is totally confident that you can faultlessly deliver what you have learnt. The only way to make this possible is when you physically repeat the action over and over again, be it presenting to a customer, writing a document, driving a golf ball straight and long down the fairway, or executing a slick cross-court volley at tennis. Relentless practice will make your mind and body absolutely rehearsed, composed and synchronised to deliver the desired outcome. Practicing over and over will also convince your inner being that you can do it. It gives the power to the mind to play the video of perfect execution, picking up pieces from the hard work it saw you do while you were building and rehearsing the skill. That's why practice is an irreplaceable asset—if the mind is unable to pick up an existing video recording of you practicing the skill over and over again with successful outcomes, then it is unable to play it back when you need it during the 'live' execution. After all, your mind is not programmed to play someone else's video. The larger your mental video library to borrow visuals from, the higher is your probability to execute perfection when called upon in the real world.

Assuming your skill gathering, experimentation, and practice are adequate, what unfolds next is brilliant. You stand in front of your audience, preparing to do what you are supposed to, and the eyes of your audience (customers, colleagues, friends, adversaries) are trained on you. You know your stuff and are fully prepared with countless hours of learning and practice. Now start playing that mental video right from your practice sessions. Then visualize the end result. You have delivered a brilliant performance in front of a captivated audience who have hung onto your every word, admired the construction of your logic, and have hugely benefited from the information that you have provided. As you close your session, your audience erupts in thunderous applause followed by handshakes, fist pumps, and high fives as you walk away from the podium.

Having completely soaked in the visual, next, take every other restraining thought out your head and execute in the physical world. You have done it.

I am doing the same here, visualizing that you will have benefited from the perspective of this chapter and reaping the enormous benefits of the technique that are rightfully yours. I am sure you have.

So lets take a break now and take a swig of the 'Fire Water' . . . Tequila!

The Art of Tequila at Work and Play: Lick—Slam—Suck

Without wanting to sound too presumptuous, I think most people slam tequila as a symbolic act to celebrate success, demonstrate machismo, and even as a means to get that quick headiness prior to heading for the dance floor.

Even at the workplace, the same pattern follows. Folks, often high achievers, start at new organizations or in new roles within their current organization, slam down a snifter of high adrenaline, and head out to the dance floor without looking out for oncoming traffic. Casualties are commonplace. Read on, and I will show you how the Art of Tequila showed me an important trail to workplace and leadership success.

In late November some years ago, I took in a 2,000-mile road trip up the California coast with a couple of colleagues from work. We called it the "Wild Hoggers' Drive." What is a drive through the coast of California worth without time spent in the breathtaking Monterey peninsula? I have always admired the region for its natural beauty that merges land, sea, and the sky. I am also drawn to the region's history and its standing as a center for art, education, and culture, dating back to the eighteenth century. The means by which tourism evolved in the region is also of interest to me. The fabled Del Monte hotel that played host to Theodore Roosevelt, Ernest Hemingway, and other Hollywood royalty of the day is still very much a part of the region's historical fabric. Today, it stands as the US Navy Post Graduate School, after the Navy requisitioned the hotel during World War II. Perhaps of greater contemporary interest is the hotel's park reservation, which was used for hunting and other outdoor activities by the hotel's guests. This hunting ground has now evolved into the Pebble Beach facility, an unincorporated community and a world-famous golf resort that annually hosts one of the most prominent golf tournaments in the world.

Somewhere on the trail, we chanced upon this Mexican cantina nestled in the gorgeous rolling hills of Carmel that lead on to the exotic waterfront of the Monterey Peninsula. (For the Clint Eastwood fans, he was the mayor of this city for a while and also sits on the board of the Pebble Beach Golf facility not too far away.)

Baja Cantina. 7166 Carmel Valley Road. Carmel. CA 93923
http://www.bajacantinacarmel.com/index.html
(Manager: Ian Penniman. Look him up if you are there; he is quite a character.)

Besides gorging on the fantastic Mexican fare of succulent meats on the sizzler, freshly toasted tortillas, gorgeous burritos and enchiladas, and my personal favorite, the chimichanga. I actually got an impromptu lesson on the art of tequila appreciation. So here goes . . .

Tequila according to the Wiki . . .

***Tequila** is an agave-based spirit made in the area surrounding Tequila, sixty-five kilometers in the northwest of Guadalajara and in the highlands (Los Altos) of the western Mexican state of Jalisco. Tequila is most often* *made at a 38-40% alcohol content (76-80 proof), but there are more potent types of tequila produced with 43-46% alcohol content (86-92 proof). It is a common misconception that tequila is fermented from cactus. Agaves and cacti are unrelated. The Aztec had previously made a fermented beverage from the agave plant, which they called Octli. When the Spanish conquistadors ran out of their own brandy, they began to distill this agave drink to produce North America's first indigenous distilled spirit. The tequila that is popular today was first mass-produced in the early 1800s in Guadalajara, Mexico.*

There are two basic categories of tequila: Mixtos and 100% Agave. Mixtos uses up to 49% of other sugars in the fermentation process, with Agave taking up the remainder. Agave sugar is fructose-based and is easier for the human body to break down. Mixtos uses both glucose and fructose sugars.

With 100% agave tequila, Tequila Blanco is harsher with the bold flavors of the distilled agave up front, while Reposado and Añejo are smoother, subtler, and more complex. As with other spirits that are aged in casks, tequila takes on the flavors of the wood, while the harshness of the alcohol mellows.

A Dummy's Guide to Drinking the Potion at Play and Work

Play First . . .

Where it comes from, Mexico, tequila is drunk straight, without salt and lime. In the most popular style of consumption, a single shot of tequila is often served with salt and a slice of lime, called "tequila cruda", and follows the "lick-slam-suck" routine. The drinker moistens the back of his or her hand below the index finger (usually by licking) and pours on the salt. The salt is then licked off the hand, the tequila is then slammed down the throat, and the fruit slice is quickly sucked. It is common for groups of drinkers to do this simultaneously. The salt lessens the "burn" of the tequila, and the sour lime fruit balances and enhances the flavor. Should you be drinking higher-quality tequila, this operating procedure does not work. Salt and lime remove much of the flavor of 100% agave tequila.

When served neat (without any additional ingredients), tequila is most often served in a narrow shot glass called a *caballito* ("little horse" in Spanish). The margarita glass, rimmed with salt, sugar, or plain is a staple for the entire tequila/fruit mixed drink genre, including the margarita itself.

Tequila—Meal Combination

Tequila is commonly bottled in three to five categories:

Tequila Blanco ("white") or ***Tequila Plata*** ("silver") or ***Tequila Oro*** ("gold")—This is a white spirit, un-aged and bottled or stored immediately after distillation. Else, it is aged less than two months in oak barrels. Jose Cuervo (the brand that you have most likely consumed if you have tasted this potion) is usually consumed as a cocktail or a pre dinner drink.

Tequila Reposado ("rested")—aged a minimum of two months but less than a year in oak barrels. Usually served with the main course in a multicourse menu. We tried out the Cabo Wabo from Sammy Hagar's (of Van Halen fame) distillery and actually fancied it more than his music. Check www.cabowabo.com.

Tequila Añejo ("aged" or "vintage") and *Extra añejo* ("extra aged" or "ultra aged") is normally aged between one and three years in oak barrels. This is the post-dinner cognac-category. Ian, our restaurant host, strongly recommended Don Julio 1942 (Premium vatted—five years from a numbered bottle) to titillate our taste buds and give us that warm, settling post-meal feeling, which it did incredibly well. *http://www.tequila.net/tequila_reviews/anejos/don_julio_1942_anejo.html.*

Lesson learnt . . . Tequila and its consumption is a fine piece of art that needs study and understanding similar to other fine forms of classical fermentation—wines and single malt whiskies. It is much more than a strong shot that needs to be slammed down to kick up the mood in hip nightspots with funky music playing in the background.

Now about Work . . .

Work life is not any different from learning how to drink tequila, as we get into a new organization or a new role.

Let's measure up the environment first and understand the moving pieces, the priorities, the influencers, and the personalities. Let's not rush to the "dance floor" first. Instead, let's determine the areas where we can immediately add value, seek buy-in from the primary stakeholders, be comfortable in our base, identify the leverage points, and then execute. This is similar to the process of downing tequila blanco. Make sure that you "lick the salt" to prepare the environment and level off the intensity of the new actions and changes that you will likely enforce. Next, "slam" it in and get into execution mode with resolve, commitment, and intensity. If change is involved, it needs to be introduced quickly; gradual changes are fraught with risks. Finally, "suck" in the results of your execution (like the sour lime you suck after downing the potion) to balance the outcome and enhance the flavor of the results. Constant communication with the rest of the team and candid feedback on what is working, what is not and what adjustments to the plan are being made and why are great flavor enhancers.

As you cement your initial wins and move to the next hierarchical level, your strategy should be more in line with the tequila reposado. You are more seasoned and so are your actions: you start to build long-term plans, a strong team, determine what you need to delegate, and what can happen if you do not do it. All the while you watch the near-term executions that you have delegated to the next level like a hawk—no misses here. As your successes line up, broaden up your stakeholder support. You are the primary conduit for your group to the rest of the organization: add value at both ends.

The next level is the tequila anejo territory—you have now attained "vintage" status in your role. You develop the long-term strategy for your unit that will eventually impact the broader organization, and you grow your people into bigger positions with broader responsibilities and build succession plans at all levels. You start planning your move to the next level while being fully committed in leaving your unit better than when you took it on.

Wonderful education from an exciting form of alcohol. Enough said . . . viva la Mexico.

Tequila Trivia

- There are over 100 distilleries making over 600 brands of tequila in Mexico.
- Over 2,000 tequila brand names have been registered. Due to this, each bottle of tequila contains a serial number depicting

which distillery the tequila was brewed and bottled in. Since there are only so many distilleries, multiple brands of tequila come from the same place.

- A one-liter bottle of limited-edition premium tequila was sold for $225,000 in July 2006 in Tequila, Jalisco, by the company Tequila Ley 925. The bottle is a two-kilo display of platinum and gold. The manufacturer received a certificate from Guinness Book of World Records for the most expensive bottle of liquor ever sold.
- In 2008, Mexican scientists discovered a method to transform 80-proof (40% alcohol) tequila into diamonds. This process requires heating the tequila to over 800 degrees C (1,400 degrees F) to vaporize the tequila. The tequila particles are then cooled and settled upon steel or silicon trays in an even, pure layer and then you have them . . . diamonds.

Sammy Hagar, rock star (singer of the bar anthem "Mas Tequila") and owner of *Cabo Wabo* Tequila, described tequila's stigma as, "The stuff that you go, 'I will never drink that as long as I live,' and you have gotten sick in college on rot-gut tequila." This image of tequila as the instigator of particularly egregious intoxication and *hangovers* is pervasive.

In music, singer-songwriter *Alanis Morissette* wrote an ode to tequila entitled "On the Tequila" for the *Flavors of Entanglement* sessions and says tequila has helped her balance things out in her life.

In the United States, 24 July is selectively in some quarters celebrated as the National Tequila Day. It is not a national holiday though.

Now lets get back to work and talk about the starting point . . . People!

Hiring "Great" and Hiring "Right"

Responding to those who suggest, "In a typical startup company, a manager may not always have the time to spend recruiting great talent," Steve Jobs (God bless his soul!), the enigmatic cofounder of Apple, said, "I disagree totally. I think it's his most important job. Assume you're by yourself in a startup and you want a partner. You'd take a lot of time finding the partner, right? He would be half of your company. Why should you take any less time finding a third of your company or a fourth of your company or a fifth of your company? When you're in a startup, the first ten people will determine whether the company succeeds or not. So each is 10% of the company. So why wouldn't you take as much time as necessary to find all the A players? If three were not so great, why would you want a company where 30% of your people are not so great?"

"When recruiting the top talent, ask yourself, 'Is this the best job opportunity this person has?' If you believe—really believe—the answer is yes, that person will end up working with you." When the company and the candidate have the same goals—perfection—the right hire will be made. (What the Recruiting Industry Should Learn From Steve Jobs by David Smooke (www.smartrecruiters.com))

Organization and team success and failures are mostly driven by a collection of people. Their experiences, talent, knowledge, and attitude all play critical roles in the result. A lack in one area cannot commonly be made up for in another. The best employees cannot do their best work if they are in the wrong position, wrong department, wrong organization, or have not received sufficient training and support.

A leader's capability starts with the quality of people the leader brings into the team and organization, as Jobs forcefully states. Hiring the right skills and attitudes not only gets the job done with minimal conflict while exceeding expectations but also frees up the manager/leader to use his or her intellectual and physical bandwidth on more impactful matters. Once supplied with a goal and a plan, an A-team should understand expectations, clarify doubts and/or concerns, and then be able to run itself and deliver the desired outcome, irrespective of where they are, irrespective of whether they are working independently or within a team or within the office or away from it. They do not need constant maintenance and guidance by their supervisor and deliver consistent performance, whether the supervisor is around or not. B and C-listers end up being high maintenance, taking up more of their leaders' time, delay schedules, and generally lower the morale and performance of the entire team.

Generally, education, skill, and capability levels may have grown in the community and the workplace, but this growth is not enough to meet the increase in the demand for these skills—organizations are competing more than ever for a relatively small talent pool. Hiring top talent requires the organization to get into the DNA of a prospective employee—find out what are the hot buttons that need to be pressed to get a top talent to join your organization versus your competitor. Well, differentiation is key!

Differentiate, Differentiate, Differentiate

Differentiation can take many forms: It is not compensation, in most cases. Work culture that promotes personal growth, exciting products, work-life balance tools, education support, and flexible work hours often are crucial differentiators. When Yahoo! recently eliminated the option for employees to work from home, the understanding across the market was that they were visibly giving up one of the standard fixtures of the modern-day corporation and standing apart from convention. I wait with interest to see whether this decision has any impact on Yahoo's end goal of growing revenue, profitability, share, and shareholder value. On the other hand, Johnson & Johnson's productivity-infusing, employee-friendly culture underlines the company's focus on the well-being of not just the employee but his family as well. Also, Google has spread in-campus meals, wacky work hard—play-hard—culture with workplace toys and recreation options. These choices have drawn and retained talent in these organizations and created financial and non financial results that are incredibly impressive.

Be on the Hunt—Always!

Given the supply crunch of top talent, I have always encouraged the teams I led to seek out talent as a habit all the time—even when there are no open positions to fill. In the hypercompetitive world of talent search, a search cannot start when you need to hire; by constantly meeting people, top talent is bound to show up. In some instances, the talent is so outstanding that it makes sense for us to create a position and find the budget just to get them in. If you were able to purchase a new, larger home in a better neighborhood at a low price, the fact that you are content with your current home isn't particularly an issue. The new home is larger, and it is a better investment at that low price. Spending more money on a better education follows the same logic; yes, it's more money now, but the downstream payoff makes it worth it many times over. Invest in top talent just as you would in any other lucrative asset with good underlying value.

Leverage Employees

Leverage your current employees while seeking talent. It's cheaper and more reliable to hire through internal references rather than looking out using external agencies. I have benefited by setting up financially attractive internal referral bonuses for the employees and by aggressively market the initiative internally. I have seen organizations where employees are unaware of this "easy money" because internal marketing is poor. If an internal reference leads to hiring, make sure that the employee who referred gets paid on time. Organizational credibility can be built or destroyed depending on how long it takes to respond to its commitment—in this case, getting the employee paid promptly. Many large companies fail to do this.

Make an Impression—Treat Candidates Like Customers

I try and make a "first class" impression about my organization and myself the moment I meet the candidate, whether internal or external. Don't take internal candidates for granted; sell the organization and the role to them as you would an external candidate, even though they are already familiar with it. Most candidate perceptions about organizations and individuals are made in the first thirty seconds following an introduction. Treat the candidate as you would treat a top customer, and watch the magic of the chemistry unfold.

Many hiring managers forget that the interview process is a two-way evaluation and are too intent to use their positional power as the hiring manager to "interrogate" the candidate—I do not think this is terribly smart. The best interviews happen when the people involved are relaxed and at ease—the environment brings the best out of both the participants. A candidate with a sense of having been interrogated will leave with an impression of the organization that you might not intend. Alternately, they might have good feelings for the company but will still reject the opportunity because of their impression of the hiring manager.

Make Onboarding Classy!

Believe me . . . everyone notices "class" when they see it and it is really worth it! Once you have hired the candidate, ensure that you have the right on-boarding procedure right from the time the employee shows for the first day at work. I have seen and heard of many established organizations with absolutely pathetic on-boarding procedures. Many do not have one! Often, pumped up new hires looking forward to an exciting stint in the organisation are led to mediocrity or worse because of the way they were treated during the first couple of weeks at work. New hires should feel welcomed, be clear about their role, and made aware that the department or the organization values their efforts.

Let's ensure that the new hire understands the on-boarding procedure, is guided through it by a nominated internal "buddy," and that the whole process is reviewed through a two-way communication at preset milestones and at the completion of the process. No one likes to be thrown into the deep end of the pool without having been taught how to swim, though this is all too common in organizations that should know better. The right on-boarding will bring out the best in the new hire and reduce the time to productivity. It will also help avoid a situation in which someone with promise and talent loses their motivation because they feel they haven't been welcomed and supported.

As critical as talent and experience are, the best new hires must also have the right attitude. A poor attitude can easily negate talent and experience, so it's important that candidates understand the way an organization works, and it's as important that the organization understands the way the candidate works. Someone who is comfortable in the driven, dog-eat-dog atmosphere of stock trading might not be able to adapt to an office setting in which collaboration is more important than individual achievement, and vice versa. This, again, brings up the virtue of habitual, proactive interviewing. A consistent, methodical habit of continually interviewing people creates a pool of candidates who are screened to fit the organization's culture. When a position opens, the hiring manager needs to merely dip into this ready pool. Most mismatches between individuals and roles/organizational culture happen when a hiring manager hires a candidate in a mad rush to fill the position. What follows is predictable.

Hiring Great and Right can start from the individual hiring manager. If that hiring manager is the CEO, then the culture spreads rapidly across the company like it did at Apple and A-players flock in. And rightly so because a company full of A-players makes the CEO's job easier not only in the good times but also when the "chips are down."

Leadership When the Chips Are Down

This is one of the earlier chapters that I had written. As things turned out, I like to think my predictions have been borne out fairly well since then.

The economic abyss that we are all in will eventually level off just like the eighteen recessions and the three depressions that have come and gone in the last 100 years. Meanwhile, organizations will face persistent uncertainty and will have to adapt to rapidly fluctuating fiscal and monetary situations. Anyone who leads in these times will be faced with the opportunity to demonstrate core abilities or the lack of them. Organizations that are used to regular home runs will also not be spared; big names like Lehman Brothers and AIG have already sunk in the dark choppy waters of 2008, and household names like GE and Citibank have taken a beating. This negative shift in paradigm will question employee and customer loyalty, security, operating budgets and everyday organizational decisions.

It is easy to find leaders who know how to cope with success rather than those who can cope with success and failure alike and still triumph. Knowing how to function during these times of uncertainty can help organizations maintain their leadership advantage, weather the immediate storms and emerge stronger in the process. This leadership doesn't only apply to a corporate environment and does not need to be demonstrated by an organization leader. The fundamental of stepping up and leading with intent during tough times applies to every individual in every walk of life. Every homeowner faced with the uncertainties of making the next mortgage payment, every student struggling to put together the next term fees will benefit from learning to manage themselves during tough times. This is a key weapon in every successful person's arsenal.

Make Caring People Decisions

Downturns normally herald missed revenue and productivity goals. As organizations review their financial statements, leaders are often tempted to scale down or eliminate employees and employee-development initiatives. While this may be necessary (not that I absolutely subscribe to them outside of sheer practicality), utmost care must be taken to communicate and implement the decision in a way that will still reinforce the organization's commitment to its workforce. If done poorly, it may seem like a "panic attack" to the workforce that can fragment the bonds of loyalty across the business.

Poor or un-weighted decisions at this stage can very adversely impact immediate priorities and have larger long-term ramifications. These unbaked decisions can also dent the organization's credibility. At the end, all these dark clouds will go away—the way in which the organization and its leaders have dealt with this period will largely determine how strongly the organization shines when the sun comes out.

Lead Well in Tough Times

Leadership is about rallying people behind shared vision, mission and goals through awareness, collaboration, accountability and empowerment.

It is about connecting human action with specific objectives and aligning people and groups to work together toward those ends.

In the midst of circumstances that spell fear, uncertainty and doubt, leaders are responsible to ensure calmness while providing clear guidance and directions to the teams that they lead. They are responsible for keeping the team focused on its immediate short to medium term objectives. The leader ensures that the team is on the lookout for changes in the circumstances, that requires them to reassess their course and flag any associated risks. The leader's ability to generate a collective feeling of belonging and accomplishment within the team is crucial.

Align Talent to Strategy

An organization needs to strengthen the link between its business strategy and its talent pools. The commander of the ship needs to consider: are short to mid-term commitments at risk due to lack of talent? Are the right people in the critical roles? How are they being retained?

Successful leaders focus their teams to address the short to mid-term exigencies. They question and closely review status quo while identifying and considering changes that need to be ushered. All this is best done by enabling collaboration between smart staffers rather than by an autocratic mandate. Collaboration drives buy-in, accountability and better execution.

The resurrection might call for attainment of multiple targets. This will demand a sense of balance. People will need to be explained the "why" and encouraged to find ways to determine how their goals can be connected without the need for a binary choice. Most leaders and teams struggle with this balance. While there is no perfect solution, the desire to question status quo, adopting a change in how things are, while aiming for the best possible solution for the current situation sounds pretty darn good to me.

If people layoffs are unavoidable, good leadership always sets progressive expectations to reengage retained employees. A leader starts to earn respect when they acknowledge and empathize with the pain and frustration of the cuts and ask teams what they believe are the top priorities during the time. Good results follow when retained employees feel themselves to be the "soldiers of resurrection" rather than consider themselves as "survivors".

Treat Employees and Customers Right

Know your people very well. Tough times (as goes the adage) bring out the best in many people. High-potential staffers and teams may step up sooner than expected. This is a time to help people learn from experience and to let the capable ones soar. This is the time to share the best practices that demonstrate the depth of the talent already on board.

Strong leadership retains top performers at any cost. Besides delivering the results, performers are capable of setting and driving the right attitude, mood, and tone across the whole organization. Get closer to these people, show your respect and support for what they are doing.

Customer loyalty is a precious commodity at all times—more so during tough times. Let's find proactive ways to anticipate what the customer wants as the environment, industry and markets change. Let's leverage technology and skill to make these changes faster than others. Reinvent the depth and breadth of the relationship with top customers by disrupting your own practices if need be, before your competitor does it.

Overdo the Communication

There is a reason why we have two ears and one mouth. Let's spend twice the time listening rather than talking. By the way, do not do both at the same time. Tough times require leaders to listen to their teams and provide them the right guidance, advise, encouragement and inspiration.

Communicate business challenges and expectations from the team with absolute candour. It is crucial to communicate even when there is nothing to communicate—employees are then reassured that communication channels are open. Forums to host collaborative discussions regarding the future state of the company spreads hope, a sense of belonging, and perceived continuity among the employees. These forums should also dispense best practices regarding employee collaboration, customer satisfaction, employee-driven initiatives, skills development and so on. This motivates the doers and educates the others.

Set a GPS for the Future

An organization becomes what its people and its leaders guide it to be.

Success happens to organizations despite uncertain circumstances and macroeconomic storms when there is proper alignment between the organization's business strategy and the . . .

- Internal or outsourced talent that it has access to,
- Relationship between the organization leaders, employees, and customers,
- Honest, clear and open communication within the organization.

As the dust begins to settle and the situation improves, the path to a fundamentally stronger future becomes clearer, so long as the leadership is in place when things are at their worst.

Who Bombed My Company? Preparing for the Inevitable

Many years ago, I started my journey as a financial investor by constructing my first investment portfolio. The "analyst DNA" in me (from my Economics and Finance courseware at college) helped. I also knew that I had to learn the game from the masters before fielding my hard-earned money. I picked up a Warren Buffet book at the airport during a business trip (like most budding investors do—check.) and read it from cover to cover, understanding most of Mr. Buffet's philosophy, if not all. As my knowledge grew, I learnt of Benjamin Graham (the man Mr. Buffet attributes his financial market education to) and his famous narrative, *The Intelligent Investor*.

These masters taught me the fundamentals of value investing and the art of profiting from market follies and disruptions rather than by participating in them. How do we identify and buy into "value" companies and invest in them for the long haul? How do we stay away from speculating in organizations and businesses we are not familiar with, irrespective of how lucrative their valuation and upside seem to be? How do we stop trying to time the market? How do we keep an eye to buying into and building a valuable portfolio when the price tag is low? How do we master seeking out option trades that most investors perceive as "risky"? There are many other anecdotes and advice that I have come to understand and appreciate. I actually followed up by reviewing Berkshire Hathaway's famed "Letter to the Shareholders" that Mr. Buffet writes every year. (*http://www.berkshirehathaway.com/letters/letters.html*).

Along the way, I got insight into the Mr. Buffet's own stock picks and other well-regarded recommendations, and then, feeling fairly well-covered, I put my money in the market.

Despite this guidance and attention, all my famed and well-researched blue chips were significantly down over the next ten weeks—partly due to the market's whims and partly due to my own! Mr. Buffet and Berkshire were not spared either. In the 2008 Letter to Shareholders, he wrote, *Our decrease in net worth during 2008 was $11.5 billion, which reduced the per-share book value of both our Class A and Class B stock by 9.6%. Over the last forty-four years, book value has grown from $19 to $70,530, a rate of 20.3% compounded annually. As the year progressed, a series of life-threatening problems within many of the world's great financial institutions was unveiled. This led to a dysfunctional credit market that in important respects soon turned non-functional. The watchword throughout the country became the creed I saw on restaurant walls when I was young: 'In God we trust; all others pay cash.'*

While I trust in God, Mr. Graham, and Mr. Buffet like the rest of the investor planet, I begin to wonder why these famed organizations that I trusted my money with actually failed to perform as the financial markets went south (which is inevitable eventually)? What can other established and upcoming organizations learn from them? Once you think about it . . . there are plenty of lessons.

All organizations are destined to face market disruptions and conflicting and negative internal forces at some stage of their evolution that will force them to take dramatic measures to survive and hold on to their positions of leadership. When this situation is coupled with larger macroeconomic slowdowns, the impact is amplified. Unlike the norm, I do not blame the management team alone when an organization falters, though this is easiest to do. The lackluster results are hardly because of a single wrong strategy that the leadership has implemented or a specific move of the competitor that the organization failed to see. Rather, the root cause is a sum of many different factors—inability to see a prominent market shift early enough (normally called a "disruption"), unwillingness to change the way of doing things, inability of hiring the right skills into the company, and the inability to see an emerging competitor who disrupts and changes the game for the incumbent market leader.

Let's be realistic: this will happen to every organization—not just once, but many times in the history of the organization. It will happen despite the skill, diligence, and track record of the management team—no exceptions. The forces that make these happen are far more diabolical than the people who are impacted by it. So the end game is not about prevention; it is about how to respond to these circumstances.

I see organizations and their leadership undergo knee-jerk reflexes, trying hard to do things that make them look effective in the short-term to their boards and shareholders. Sometimes these quick-silver reflexes work, sometimes they do not. However, given the choice, here is my pick of pointed actions by the leadership team when the going gets really tough:

- **Stay the course, show that you know what you are doing—** Demonstration of confidence is a "healer". It is natural for leaders to be concerned, but they need to face their troops, stakeholders, and customers with confidence. Confidence has to be communicated regarding their ability to deal with the situation, however bad it might be. While doing so, they can be vocal about what is unknown to them—taking this position does not weaken them; on the contrary, this makes them more credible and human. While committing to a course of action, constantly check outcomes and measure any variance with the expected results. If the variance seeps beyond a preset watermark, then review and re-chart the course, if needed, without delay.

- **Ensure consensus within the leadership team; consistent and extensive communication, both internal and external**—A classic type of fallout during a crisis is a flurry of misguided, disjointed activities by executives to demonstrate that there is "action". These actions are not products of collaboration or consensus and in many instances, are conflicting and counterproductive. Hard times call for stronger consensus among the leadership. Resources and time are scarce, more so in troubled times. It is absolutely ridiculous to squander this due to irresponsible and unsynchronized planning by management. Once leadership gets around the table and determines a common action, consistent and regular internal and external communication is a must. Constant, clear communication gives people the comfort that things are progressing and will hopefully be in control. Positive data, if available, heightens this optimism.

- **Focus on customers more than ever before**—Customers often make or break organizations. During the tough times, it is great to have customers help pull some weight and back the organization. Do not just be happy satisfying them; wow them out of their shoes. Knowing the situation that your organization and the economy is in, they will admire your gesture even more than they did during the sweet times.

- **Focus on areas of strength while fixing your gaps**—Despite crisis ushering a flurry of unorchestrated activities, the leadership has to agree on some key areas to focus the limited resources on. These done, a downturn is a great time to let the bottom open out to discard wrong products, processes and people. Eliminate the laggards that are preventing the organization from moving forward. This is as good an opportunity as any that will come along.

- **Find every opportunity to differentiate**—Leadership in revenue, margins and share is driven by differentiation. In a world where information is readily available, it is hard to do anything that someone else has not already done or is not in the process of doing. Yet, a Yahoo! happened despite an Alta Vista, a Google happened despite a Yahoo!, a Kik is happening despite Facebook, an iPad came along despite the failed legacy of the Apple Newton or the Microsoft tablet from a few years past, and the last I checked, the Samsung Galaxy Note 8 was taking potshots at the iPad Mini. You get the plot—great examples of differentiation and value creation. Do it better, faster, cheaper and easier than anything anybody has ever done before, and you have a chance to win. Differentiation comes out of innovation, and innovation is a product of attitude. Good times or bad, this attitude and commitment at every level of the organization are an absolute must for any organization to turn the corner, especially when the chips are down!

Two investment criteria for portfolio companies that Mr. Buffet and Berkshire invest in are simplicity of their business proposition and a first-class executive team. I am quite hopeful that these high-quality executives have a checklist similar to the one I have listed in this section as they grind through murky economic waters. If they do, then my investment and those of millions of other individuals and funds that ape Berkshire's portfolio will stand protected and return back to where they were when the tides rise again.

My habit of reading Mr. Buffet's letter to the Berkshire's shareholders has continued, and I have no doubt it will be a lot more optimistic in years to come.

Is Changing a Habit Even Worth It?

It was the summer of 2003, and I was standing on the kerbside of Newark International Airport in New Jersey with my brother-in-law, puffing furiously on the last inch of my cigarette. I felt as if my life depended on it, before boarding my nine-hour nonsmoking flight to Amsterdam en route to Singapore. It had been a hell of a busy week that started in California and then took me to the East Coast. We decided to wind down over the weekend and so drove out to Atlantic City to roll some dice, throw some cards and hope to hit some 21s. And what is a downtime without a few vodka martinis and some greasy junk that often ends up being called food? So there I was, loaded with greasy meat, alcohol, nicotine, and sleep deprivation, barely making it to the airport on time, feeling more drained than rejuvenated. Security check was announced, and we hugged and said our good-byes. I vividly remember my cigarette butt still clasped between my fingers as I did so; then as I turned toward the trash bin and flicked my cigarette into it like I had done a thousand times prior, the haze suddenly cleared, and in that nanosecond, I faced my "aha" moment. *Let this be my last cigarette*, I thought—just like that, clear and loud.

I rushed through immigration and security and boarded the plane. Tired to the bones, I dozed off even before the seat belt signs came on. Daylight and awareness finally shone through my lids as the airplane thudded onto the tarmac at the Schiphol in Amsterdam. The first thought that blazed in was, *Gosh, I quit smoking.* A swell of emotional pain followed soon . . . the pain of parting with a twenty-four-year-old habit is never an easy one. I slept through the Amsterdam stopover (yes, this was when global security did not require passengers to deplane in every stopover) and most of the next fourteen hours into Singapore. By the time I woke up again, most of the fatigue had washed away, my mind had cleared, and I was able to reflect on what I had done more objectively. By the time I was clearing immigration in Singapore, I was getting comfortable with my decision and almost had a plan to deal with it and make it happen.

For many years, and very much like Mark Twain, I believed that *Giving up smoking is the easiest thing in the world. I know because I've done it thousands of times . . . . only to start again.* Smoking did not do me any good at sports. My clothes and hair must have borne the tobacco stink that I knew was not pleasant for any nonsmoker in proximity; it was not good for my health and, most importantly, would leave me feeling embarrassed and awkward when my daughter (seven years old then) asked me pointed questions about why I smoked and when I would quit. I never did have a confident answer that would satisfy her or any other well-wisher of mine when it came to defending my nicotine habit.

All that changed in that nanosecond . . . that moment in time when all the past thoughts, awareness, questions, and everything in my subconscious mind snowballed into a critical mass that made me take a decision to change it all. I write this in such great detail because it is indeed one of the most impactful, life-changing, and fulfilling decisions I have taken—it impacted my life in more ways than one. It also taught me how to successfully make massive changes in life that initially looked too monstrous to overcome.

We live in a changing world where change is indeed the "only constant." Easier said than done, really. Change when properly instituted requires resolve, courage, determination and massive actions. While many people resist change (which, by the way, I do not endorse), I am alarmed to see people or even organizations trying to change things without a clear purpose or a need. A half-baked, emotional drive for a change that is not well thought out does not cut it. The actions that will drive the planned change need solid commitment, and commitments need resources (time, effort and in many cases, money) to bring the right results. If the expectation about results is improperly set or if the results do not show due to poor or inadequate execution, the "change exercise" often does more harm than good.

All I am asking of you is to pick your battles (read "changes") wisely. If you think there are things you need to change in yourself or your professional or social space, list and prioritize them. Be absolutely certain why you need to change in each of these aspects. Where are you falling behind in your life by holding on to these habits, and how will you benefit if you let them go? What is your net gain through this transformation, and how will it impact the people around you? Your findings need to be pretty dramatic to make the commitment that will follow to be sustainable.

Once this is done, talk to someone you trust: friend, family member, or if it is a work situation, then with your supervisor and a teammate on the changes that you are planning to effect. Choose someone who will candidly tell you the way things are rather than say things to make you feel happy. Seek their opinion on your list and how you have stacked them. Very often, we are overcritical toward ourselves; we lead ourselves to think that the more faults we identify in us and resolutely go about fixing them, the more likely are we to be successful! Talking to others often extinguishes this overcritical bearing through simple logic. Dialog also helps identify other areas that might need attention though they do not show up in our radar. During these "tell me about me" sessions, be aware that all you need is their opinion only. The final decision is yours alone—do not let others do this for you.

I ask you to choose very carefully because as I have said earlier, successful change will need incredible commitment and massive actions. Being able to manage this is never easy as you go through the following stages:

- Commit to dramatically transforming a deep-rooted behavior rather than progressively replacing it. At the Newark airport that evening, I firmly believed that my kerbside cigarette would be the last cigarette I would smoke. I did not decide to slow down on my daily intake and progressively wean myself off like many plan to do—I just stopped smoking!
- Next, build walls around the change-related actions so that initial hardships do not make the resolve weak. I would, at every opportunity, speak to people around me about how comfortable I was getting without a cigarette and how I was absolutely convinced that I would never have to get back to it. I also placed some wagers with the naysayers who believed that I would get sucked back into the habit. Every time I spoke those words, I strengthened my resolve and strengthened the wall around the change that I was driving.
- Finally, supplement your change-related actions with other parallel actions that are empowering. These actions should support and reflect in a positive light the change that you are implementing. I revved up my gym work, leaned more on sports, improved my eating habits and felt my energy levels

> soar. I felt calmer and started to relate better to people around me. My confidence skyrocketed with the awareness that I had accomplished quite easily what others had struggled to do in their entire lifetime.

The steps I have laid out are no rocket science and can be accomplished. If the desire and resolve exists, voila! You will see the magic unfold.

This method for change applies to any area of life that you feel needs improvement. It can defeat smoking, overeating, procrastination, overspending, under-performance, relationship problems, lack of fitness, and the list goes on.

The human mind and intent is indeed more powerful than what we normally give it credit for. Use this amazing force wisely, whether you are changing a habit, starting a company, or asking for that 'pay raise'.

Asking for that Raise Is Fantastic, but Do You Deserve It?

Growing at work, earning more than the previous year is great. I see many people focused on this. Nothing wrong here—between basic needs, some conspicuous consumption, charity work etc. you have an ever-growing spending list. All this needs money.

So how do you go about making more money? Seeking a pay rise, of course. It first starts within the organization that employs the individual, and when that does not work out, employees are quick to look at new places of employment for even a few dollars more. Most of these ad hoc employment changes do not serve the individual well.

At the onset, the employee seeks a pay rise without a proper plan that justifies their intent. Supervisors at work are often confronted with these demands and often are at a loss in how to respond to them. This makes matters worse. Employee dissatisfaction starts to build. A dip in productivity follows. Then there is the other type of employee who will suffer in silence; they come to work every day with that miserable feeling that they are worth more than what they get paid. Very often, they are unable to articulate why they deserve more money than what shows on their paychecks. Many are gripped by fear at the thought of standing up and making their demands, only to be rejected. For others, the company culture does not encourage them to speak out. Naturally, this affects their performance as they keep reaching out for their next employer, even if the new job pays just a little bit more that what they currently make. They are willing to bail out and leave behind everything that they have worked for and accomplished within their current employment over the years for a few dollars more. None of this is desirable for the employee or the employer. There has to be a way to fix this . . . but how?

First, compensation is a topic that should not be approached emotionally—neither by the employee nor by the employer. Today's businesses often use very sophisticated, specialist third-party-developed compensation models that classify the employee by skill type (e.g. sales, technical, marketing, administration, etc.), skill level (years of relevant experience), work impact bands (low, medium, high), location of employment (country, cost of living index), and other data/consultation services. These published industry standard models are the tool to logically determine the targeted compensation for any employee and should help provide guidelines for fixed and variable compensation and benefits. The publishers of these models do ongoing market research and regularly update the data based on changing economic parameters. Towers Watson (*http://www.towerswatson.com*), Mercer (*http://www.mercer.com*), and Culpepper (*http://www.culpepper.com*) are some prominent names in this space. Organizations and hiring managers are strongly advised to use this data with confidence during workforce planning, budgeting and determining employee compensations. Employees should also be proactive in making themselves generally familiar with how their skills are compensated in their geographical location. There is plenty of public domain information that is freely available to those who seek.

Now let's consider the employee. If you, the employee really want to know how your employer rates you, look at your pay slip . . . period! You receive the sum on your paycheck specifically because of the skills, track record and reputation that you have built over the years. Your paycheck is not higher than what it is today because you do not posses (or choose not to possess) the skills or attributes that are needed to get you there. Identify these skills, choose to practice and perfect them with commitment, and publish the proof points with intent. I can assure you that you will see your compensation curve change within a practical range. So let us get this clear: our compensation is a scorecard—it shows our standing in our profession relative to others. Successful professionals do not spend time and emotions on the score other than using it to judge where they presently stand and set their next goal. They focus, plan and implement their efforts around the causes that they have previously identified that will lead them to their new targeted score, be it position, responsibility or compensation.

While it is absolutely fantastic to look at your paycheck and then target what it needs to be in the near future and work at building the missing pieces that will take you there, greed (not the "Greed is Good" kind of greed that is explained in another chapter) is the biggest derailer to this process. I have seen individuals come across and get considered for opportunities that are either well above their capabilities or get considered for a position that matches their skills but pays far more than what they are worth. Both these situations are career traps that you should look out for and avoid.

The first situation happens where an employee goes through an imperfect recruitment process (it is common to see this in target companies ahead of hostile takeovers) or have internal influencers within the organization who find them suitable for a position that in all probability the hiring manager is incapable to fill. In the first situation, this inadequacy of the candidate becomes visible very quickly, and the consequences are never pleasant. It however serves the purpose of the acquired company in the form of financial payouts that the acquiring company has to fork out to get rid of the inadequate employee (also called a "poison pill"), according to the terms of the contract. In today's connected world, news travels faster than we can imagine, and the credibility and integrity of people who take part in these situations gets deeply dented, though they walk away with hefty separation payments. The second situation is more common, and this is how it unfolds. An organization might be a new player in a specific market segment and might be in an urgent need to hire someone with the skill to help them get going. The easiest way in is to lure an employee from a competitor whose skill matches the new business need—a higher than market offer usually follows to get this person in quickly.

The organization sees this as a short-term tactical move, but the impact on the employee is long-term. The business priorities that led to the hiring of this individual at a premium sometimes stays. At other times, the priority tapers off as the business needs change. The employee who is hired might sometimes do well or get moved to another position, but sometimes stays and stagnates in the position, which is not anymore a priority in the company. Many of these situations then lead to a termination as the position becomes redundant, leaving the employee without a job but with a more expensive lifestyle that cannot be funded by what the market is willing to pay him. What a tragedy!

Many a career has been destroyed by this unnecessary greed of seeking something that we are not worthy of. Some of these unfortunate victims are forced to take job openings that come along but are not able to cope with a reduction in compensation even though they try hard. The employee starts work at the new organization disillusioned, demotivated, and disgruntled from day one. From there on, his future in this new role is a self-fulfilling prophecy.

I am forever a big fan of ambition and enterprise in all humans to reach for greater heights and larger achievements. While we set our sights high and drive toward our goals, just be wary and constantly watchful of the small rocks and potholes strewn along the way. Some of them will be very well camouflaged. Make sure that you drive your car with care, avoid these pitfalls; else, you will have to kiss your bigger dreams good-bye.

You Read the Driver's Manual—Now Take the Keys and Drive the Car

It was an early week of a wet August in 2009 as I boarded a plane to Manila. As the Singapore Airlines flight taxied down the rain-drenched Ninoy Aquino International Airport's tarmac, I looked around into the gathering dusk at the hazy silhouette of the neon-lit airport terminal—nothing much had changed in the ten years I had been traveling to this country. As I disembarked, I am bundled through immigration and customs. I thanked my lucky stars that it was early in the week, or was it that the efficiency of the airport had just got better? I had to find out. I have had my trysts with destiny while trudging through the crowd at this airport during previous visits and they have indeed been a challenge. My last visit was a year previous—I half-expectedly started peering out of the window of the hotel car that whisked me from the kerbside lounge as I was chauffeured down the well-lit streets by a chauffer whose infectious exuberance that characterizes every Filipino had thankfully not altered one bit.

Manila did surprise me. The streets were cleaner, the traffic more orderly, and as I discovered in the two days I spent there, a tremendous focus on urbanization, infrastructure development and employment had taken effect. Singapore has always been an influence on the South East Asia region. A visit to the Fort Bonifacio, a highly urbanized office, entertainment and residential district in *Taguig City* within metro Manila, is a great example of this influence. I was at the Fort to meet a business contact ten years ago, and all there was at that time was rolling, dusty and barren land left behind by an army garrison. What I see today is a shining metropolis, tree-lined boulevards, commercial and residential high-rises with glittering glass facades and enough dining and wining options to keep a social animal spoilt for choice and occupied for a year. The place does reflect the orderliness, completeness, and structure of a very modern metropolis. Well done, Ayala Corporation and Evergreen Holdings, the two conglomerates who made this happen! Well done, Philippines!

During a couple of days in Manila, my agenda was peppered with speaking assignments with customers and business partners and in getting seduced by the lucrative infrastructure development opportunities that the country presents that our organization's technology can address. I took the time to meet some business associates who I have learned to trust as friends over the ten years that I have known them. It was great to meet them over a drink or a meal, be humbled by their progress and take a moment to talk nostalgically about the past and discuss the exciting future. Absolutely brilliant!

Manuel Bobiles, Chairman and CEO of a growing tech company and a leading network system integrator, is a man I have known and respected for a long time. Manuel came to the Philippines years ago as a student, started his company, and grew it over the years into a multimillion-dollar technology corporation. One of the cornerstones of Manuel and his organization's progress is the way the organization hires, trains, grooms and evolves employees while preparing them to take on the challenges and opportunities that the ever-changing contemporary world presents. What Manuel does within his organization is also a subject very close to my heart.

I have been preaching the need to bring our workforce up to speed on workplace readiness and leadership development. I do believe that this is the single largest impediment that we face as a society to tackle the challenges that an increasingly complex workplace is incessantly throwing at us. As I travel around and ask any business leader what their primary challenge at work is, they do not blink an eyelid before saying, "People." Well, Asia has no problem with quantity—it is the quality that is the concern. I am not downplaying the credentials or the capabilities of our educational institutions; there are many good ones and a few outstanding establishments in Asia. It is just that there is a very large divide between the environment that the typical Asian educational institution provides that an average student grows up in and the work world environment that they face the first day they start at work. While the specialized tertiary institutes arm the employee with the hard skills to pursue the careers that they seek, the real gaps are in the soft skills department. Unfortunately, these soft skills (or the lack of them) within the new employees become glaringly visible as they start work and get them off on the wrong foot in the workplace. Many never recover from this less-than-desirable start, while others pick up some steam as they go along but never attain their full potential.

The trick to get the best out of the people we hire is to choose the ones with the best hard skills needed for the roles that they are hired for: academic accomplishment and documented grades are good measures of these skills. In addition to these hard attributes, we look out for at least some soft skills. Attitude, passion, and communication are some that I rate very highly. I will double down and take on an outsider with an unproven skillset in my team as long as they come with a first-class attitude. Trust me, everything else builds from there. I have seen many a relative outsider make it big despite multiple shortcomings riding on that priceless attribute: their attitude. On the contrary, show me one single achiever with a lousy attitude toward their trade, and I will show you polar ice caps in the midst of the Sahara.

Having practiced the concept within my own organization, I am recommending the business leadership community to spend time and effort in getting their people workplace ready as quickly as possible and reduce their time to productivity. The exercise routine that is needed to accomplish this is split into two logical parts. One, provide every employee with an opportunity to master the soft skills that they need to excel in their chosen profession. These could be interpersonal skills, operating in a crisis, managing and delivering on expectations, communicating upward, leveraging executives, goal setting—you know there are many. I prefer an analysis on the individual based on feedback from the supervisor, coworkers, and the individual himself or herself to determine the areas that need the most development, rather than adopting a "one size fits all" approach.

This analysis should be followed by a rigorous courseware—instruction set and group activities followed by an evaluation process to determine sequential progress. The courseware and its implementation can be developed and implemented within the organization (not the best choice unless you have the breadth, total commitment, and the bandwidth to do so), or help from external providers with first-class content and delivery consultants can be solicited. This done, most organizations stop at this stage and conclude that they have done a great job. Hardly.

Analysis and development exercises are like taking a budding driver through a well-documented driving manual and then throwing the car keys at them, expecting them to drive effortlessly on the rain-soaked streets of Manila. This should hardly be the right expectation. The missing link that most organizations overlook is a stint of mentorship.

Having an experienced campaigner who has all the battle scars sitting next to the newly minted, instruction-manual-trained rookie driver showing the tricks while pointing out the pitfalls seems to me what makes the real difference. A good golf instructor will take his rookie student out to the golf course for a round of golf in real settings after the swing analysis, theory and driving range, chipping and putting green lessons are done. It is on the course that the turf is uneven, where the depth of the grass varies, sand traps are laid out and obstacles block the target. That's where the real learning happens—where course management, adjustments and shot or club selection is learnt. Without this practical exposure, learning is incomplete and often not fully relevant.

The more sincere the mentor and the mutual engagement he drives with the student, the more complete the education and the skill development of the student. Mentorship is not about a single session or even one involving days and weeks—it is an ongoing commitment that the student and the teacher need to sign off on to be able to see real results. It is fabulously fulfilling.

Manuel and his Filipino leadership team are committed to the development of the people they hire. They eliminate elementary employee concerns around healthcare for the employee and his family, basic amenities of life, small interest free loans for life's little joys and so forth. Employees who are now free of these little concerns and consumed by the care that the organization showers on them show up for work with absolute commitment toward their roles and responsibilities. What follow are high-quality projects and services for Manuel's customers that naturally lead to revenue and profitability. A very simple formula.

As we slug our last dirty martinis for the night, laden with plump olives with stuffed pepper at the chic Prive nightclub in Fort Bonifacio,

Manuel emphasizes that by asking his people to read a manual and drive a car would never deliver the results that his team is producing. It is the mentors in his executive team who are jumping in the car beside the drivers and passionately sharing and helping elevate the young Turks to the next level.

I am hoping that more organizations, especially in the rapidly developing countries in Asia, Latin America, Eastern Europe and the Middle East are following the trajectory that Manuel's organization is. I am also hoping that employees who work within these organizations take ownership in seeking out top performers within and build formal and informal mentoring relationships. This will help accelerate their development and avoid the inevitable potholes.

If so, these businesses and the people within will not only symbolize loyalty like Manuel's team but very soon start to operate in a manner as slick as in the glittering business districts of Tokyo, Hong Kong, Singapore or even Fort Bonifacio.

Now let's move on to more on loyalty . . .

Loyalty—Is it Only about Dogs?

I would often walk over to our Human Resources area and read through job description documents that propagate a search. I also discuss with our hiring managers regarding the customer-facing and back-office roles that will enable us to execute our organizational and revenue goals. We did this as a part of our Workforce Planning process. I also got into brief conversations with prospective employees who came to interview with us. In all these situations, a point of discussion is, "What are the key qualities that will make the new hire succeed?"

The flavors of the response are varied. The MBA types will call out education, communication, integrity, concepts, leadership, intellect, analytics, execution and so on. Others will categorize effort, relationships, knowledge and quality of work as key attributes for success.

All these assumptions are true—and why not? Possessing these skills requires tremendous resolve, focus, and discipline. These make up the professional's arsenal—the tools for success. However, what is the quality that plays an equally crucial role, if not more—an attribute that all organizations look forward to in the employees and test them over time? No glib talker gets away talking through this—the proof lies in the actions of the employee and takes time to judge.

I do not want to leave you hanging, but let us look at this from another perspective. The greatest professional and individual successes (Gates, Jobs, Buffet, Grove, Iacocca, Ellison, Welch, Bezos) have happened after these individuals focused their attention and effort on one single company over many years. Granted that some happened to be the founders of the organizations that they worked for, but still, it is undeniable that they worked hard, demonstrated commitment, patience, and passion, earned the loyalty and trust of the employees within the organization, and progressively earned their stripes while putting their paw marks on more than one initiative where their involvement largely contributed to the success. The organizations recognized the capability of these individuals, the sincerity of their intent, and progressively entrusted them with more authority, knowing well that these individuals had the capability to carry the accountability that comes along with it. And boy, did they, and some of them are even doing so today.

The missing attribute for success I am talking about is "loyalty," a quality not discussed or probed much in most interview sessions. In a professional world that is talent starved, material and frequent employment changes are more of a norm than an exception. You cannot talk someone into believing that you are a loyalist. You have to demonstrate it over time—not just in fair weather, but when the going gets tough, the adversities run high and when the organization needs believers. That is when true loyalty shows up, and believe you me, there are people looking out and checking in to see who are the ones demonstrating this trait and sticking with the company.

In fact, this is so not just at the corporation level, but equally so even within departments, workgroups, and neighborhood sports teams. Loyalty is an attribute that does not go unnoticed. It does not really matter how capable, experienced, influential, or connected an individual is. Any demonstration of lack in loyalty will certainly not be an ingredient that will propel professional success. Take this as a rule of thumb, whether in small, family-run businesses or global multinational corporations. Many organizations will state this in their manifesto, many will not . . . instead they will bracket the skill as the "ability to align with the corporation," "be committed to the corporate culture," etc. The verbal flavors are many, but the expectation is the same.

Put yourself in the shoes of the powers that be within the organization, most of who have risen to their high offices after having contributed to the development of the organization over the years. When they are ready to look around to hand over the mantle to someone to lead a function, department, or the entire organization and take it to the next level of success, what competency will they seek in the individual after all the "ticket to entry" qualities have been checked out? They will without doubt seek out for their trust in the individual's ability of carrying out the mission as closely as possible to what they would have done themselves—an individual who, while shouldering the responsibilities of the organization, will also keep an ear out for the recommendations and suggestions of the old guard, an individual who gives the confidence that he will honor the past legacy and preserve the building blocks on which the organization was built, while driving the next level of growth, playing by the prevailing rules for success.

Any career-guidance session that I speak in is always laced with ample discussions about patience and commitment toward the organization. If your job is a downright drag, and you are gaining nothing from it, then move on. Go some place which will serve your career and your personal growth better. Else, patience is your best friend as you progress through your organization. Remember to demonstrate loyalty to your team, region, function, supervisor, and the company at large in every instance along with demonstration of your capability in the role you play.

Be assured that people are watching you and the rewards will come when the time is right. Be loyal and be prepared. Let everyone see it. Things will begin to happen for you.

How Come it Didn't Happen? How Come it Did?

Do you know how a modern-day automobile is assembled? The assembly task is split among multiple assembly stations. Each station sequentially installs the engine, the hood, the doors, and the wheels. Only one of these steps can be done at a time, so in traditional production, only one car would be assembled at a time. If the engine is installed in twenty minutes, the hood in five minutes, and wheel in ten minutes, then a car should pop out every thirty-five minutes plus some transition between assemblies. When the assembly line was commissioned, the car assembly was split between several simultaneously operating assembly stations, which passed on the unit to the next station once each had done its job. The four stations worked on four cars simultaneously but discretely.

With the assembly line in place, the longest stage on the assembly line, that is twenty minutes for the engine install, will determine the throughput. A car can now be churned out every twenty minutes, once the first car is manufactured in thirty minutes. This is an efficiency milestone for the human race. Collaboration is very powerful, but often, one end of the chain does not know what the other end is doing.

Philosophically speaking, all individuals belong to something bigger—an institution, a social group, an organization, or the universe at large. What we are asked to do or what we volunteer to do is a part of a bigger plan or a larger cause. That does not make our effort any smaller; on the contrary, our actions are a crucial component of the larger design, which could very well fail without our contributions. Not every project is green lit in the end, and most of us won't get the kind of credit we deserve. Nevertheless, let's do our part and take pride in it.

The reason I write this is because I have been in collaborative situations (especially in the early stages of my career) where I worked diligently to complete tasks assigned to me, submitted my assignment on time, and waited in anticipation to see the rollout of the overall project. Alas, many never reached that point. And, I went off thinking . . . *Gosh, how come it did not happen?* On the flip side, there have also been instances where, after having provided research, analysis, and recommendations on an initiative and seeing nothing emerge some months later (or even a year later), the project started being implemented and then I went, "Gosh, where did that come from? And just when I had almost forgotten about it!"

What is happening behind the scene that causes these two eventualities? Our contribution, however crucial, is not the end product. The end product is the complete initiative, the sum total of several "microelements" that others like us are responsible for. To make the overall initiative successful, not only must all the microelements be completed, but also their individual execution needs to be timely. Each microelement needs the right environment to be able to provide maximum impact to the overall initiative. The larger the number of these microelements, the more complicated the rollout. So there you are, armed with your complete microelement, ready to go while others are not ready or everyone is ready but the timing of the overall execution is not appropriate. The initiative in all probability is going to be held back from a rollout. Let's understand this and manage our expectations accordingly.

Even if the initiative is ready to roll, sometimes a higher priority or a dramatic shift in the external conditions gets in the way. Therefore, it is not about you, your efforts, your sincerity, or your readiness—it is a sum total of preparedness of every cog in the wheel and the readiness of the wheel itself to roll that sets the machinery in motion.

With these uncertainties, how do we make the environment predictable? Communication. Frank and honest communication among participants and leaders resolves anxiety and disappointments. It also sets expectations when the outcome is not in the hands of the participants or even the leader. It helps participating troops understand where they stand or what to look forward to or what not to expect. It gives them support when they are groping in the dark.

People programmed for success are proactive and regular in communication, when business is as usual and even more so when the business is NOT usual—in the face of massive challenges. Actions like this breed confidence and a sense of predictability among their team members and ease their emotions—a prized outcome in times of uncertainty.

Like David standing in the face of the Goliath of competitive challenges and economic downturns.

Go, David, Go!
10 Bullets for Winning Professional Combats

Most of us grew up pretty awestruck, hearing David's biblical victory over Goliath—not a commonplace street fight at all, we think.

Ivan Arreguín-Toft, a political scientist, "looked at every war fought in the past 200 years between strong and relatively weak combatants. The Goliaths, he found, won in 71.5% of the cases while the Davids won 28.5%. Arreguín-Toft was analyzing conflicts in which one side was at least ten times as powerful—in terms of armed might and population—as its opponent, and even in those lopsided contests, the underdog won almost a third of the time." While the statistics were startling, somehow I was not surprised; I always felt that way in my guts. I read on: "In the biblical story of David and Goliath, David initially put on a coat of mail and a brass helmet and girded himself with a sword: he prepared to wage a conventional battle of swords against Goliath. But then he stopped. 'I cannot walk in these, for I am unused to it,' he said (in Robert Alter's translation) and picked up those five smooth stones." What happened, Arreguín-Toft wondered, when the underdogs likewise acknowledged their weakness and chose an unconventional strategy that supports their position? He went back and reanalyzed his data. In those cases, David's winning percentage went from 28.5 to 63.6. Arreguín-Toft concluded that when underdogs choose not to play by Goliath's rules, they win "even when everything we think we know about power says they shouldn't." Having doffed his armor and put down his sword, David braced himself, loaded one of the smooth stones in his sling, aimed between Goliath's eyes, and unleashed the projectile with deadly accuracy. The rest is history.

Ever since childhood, I have strangely fancied competing with forces that are larger than me. I always found that adrenaline rush every time I did it. I am not so sure it always worked out. There were times when I was a tad too late in calling out to the other guy to "take on someone his own size"—the inevitable damage would be done by then, and I would sneak back home through the back door battered and bruised and blame it all on the rough soccer game when my mom enquired. As I started to grow, got into sports, and even saw clusters of muscles start to peep out and take shape, I realized that strategy is more crucial than might in even the most basic hand-to-hand combat. Shinbones, ankles, and the lower abdomen were more susceptible to even light knocks than rigorous wrestles with arms, shoulders, and torsos. No more graphic descriptions of my formative years needed . . . you know what I mean.

As I came into work life, I have had to contend with similar circumstances clothed in more professional attire and with more at stake than just an ego boost that comes from felling somebody. The Goliaths have showed up in different forms and circumstances, from office bullies to competitors, preventing me from going after what they have—market share, influence, power, or just plain ego. Instead of being overawed, my adrenaline rush from my childhood days still persists, shines through, and carries me to strike at the jugular of the foe. The years of hard knocks have helped me construct powerful bullets—abilities to differentiate, negotiate, communicate, empathy, subtlety, self awareness and confidence. These when intelligently combined, create a force as lethal as David's smooth stones in any professional combat. Use them well and you have game, set and match. No more low, hard kicks on the shinbones needed. Now, let me take you briefly through the Ten Bullets for professional combat:

Differentiation: When faced with a bigger foe, seek out the strengths and advantages you have that your rival does not. Do not fight on equal terms, and do not fight the way your enemy wants you to. You see, David discarded the coat of mail and brass helmet that restricted his movements. He knew that speed was a differentiator against the larger being. He used speed to his advantage. He knew that he would have a problem of reach with the Goliath, so he used a projectile weapon, the slingshot, as a differentiator.

Reasoning: Put your emotions in the cooler—do not let them guide you. You will be misled. Never respond immediately to an external stimulus. Take your time. The quality of your decision when you allow your mind the space to reason will be infinitesimally better than sudden, knee-jerk responses.

Surprise: Any form of response usually becomes more intense when it is mixed with an 'element of surprise' (as the Pink Panther would say). Use surprise as your ally, especially when your bigger enemy is normally used to dealing with a pattern. David broke out from the file and charged at Goliath. He took aim and fired his slingshot on an improbable trajectory that took Goliath by surprise.

Leverage: Irrespective of your individual strength, seek every leverage you possibly can. Leverages are adjacent forces or influences that have reason to collaborate and align with you against your rival. Carefully culture these influences—they are not developed overnight. Seek out vectors built over time—these are supportive elements (skills, changes, new technology, etc.) that will develop over time due to no effort of yours that you can leverage to your advantage.

Communication: You need to be perceived as the good guy, the underdog, and the challenger both going in and coming out of the combat, irrespective of the result. It is human nature to root for the underdog. History is laced with examples of underdogs who might lose a skirmish but end up winning the war—Vietnam, Apple Computers, and Peet's Coffee; even Tiger Woods entered PGA as an underdog and then made it big—you get the idea. Nothing puts you more into that position than great communication. Lobby people, make people aware of the war you are bravely fighting and get them on your side, and make them root for you.

Timing: Just because you have your missiles ready does not mean that you fire them. Timing is key. Behaviorally speaking, the Goliath will be overconfident. Eventually, he will let his guard down and take his eyes off you. That's when you strike . . . and strike hard. You may not get another chance, but remember, David needed just one stone—though he had five!

Subtlety: Preparing a punch does not mean that you need to get all worked up before you do so. When you are worked up, it shows, and you are unnecessarily alerting the enemy and letting precious energy drain away. Subtlety is powerful; it does not demean the intent but cloaks it intelligently and most often delivers more damage on the target. Those of you familiar with Bruce Lee and his legendary motion picture *Enter the Dragon* that heralded Chinese martial arts to the global audience will know what subtlety in offensive is all about. See the movie if you have not—for those of you in your 20s and 30s, trust me, it is not old fashioned and will be worth your viewing time.

Confidence: David did not, for a second, doubt his sling or his aim. Neither should you. After the earlier actions have led you to form your strategy and your communication, once you know the timing is right, do not hesitate anymore. Trust your judgment, and pull the trigger . . . you might not have a second chance.

Empathy: As I have grown, I have learnt to be gracious in victory. I empathize with the fallen and do a mental check of what I did right and what the close shaves were that could have turned the tables on me. Winning is a great feeling—understanding why you did and treating your vanquished foe with respect is a greater one. If you do lose (remember, Arreguín-Toft says there is a 36% chance that you will despite doing all the above), regroup, ask yourself why you lost, and more importantly, what you learnt. Live to fight another day.

Self-Awareness: This is an incredible skill to build, and the benefits are immense—more so when you start to use it subconsciously. Self-awareness is about being aware of the impact of your actions on others—not just on your rivals, but on everyone who is in any way linked to the battle, even people who are watching from the sidelines. Not only do you need to win, but you also need to leave a lasting impression of what you stood for and how you won in the eyes of everyone involved. Your actions before, during, and after the battle will determine this.

To all the Davids out there: happy hunting! Keep those slingshots coming strong. Make a solid impression on others, and they will sell the stories of your victory forever. Just like what Ivan Arreguín-Toft and I are doing for David.

But where are the rest of the salesmen?

Where Have All the Salesmen Gone?

For years I have built the habit of socializing with my industry peers about pressing topics at the beginning of the year. Besides gaining valuable perspectives, I find these discussions incredibly entertaining, especially over a couple of bottles of fine wine. At the end of one of those conversations, I concluded that a large risk threatening to plague most businesses is not lack of innovation, not eroding margins, not trade unions—it is a rapidly diminishing quantity and quality of the sales pipeline. This is not a surprise to me. In the age of big budget field marketing, telemarketing, social media communities, e-mail-based demand generation campaigns, and channel partner-led sales coverage, cold calling and pipeline development is not a high priority in a typical sales rep's daily routine anymore.

It was not like that some twenty years ago. I remember my early years in frontline field sales in the late '80s and early '90s when the technology industry was in its infancy. The drill was strict and purely arithmetical: a rep needed to own a qualified sales pipeline for his territory that was at least three to four times the sales target. A qualified sales opportunity was where there was a genuine customer need for the product or service, an approved budget to fund the need, and the priority and willingness regarding the procurement in the person authorized to make the purchase decision. The sales supervisor would inspect the sales rep's field activity, and any time his pipeline dipped below the 3×-4× multiplier watermark, the rep would get anything from a firm reminder to a dressing down, depending on his past performance or his level of shortfall. We all followed this mantra, and whoever did so, diligently performed and prospered. Period.

The companies that we worked for had hardly any other choice. Technology products were sold as a pricey "niche market" offering—far removed from the commoditization that has happened today. This included personal computing hardware, system software, and clunky desktop printing equipment. With the high prevailing price point and the early stage of the technology evolution, no customer would want to buy products from anyone else but the original manufacturer—there was almost no partner channel. The fat margins that the vendors made, thanks to the limitation of available options, made it possible to retain all sales activity in-house. The "pipeline factor" lived on and the sales force was kept disciplined. The result—both revenue and margin stayed prosperous and predictable.

As the technology business commoditized with the maturity and dramatic growth in the number of users and the arrival of more providers, as innovation opened the doors for differentiated offerings, price and margins both went into a free fall. You just had to sell more and crank the top-line revenue to make the same level of profit as you did in the past. A direct sales approach was neither good enough to generate the volumes that were needed nor was it able to handle the burgeoning demand for technology. Enter two new categories of business weaponry: aggressive branding and product marketing and the channel partner who helped the vendor sell more units to more customers in exchange of a sales margin. The vendor viewed this margin as cost of sales. The more work the partner did, the more lucrative the margin was. Innovative marketing programs were unleashed to drive consumer and corporate demand, and channel partners were cleverly planted to fulfill the customer demand on behalf of the vendor. For a while, things went well, but as technology further commoditized and the burden on price and margins further intensified, the margins that were offered by vendors to their channel started to trickle down. So what next?

The channel partners, who were by now the primary drivers of an organization's sales pipeline, started to sign up other vendors (albeit in complimentary segments), and their focus for individual vendors dropped or was directly proportional to the margin (share of the profit the vendor was willing to provide) or the ease of the sale. In a commoditized marketplace, only a few could differentiate themselves or were able to build brand equity to leverage the marketing effort dramatically. Meanwhile, a new generation of sales force had arrived, one that was used to playing evangelist for their products rather than selling it, comfortable in building relationships with the channel for pipeline and sales rather than doing the hard work themselves. Organizations with market share leadership and a solid brand were okay—their hard work had got them to the stage where customers naturally demanded their products and the channel gleefully fulfilled this demand even at meager margins for two reasons. The products had brand equity, customer pull and therefore were easier to sell. Even if they did not make big margins as the product commoditized, their top-line revenue was taken care of. For lesser organizations, the situation was more acute—put together dwindling channel loyalty in the face of eroding margins and an internal sales force that is not trained to build a direct pipeline and close a sale and you have a dangerous concoction that starts a chain reaction that puts severe pressure on revenue and business viability.

So here is my advice for sales people in organizations who do not have market share leadership or a strongly prevailing brand position and actually have to sell their stuff:

Use the channel partner as a scalable go-to-market avenue for sure, but do not expect the channel to build your business, especially if you are a new entrant or an underdog trying to take on a market leader. Your primary focus needs to be the customer, nothing less. You, as the vendor, are responsible for aggressively and consistently building your brand, marketing your technology, explaining how your offering differentiates itself from others, and addressing the customers' needs or their problems.

Next, leverage this awareness by having your channel partner accompany you to connect with your target customer, qualify the customers' needs and their intention to buy (i.e. build a qualified sales pipeline), then set up and monitor the sales cycle that your partner front ends till the deal closes. This way, you own your destiny and stay in touch with your customer while making the association rewarding for the channel partner and enabling yourself to engage with a large number of opportunities.

Every sales win that the vendor engineers enhances the vendor's brand amongst customers and partners. Every new transaction or installation footprint increases the awareness of the vendor's proposition and makes all parties familiar with the vendor's offerings. Every new sales transaction brings the channel partner closer to the vendor while developing two crucial attributes: mutual loyalty and trust. It starts small but progressively snowballs to giant proportions, building loyal, trained and capable channel partners all intent on driving revenue for vendors that they can both benefit from.

I bet you that every organization that you enviously look at today—organizations and brands that you think have an easy sale, with customers and channel partners flocking at their doorstep—have all gone through this pain.

Do it yourself, deliver value, and you will be there among the clouds in a not-too-distant future.

The V-Word Unleashed

At the end of March, I planted another candle on my birthday cake. It was a fun, relaxing day that I got to spend with family, friends, and food (the ultimate indulgence for people like me). I have picked up the annual habit of observing the birthday greetings that I receive and where they come from. There are the constants—family, old friends, and very close business associates who have become friends over the years—they and their greetings will show up, nevertheless. While I do not take their warmth and feelings for granted, I expect them regardless. Then there are the social network platforms, a new source of warm gestures from distant friends, acquaintances, and even strangers. It is amazing how some people make the effort to write a note and wish you when Plaxo, LinkedIn, or Facebook pops up a reminder. Well, what can you say? Thank you very much to all the kind and thoughtful souls out there—your good wishes are greatly appreciated.

The category of greetings that surprises me and gets me thinking are the outliers. These are individuals who normally do not write in and neither do I expect them to. However, the outliers write in out of the blue because there is something going on between them and me at that specific point in time that makes it polite for them to do so. After observing this trend closely, I have concluded that these niceties often stem from some sort of value that I have delivered to them in the recent past or that they expect me to do so in the near future. Value or lack of it has had an incredible impact on relationships in homes, work, and social circles. Individual values generate interest, trust, and collaboration. Value has the power to level out color, race, religion, or sex. It powerfully normalizes all the differences within a heterogeneous society. So do not ignore the power of the V-word.

Let me cite some examples: Steve Jobs and his band of merry men at Apple Computers and Pixar Animation (now a division of Disney) are perhaps some of the greatest sources of "value" in the twenty-first century. Their ability to deliver consistent streams of innovative products have revolutionized the world of personal computing, mobile communication, music, and digital animation while delivering an incredible user experience in every corner of the world. This is a very powerful form of value. Look at what this has done for both Apple and Pixar in terms of brand, market share, revenue, and market capitalization over the last ten years—simply brilliant results.

Five Guys (*http://www.fiveguys.com/*) is another example in the food and beverage industry. It is incredible how a homegrown Arlington, Virginia franchise can reinvent commoditized fast food—burgers, hot dogs, and fries—and serve customers free peanuts while they wait for their orders at 300 outlets in the last five years that sell over 250,000 burgers a day. Five Guys have used "niche value" to differentiate themselves from the global chains and have created a place for themselves in a very crowded industry.

So if value is so important, how do you go about building it? Well, I think it is hard to build value. You see, value is not a specific attribute. It is a combination of skill, experience, and creativity that produces an end result for others to see, appreciate, respond to, and adopt. So rather than focusing on value itself, I will dwell on the underlying factors that surround it. So here goes . . .

Be knowledgeable: To add any value to anybody on a specific subject, knowledge on the subject is paramount. Period. While general knowledge generally helps, it does not extend beyond a point. Core competence in the subject matter is needed to deliver value that is visible and sustainable. It is one of the givens of the new marketing that one should position oneself as an "expert" in order to convert interested parties into customers. But all too often these days, a claim of expertise is just that: a claim, and with little to back it up. Overstating your experience and knowledge is a good way to erode your reputation in any environment, whether personal or professional.

Connect with reality: While knowledge is the fundamental platform, a keen understanding and experience of applying that knowledge in the real world with real results that others can relate to and endorse dramatically enhances the level of value. Without this built-in reality check, knowledge is merely a theoretical parade of ideas. Linking knowledge and reality often gives rise to innovation—a key attribute of value.

Empathize with the receiver: Being in a position to deliver value does not give the license to assume how smart the provider is. On the contrary, empathy regarding the receiver's ability to take in the value and derive measurable benefit from it further enhances the value of the provider. So if you do wish to deliver value, then deliver it with humility while keeping the receiver's interests in mind. If the receiver's interests are met, yours will be as well.

Spot linkages: Nothing drives a "value" home better than live examples, which are factually or logically close to the receiver's personal situation at that point in time. I try and spot these linkages with my audience right at the beginning of a communication and tailor my pitch, the references, or examples I provide, as close to their circumstances as possible. If I do not, then my audience will quickly disconnect with me. All I say will head into deaf ears, irrespective of what the "value" is.

Honesty: Be honest and upfront about what you can or cannot deliver. Let's be honest if our ability to deliver and the receiver's ability to absorb actually match or not. The value of any effort drops dramatically if it is based on wrong expectations and beliefs. We've all experienced this after being disappointed by a badly made film. We are experienced consumers of narrative, and we have the ability to spot a bad movie a mile away. Knowing this, the big studios have special editing teams that create the trailers used in the marketing of movies. These guys are rock stars; they can extract the best parts of a mediocre movie and present them in a way that entices the audience. Despite all the added seasoning, bad films always deliver the same experience: halfway through, you realize you've already seen the best parts in the trailer, and it doesn't get any better.

Drive conclusions: Close the loop by explaining how what you have offered helps the receiver to deal with a situation that he is normally faced with and does not usually deal with very well. Explain clearly, by demonstrating if possible, how your offering will help him deal with the situation better than he has thus far.

If you want to visualize any of this to get a deeper feel, make your way to an Apple product launch live or online or queue up for a Five Guys burger—nibble on their peanuts and see how they have 'transformed' the customer experiences for us in unique ways and made us used to and comfortable with their style. We cannot define it always, but we miss it when we deal with their competitors. Therein lies their competitive advantage; therein lies their niche.

Energize a Teen, Transform the World

There is always a first time.

As long as I am doing anything that is meaningful to those involved and to myself, I try having fun doing it. There are times when what I have to do is outside my comfort zone; this happens often. I have conditioned myself to go ahead and give it a shot anyway and pat myself on the back afterward and say, "Congrats! I just grew my myself some—I did something meaningful that I have never done before." Sounds like a bit of a scare, but once you get into the groove, it can be fun. No big deal. After all, nothing worth doing is ever easy to start.

In early August 2010, an administrator and teacher of a progressive local school in Singapore expressed interest to have me speak to grade nine and ten students. The school lends a lot of focus on development beyond the curriculum, instilling character for the years that will follow in life and work life. They host an annual lecture series where leaders from society, business, and government are invited to share experiences and deliver motivational messages and thoughts to the students and staff.

I was very humbled by the invitation and gladly accepted, but on afterthought, I went, "Wow! What a difference 'communication' has made in my life." Following a childhood where I was quiet and reserved, I started taking interest in people and in communicating with them as I grew up. Chatting up with people, even walking up to a group of unknown people and striking up a conversation, now comes naturally to me, and I enjoy it. But this was different. Try visualizing today's fourteen—to fifteen-year-olds: opinionated, impatient, informed, and intelligent with zillions of energy pulses zipping through their neurons. If you have parented adolescents and teenagers in the twenty-first century, you know exactly what I mean. And here I was . . . about to address not one, ten, or fifty but 200 of them.

I prepared hard with three goals that I felt would work:

> One, I would not preach to them. All of them have enough preachers around in the school and definitely at home, of which I was certain. I planned to converse, not lecture.
>
> Two, I would not bore them. I wanted to keep them engaged with each other and with me throughout the time we were to spend together.
>
> Three, I would leave them with a couple of takeaways—implants from stories and experiences (theirs, mine, and others who they could associate with). You see, stories are easy to remember and learn from. Know anyone who does not like stories? Parents, family, and teachers who told us stories buoyed our earliest interests. We are all suckers for stories.

What mattered most was to first connect with this bunch and keep that connection alive throughout. I had to have all 200 of them with me, all the way through. I chose words, gestures, humor, and histrionics that would rivet them to the session and keep them connected to me. Do not bore your audience, and you have a real shot at accomplishing this. Every audience comes with an expectation of the obvious in any session. Break that convention, get their attention early, and you are off to a good start. Read their eyes (you know the eyes never lie). Once the eyes start to shift, you have lost them.

Think about it this way—speaking in front of an audience is a mutual commitment between the speaker and the audience to keep each other engaged. The audience has a much harder task in that association. They are the ones listening; they are on the receiving end with no control over how the session flows, the ones with the largest likelihood of not being heard or acknowledged. Boredom creeping in is natural. I wish every speaker were aware of this. Does it not make sense therefore to start a session by at least communicating to your audience what they are in for . . . just so that they are aware? Another way to engage the audience is through involvement. I try to insert a dialog or even a "multilogue" with multiple people in the audience wherever possible. If I am faced with an uncommunicative audience, I will try and seek mutual acknowledgment. I make a point and ask for a show of hands if the audience agrees or disagrees; I seek their point of view. Give *them* a chance to talk. That's engagement. And after a while, audience participation begins, and things start to work out.

Stories are powerful platforms to launch the points we want to make and make them stick. Random stories might not make the cut. Look at your audience and determine who they relate to. Learning becomes easier and more effective when inspirations and examples are drawn from those we idolize. Passion and commitment is easier to explain to teens when your example is a Taylor Swift, Lady Gaga, Lewis Hamilton, Justin Beiber, or Christiano Ronaldo. Perfection becomes easy to understand when you introduce Michael Phelps, Usain Bolt, Lionel Messi or Roger Federer as examples, and the strength of the human spirit takes shape when you mention Gandhi, Martin Luther King, Nelson Mandela or Aung San Suu Kyi—you see what I mean?

One of the supervisors in my early days at work taught me the power of the question-and-answer session, a part that is mostly never utilized or leveraged. I have seen tactful and skillful speakers use this session to get the audience to reinforce key messages and bring out other perspectives that were possibly not covered. You, as the speaker, are the director of the plot; you can weave it any way you want by cleverly using the Q&A session. The Q&A session might not involve any questions at all, especially when a very self-conscious audience occupies the room. That does not mean that the presenter should not use the time set aside for this activity. I like to use the Q&A time to highlight things that come to mind, which were left out in the session. I also find these sessions to drive even more engagement, make things even more memorable, and deliver incredible impact.

In the midst of a communicative audience throwing out a hailstorm of questions, Q&A sessions do not require the presenter to answer every question. Instead, use this as an opportunity to leverage the intellect that sits in front of you—your audience. While speaking to these school kids, I was often stumped by the quality and intelligence behind the questions they asked. As I mulled over how to respond, I actually inadvertently encouraged the young audience to respond to questions set out by another member of the audience. Their answers were brilliant—probably better than anything I could have come up with. Anticipate and acknowledge brilliance and you have fueled the confidence and grown the self-esteem of another human being. Isn't that wonderful? Even more so, if the individual is a fifteen-year-old, with the horsepower to transform the world.

To round up my story, in front of those 200 young minds, I had one of the most exhilarating experiences in public speaking. I bet many of them could associate and align themselves with the stories from the lives of "their" idols that I narrated. Besides the lessons learnt, they loved the fact that these idols also had challenges and failures in their growing years, many of which were more daunting than what any of them in the audience had to deal with. Yet these idols triumphed and came up tops. They succeeded not necessarily by taking massive complex steps, but by consistently demonstrating small but brilliant behavioral patterns that turned into sustainable habits.

But most of all, the students benefited from their own awareness of the capability and promise that they held within themselves. A promise that, if skillfully unleashed, could make them change the world. I would not have been able to instill that realization within every member of the audience but tried to do so with as many of them as possible by talking, letting them talk, and waving the wand of sincere and positive reinforcement.

It was challenging, compelling and left a pleasant taste of fulfillment and personal growth in my own mouth. I felt I had done my part to help the students build a mindset for their work lives. As I drove back to my workplace with a warm glow around me, I kept thinking about how I should document this experience and share it. If nothing else, it helps me be self-aware of this reality every time I get up in front of a crowd.

Personal Branding: A Primer on Workplace Readiness

Personal branding has deftly worked its way in the workplace—it is a tricky element, though. Those who do it well will benefit greatly. Those who misuse it or inadvertently blur their personal and professional worlds will have to deal with the consequences.

Three suggestions . . .

Be Succinct

Brands in general are tightly woven. They are to-the-point representations of the services or products they represent. Similarly, your personal brand should be succinct enough to fit in one or two sentences. In business, this is the well-known "elevator pitch," and in the film industry, it's called a "logline." The logline introduces the protagonist, his goals, what stands in the way of achieving them, and how he overcomes them. The quality of the logline can determine whether the producer even reads the script. The logline for *Raiders of the Lost Ark* might look like this: "Just before the outbreak of World War II, an adventurous archaeologist named Indiana Jones races around the globe to single-handedly prevent the Nazis from turning the greatest archaeological relic of all time into a weapon of world domination." That's all!

The personal brand statement is critical in letting others know who you are, where you are heading and why, and what challenges you have overcome along the way.

Find your 'Difference'

If you and the two people next to you are all gunning for the same position and you each have the same credentials, what advantage does that lend you? Finding an area of differentiation, building on it, and articulating it effectively separates you from the crowd.

You differentiate through experience (you have worked in the relevant country or market) or by insight (you have a unique way to look at a situation and deal with it) or play a hunch. Consider the product team at Apple in 2008 that believed there was an untapped market in a computing form factor called the "tablet" despite established segments like the laptop or the smartphone. That kind of differentiation can make or break an opportunity. There are several other examples of differentiation—where you take a unique position, stand by it, and deliver on it.

Be Flexible

As you discover and start building your personal brand, maintain a loose fit that enables you to maneuver, especially if you are in the early stages of your career or about to start your work life. Cementing your brand without proof points does not lend credibility. It also somewhat restricts you from stating what else you are or want to be over time.

Emphasize multiple demonstrable skills that define who you are. For example, I might say that, "I am Deb Dutta, etc., etc . . . . I enjoy innovating and creating value. I love sports, music, and art. I love to serve social causes. I have pursued these interests <with examples> despite obstacles and challenges <with examples>. This is your logline. Now build on this.

Our lives, like those of corporations, are sprinkled with unintended discoveries that provide new and surprising opportunities. The company 3M is an excellent example. 3M was originally "Minnesota Mining and Manufacturing," a company that made crushed-rock products for grinding wheels and sandpaper. While experimenting with different glues to make better sandpaper, they invented masking tape. Innovating further, they invented cellophane tape ("Scotch tape") and later moved into the magnetic tape and then onto digital storage media. It is hard to define transformation better than this. The company took advantage of all the transformational opportunities that came their way and reinvented themselves all the way to a valuation of almost $80 billion as I write this. If a large organization can reposition itself, why can't we? And if we choose to do so, we do not do ourselves a favor by being rigid with our brand.

So don't lose sight of the big picture as you go about constructing your brand. Keep an eye out for new opportunities that come your way, even if they are not part of your current master plan—be willing to implement changes (think 3M!) if it makes sense to do so!

Build a brand that not only markets you but also inspires you . . . and progressively inspires people around you.

Think of Nelson Mandela.

In Need of an Inspiration

On one of my intercontinental flights, I happened to watch Clint Eastwood's *Invictus.* I have since etched in my mind this memorable exchange between Matt Damon's Francois Pienaar character, the captain of the Springboks rugby team, and President Nelson Mandela, brilliantly played by Morgan Freeman. President Mandela invites Pienaar for tea after a dismal performance by the Springboks against England one year ahead of the Rugby World Cup. He asks Pienaar, "What is your philosophy of leadership? How do you inspire your team to do their best?"

Pienaar, a natural leader, says, "I lead by example. I do not expect my team to do anything that I am not prepared to do myself."

President Mandela keeps probing: "How could your team be made to do better than what they think they can do? Perhaps it is through inspiration . . . by inspiring each individual to greatness where nothing less will do—by using the work and success of others. To build our nation, we need to exceed our own expectations."

President Mandela delivers the inspiration to Pienaar in the form of a Victorian poem he read while in prison. Francois Pienaar and his team respond to the president's challenge by winning the World Cup for South Africa against all odds. A team, which, until a year before, thought they were an also-ran against stronger opponents. President Mandela had used the same inspiration to stand tall, extract a nation from the throes of post-apartheid infighting, and transform the country into a developed nation of equal opportunity for people irrespective of caste, color, or creed. Both individuals demonstrate incredible persistence against stiff odds, resilience, and all the characteristics of true leadership—they connect well among themselves and definitely well with the people they lead.

Circumstances that leaders (at every level, including those who lead just themselves) often face are far from ideal. They are unknown, unfair, unreal, and often impractical—but they are crucial and have far-reaching consequences. Elements that are out of control of the leader or the team that he leads often governs them. In the face of significant odds, the team is looking up to the leader. What does he do? I have been in these situations many a time and did better in some than in others. So what was unique in the instances where my team and I fared relatively well?

An inspiration—Someone else's example of triumph over insurmountable odds, much like President Mandela's inspiration that Pienaar uses is a powerful beacon that is able to guide. History has seen the human race, and its leaders face every form of conceivable odds and triumph over them. Find one that suits your situation the most. I find myself reading voraciously when I am faced with new circumstances and change, irrespective of how complex they are. Reading often helps me find and learn things I can use in the situation. I firmly believe that knowledge and awareness of a precedent is the biggest hedge against any odd.

A vision to get the team together, committed, and focused on a common goal. A vision that is larger than life. People relate well to anything that is larger than themselves: an empowering belief, an image of the positive outcomes of their efforts that emerges out of the belief and rewards them are great examples.

Since this chapter begins with an example from the world of sport, it's useful to consider the now-famous Jamaican bobsledding team as an illustration of vision. The novelty of a tropical nation competing in a winter sport in the Olympics was always going to be a wonderful underdog story. It was the compelling power of that story—an inspiration to achieve despite the odds—and the commitment of the nation and the members of the bobsled team that saw Jamaica take the 14th place in the 1994 games, ahead of the United States, Russia, and France.

Get the "right people on the bus"—Outcomes are a reflection of the quality of people who are involved in it. Get the right skills together, and as a leader, do not flinch in importing top talent, even people smarter than you. Insecurity is the first nail in a leader's coffin. A great team elevates a leader while a poor team pulls the leader down, irrespective of the leader's personal capabilities.

In the world of professional basketball, consider that Lebron James left the Cleveland Cavaliers and signed with the Miami Heat, and he did so in part because of the talented players he knew he would be playing with. He committed to a Miami "dream team" rather than remaining in Cleveland where he was by far the most talented player. Do you want to be a big fish in a small pond or a small fish in a big pond? The latter will grow and get a shot at dominating the big pond, while the former will grow and die in a small confine. Let's make our choice.

Focus on the control points—Individuals and teams spend time, effort, and cycles, focusing on things they do not control or have zero influence over. Blaming the world, weather, inflation, taxes, and other external factors and mulling over matters that are beyond our control make little sense and are perhaps the most wasteful leakage of our energy reserves, spirit, and motivation. When President Mandela asks Pienaar how his injured ankle is doing, Pienaar replies, "You never play at 100%, Mr. President."

"In sports and in life," President Mandela adds.

We're all familiar with stories of athletes who, after having accomplished an amazing win, reveal that they went in with an injury. You never play at 100%, but if you give 100% of what is in your control, you will win. You might not succeed due to circumstances beyond your control, but if you sit on the bench and don't play, you will fail 100% of the time.

Accountability and Authority—Challenging times need teamwork chugging at its best. The sum total of the team's output needs to invariably be larger than the sum of the individual parts. Every member of the team is expected to understand his competency, role, and expectations. I cluster all this into a single word: accountability. I cannot hold team members accountable if I do not give them the authority. Conversely, I cannot give them authority if they are unsure of their accountability or are unwilling to sign up for it. Every time I have seen this packaged well by the leader and accepted well by the team, the results are invariably incredible.

This is why athletic and sports teams go after top coaches and make bids for big sums of money with multiyear contracts to rope them in. The right coach will deliver the right balance of accountability and authority (along with vision and inspiration) so that the team works together as a unit, rather than as a collection of individuals.

Finally, **balanced nonchalance**—This is the one that makes the biggest difference. It is an ability to blend and balance the state of inspiration and the commitment to the vision or end goal with the acceptance of the present: the realization and acceptance of a larger purpose rather than the immediate goal, the act of controlling stress and anger. Our best performances at work, sports, or in social settings come when we do not force things or get "over strung." Our actions flow smoothly, effortlessly, but synchronously with sophisticated grace. Yet they all happen in a seemingly nonchalant state—a state of balance. If you have watched Ernie Els's (another remarkable South African) golf swing or Roger Federer's single-handed backhand cross court returns from the baseline, you will know what I mean—graceful, unhurried, effortless but bang on target.

For those of you who have watched *Invictus*, you know the Victorian poem that inspired the emergence of not just a national rugby team to international prominence, but the vision of a new nation itself. For me, the last two lines are inspiring enough:

> "I am the master of my fate
> I am the captain of my soul."

Visualization Is Power . . . But Are You Competent to Use It?

I love playing golf. I also like watching golf pros competing against each other at the highest level of the game. I like to see their discipline, determination, and concentration as they go about their rounds. I also like the end result of the days, months, and years of hard work that has gone into perfecting their craft: the effortless swing, the whip-like whoosh generated by tremendous clubhead speed as it powers through the impact zone, the perfect divots, and the golf ball soaring majestically and landing with pinpoint precision smack in the middle of the fairway or close to the flag pin tucked in an impossible corner of the green. I also like the greenery and the soothing ambiance that all golf courses present either live or on a television screen.

Over an early May weekend, my eyes were trained on the TPC Sawgrass Players Tournament in Florida, one of the biggies in the US PGA circuit. Aaron Baddeley is a talented Australian who has been in the PGA circuit for a while; he was about to tee off on the renowned 119-meter island green on the 17th where many a pro's hope of winning the tournament are dashed as their approach shots land in the water, incurring a penalty stroke (sometimes more than one!). As Aaron completed his pre-shot routine (a set of activities that every good golfer goes through to get themselves into the groove ahead of a shot), I saw him close his eyes for a good ten seconds. The commentator and I blurted out together, “He is visualizing the shot.” Unless Aaron was dozing off under the afternoon sun (unlikely), I am quite sure that the commentator and I were both right.

I have written in another chapter about the power of visualization, the exercise of mentally viewing an action before it is physically executed. When visualization is done with sincerity after countless hours of practice in the range and practice or tournament rounds in the golf course, the human nervous and muscular systems prepare themselves by firing precisely in a similar manner to what they do when the physical action actually happens. Medical tests were conducted on Olympic athletes where they were asked to run races in their minds by visualizing themselves doing so. While they sat absolutely stationary, it was incredible that the same nerve cells and muscular tissues fired up that would have if they were actually running the race. This technique (in addition, sadly, to steroid use) was part of the reason for the Olympic success of so many Soviet Bloc teams during the Cold War era, a period in which it had not seen widespread implementation in the West.

What Is Competency?

A lot has been spoken and written about visualization. Now let me set your expectations right. Hand a three iron (a longer and more difficult to wield golf club) to a high-handicapped weekend golfer, have him stand on the fairway, and strike the golf ball 200 meters straight at the flag across water. Have him do all the visualization exercises that he cares to and then have him fire the shot. This guy will be lucky to get the ball on the green one out of ten times—a pro could possibly do it eight out of ten times. So what is the difference? It is the level of competency. Competency is a critical forerunner, a necessary dependency for visualization to work. You see, the examples I have stated above—Aaron Baddeley, a pro golfer, or Olympic runners—are finely tuned athletes who, through education and diligent practice over time, have attained a high level of capability and expertise in what they do. This is competency.

The power of visualization has a prerequisite. It relies on developed competencies (motor skills in athletics and analogous skills in other environments) to work. Visualization primes the mind to direct execution at a high level based on past experience. Visualization without competency developed by practice and experience is mere imagination. I can easily *imagine* hitting a hole in one, but the likelihood of me achieving such a feat (incredibly rare, even for the best) approaches nil if I have not developed the competency to hit a golf ball straight at its target.

Competency is fortunately quite easy to determine and is spelt out in four very prominent stages. Think of every skill that you have accomplished in your life or have not accomplished—you will be able to immediately recall how you went through the stages and where you are presently held up. Let me explain the stages through a bicycle analogy that most of us can relate to.

Stage One: Unconscious Incompetence—This is when you are in la-la land, a zone of zero awareness—like when you first rode a bicycle (or rather, attempted to ride it). You were not aware of what it takes to ride the bicycle, why balance is important, and what happens when balance fails. When you had the first fall, you did not know how to prevent the fall or what to do if you were falling. In other words, you were unaware of the techniques related to the competency or have just been introduced to them and have not have had enough hours in practicing them. This is the most frustrating phase in mastering any skill—most people give up right here.

Stage Two: Conscious Incompetence—If you are able to labor past phase one, things start to get better. As you continue learning the competency, you become more conscious and aware of what you do not know. This in itself is a progression toward mastering the skill. On the bicycle, you realize that balance is crucial, or that increasing speed improves balance and, therefore, you need to be aware where the brakes are or you know that when you are taking a steep right, you lean your body slightly to the left for balance—you get the idea? Once you are conscious of the areas that you need to master, attention flows, you start to take the necessary actions, and results show. As your incompetence starts to wear away little by little, you start to get excited by the possibilities of gaining competence.

Stage Three: Conscious Competence—As you reach this stage, you are beginning to have fun learning this skill. You are practicing the skill with consciousness, consistently in a specific sequence, and you are getting predictable outcomes. Your commitment and interest continues to grow. This is a stage where you are conscious of what you know and are able to execute the ability with confidence. On the bicycle, you start to move around while being consciously optimistic—conscious of your learning and past practice, keeping the balance in center, keeping to the speed that delivers the balance, being wary of where the brakes are and ready to extend your leg to brace a fall if that were to happen, and optimistic of pulling it off with the knowledge and practice that you have acquired through your hard work and commitment. Most people peak at this stage—the rewards are adequate. Very few have the desire, dedication, and commitment to move to stage four.

Stage Four: Unconscious Competence—This is when you have truly arrived as a master of your craft. You are like a seasoned bicyclist—pedaling away joyfully on two wheels, sometimes without your hands on the handlebars, without being aware of the motion and balance you unknowingly impart. This is a stage where knowledge and practice have intertwined, been internally programmed, and have manifested to such a level of ability where you are able to demonstrate competence without having to be aware of it. While all this sounds quite magical, very few (the top practitioners of their respective crafts) really get to attain this stage in professional fields. You may wonder what is next after this level of attainment. Well, that's why stage four is for very special people. They keep vacillating between stages three and four—learning, experimenting, discovering, and remastering the art as a lifetime pursuit.

Linking the Two . . .

Now that we understand what competence is and how it evolves, let's link it to the power of visualization. For visualization to do what it does, the subject needs to possess a level of competency in terms of knowledge and practice to be able to know what to visualize accurately in the first place. I believe that it is only in stage three that this level of awareness actually kicks in. See it this way: effective visualization requires the ability to visualize the right action and the right outcome. Both need knowledge and the practice of usage of that knowledge (competence). Without this, visualization is a futile exercise. Competence is the biggest "differentiator in odds" between a high-handicap weekend golfer and a professional tour golfer as they stand 200 meters from the green with a three iron in their hands, a golf ball on the fairway, a flag pin to aim at, and a large spread of water in between that the ball has to carry across.

To conclude Aaron Baddeley's story after his visualization exercise: he steps up to the tee box and launches into a smooth, confident, and languid swing. The club hits down on the ball accurately and picks a healthy divot as the ball soars toward the green. Halfway into the flight, the ball continues to climb. As all eyes follow the ball, it overshoots the pin and lands on the far end of the island green. The crowd sighs as the ball rolls further, catches the downward slope off the green, and trickles into the surrounding water!

Aaron loses a stroke!

Aaron is a great user of visualization, an excellent golfer, and a disciplined professional. Instances like this one on the 17th are the reason why, like others at the same level of the game, he continues the vacillations between competency stages three and four as he seeks out perfection—in his chosen profession.

This is the quest for 'greatness' that many who are 'good', seek.

Looking Out for Greatness

Joshua Bell, the acclaimed violinist, once stood in the corner of a Washington D.C. metro station during the morning rush hour in street clothes playing his violin. He belted out six of his classic masterpieces with extraordinary finesse. Bell's performance was consistent with the quality that earned him international fame but went virtually unnoticed by the thousand-odd rush hour crowd. Many of these people were music aficionados—Bell fans—and would have paid upward of 100 dollars for a seat at a Bell concert a couple nights previous, and others would have considered it the privilege of a lifetime to hear him play live.

Bell was there in the subway station as a part of an experiment on context and perception. The experiment revealed that Bell's obvious artistry and magic was hugely overshadowed by the ordinary circumstances of his appearance, the time, the place, and the mental state of the human traffic that overlooked him.

I cite this example to demonstrate the programming of the human mind to do, feel, and identify innovation, brilliance, or sheer greatness around it the way it is programmed to. Every day, genius unfolds in front of our eyes in classrooms, at work, or even in social settings, but we fail to acknowledge these incredible streaks because they do not come wrapped in appropriate packages or happen in expected settings or come from established superstars that make them visible to our predictable and programmed senses. These are the exact perceptions that hold us and bind us to the world of mediocrity.

I have spent almost my entire professional life in the world of technology. Through these years, I have rated innovation and execution as two primary differentiators that separate great organizations and individuals from the good and the good from the ordinary. Innovation is a prerequisite for execution—you obviously need to have something to execute on. Having been fortunate to operate within and lead a couple of extremely innovative organizations, I am often asked what drives innovations. This is not an easy answer, but three thoughts come to my mind immediately.

Between Zero and One

While the human mind does very well at understanding the gray areas between extremes (we understand that our elected officials hold some positions we don't agree with, but we vote for them anyway), it is most comfortable with black and white representations of situations (thus the polarized nature of political campaigns). We might understand intellectually that, for example, Saddam Hussein was a good father (I don't have the facts to know that for certain), but we think of him as a brutal dictator. John Kennedy is lionized for being an exceptional American president, but it's also well known that he had many personal failings of character, for example, his numerous extramarital affairs. We choose to focus on his excellence rather than his personal failures. In most instances (with exceptions like the one Tiger Woods faced after his personal indiscretions that led to his divorce), we like to put things in boxes, and it gets very uncomfortable for most people in perceiving anything that sits between the gray scales between black and white.

The reason for this, of course, is that this kind of binary thinking works well in almost all ordinary situations. We have to make thousands of judgments each day based on past experiences, and the most efficient way to do this is to simplify the variables. Would you send your child to a school that has a poor academic reputation? Certainly not. There might be reasons the reputation is undeserved, or there could be data that supports that the nature of the school matches the particular character and aptitudes of your child, but in general, we are justified in giving such a school a miss. Binary thinking is powerful because it works almost all the time, unless we are faced with a novel situation. One of the limitations of this kind of thinking is that it makes it difficult for us to even appreciate that the situation we are facing is a novel one that requires a different approach.

Binary thinking is fine for conventional minds, conventional groups, and conventional organizations, but I assure you that all you will find in this space is status quo or at best efficiencies that will drive a 10%-20% improvement in output. To find dramatic and incredible improvements—300% or 500% improvements or even more—disruptions are needed.

Disruptions are radical changes to the status quo that call for paradigm shifts. Shifts in the paradigm create permanent changes in the way things have been viewed or done. New products, process, and methodologies emerge through these innovations that deliver a dramatic shift in output or value. Innovation never emerges from a zone of comfortable status quo. On the contrary, it originates between the zeros and ones. Innovation serves both inventions and discoveries. Operating from black and white serves us well in everyday situations: stop the car at the red light, start driving when the light goes green. Go for the job that pays more, or for the better college. But disruptors occupy a middle ground, a place outside our usual sense of how things are and how things work.

The examples of disruptors are rife: Christopher Columbus sailing perpendicular to the shore in search of a shorter route to the new world instead of the prevailing norm of sailing along the shores, "Total Football" in the 1974 FIFA World Cup where all ten Dutch players save the goalkeeper traded positions, demonstrated dazzling ball play, and reinvented the art of modern soccer, or Thomas Edison tinkering with the light bulb that lit up the world. All these instances are innovations that did not come out of conventional thinking. They were not zeros or ones, and they were not black or white. Luckily for us, these accomplishments were not overlooked like Joshua Bell was at the subway station, and generations thereafter benefited from them.

Appetite to Fail

Our society rewards success as much as it penalizes failure. Parents, teachers, and supervisors are all chanting the mantra of a performance-based culture so unanimously that the experimentally bent human mind is fearful of pursuing the unconventional that deserves time, effort, and energy. We have built a performance-based world in which capability and skill are largely directed to individual accomplishments and not at uplifting our social, economic, and environmental communities. Take a step back and look at innovation again—it is a pathway to the unknown, a journey on an uncharted path where others have never ventured, to find dramatically superior (but still unknown) outcomes for a larger community. Does this seem like a journey that spells guaranteed success or predictable gratification to you? Definitely not!

How is it then that an individual, a community, or even an organization that is not programmed to accept failure from experimentation is even remotely likely to succeed at innovation? Let's not mix up "shareholder value" with the desire to try something unique and be ready to fail in the process. Shareholder value is about near-term accomplishments—attaining goals in revenue, profitability, market share. These have to definitely trend up. The long-term potential to retain this trend requires foresight, research, and long-term innovation that is not instantly gratifying like these short-term goals but is also a part of shareholder value. Unlike revenue and profitability, innovation cannot be viewed through the same near-term glasses. Innovations in pharmaceuticals, for instance, need years to evolve and then more years to get the necessary government certification for commercialization. If organizations do not set up the expectation of failure in this area and extend that expectation to those entrusted with the innovation, then innovation will never be a desirable trait in the organization despite whatever lip service goes around the corporate corridors.

Find the Joshua Bells . . . Anywhere

An "innovation culture" is an outcome of systematic process. It requires focused commitment, support, and very directed social engineering whether it is within a workgroup, a community, an organization, or a nation—a culture that educates, identifies, motivates, nurtures, and rewards innovators and their innovation irrespective of the outcome. Silicon Valley is a great example. Our world is littered with individuals and organizations who were largely disqualified and passed over in their initial efforts with their innovations till the world finally did "get it"—at least in some cases. The rest were left on the wayside. For those who made it, in the initial lull and periods of disillusionment, their hopes were kept alive by their own belief and the motivation and support they received from the environment around them. Innovation needs a reward system (beyond financial accolades) that drives people toward these outcomes. Creating this environment is not just a matter of effort and investment—it needs time, education, and culture. Technologies like social media are very capable to put this transformation on steroids, assuming the platform is ready.

The life lesson here is this: once the folks who are trained to look out for hints of emerging greatness (that includes all of us), begin to reprogram their minds, they will certainly start to identify the Joshua Bells in the subway. Not because how he looks, where he stands, or what he wears, but because of how he sounds.

Once we learn this Lesson—We will have arrived. Since we are talking about lessons, lets learn an interesting one next from a prominent sporting event.

Life Lessons from the Super Bowl

Chase Blackburn is a linebacker with the New York Giants in the National Football League in the United States. In Super Bowl XLII, Blackburn had a costly penalty on a punt return because he was the extra man on the field (a twelve-men-on-the-field penalty). After the game, the rival Patriots' head coach, Bill Belichick, challenged the fact that the Giants had twelve men on the field and won. The penalty led to a first down, but the Patriots did not score on that drive after a failed fourth down conversion. Consequently, the Giants improved their field position by twenty yards, and the penalty actually went on to help them to finally win the game. The New York Giants then cut Blackburn after the 2010 season, a season in which he was the captain for the special teams. So what did he do? He waited for another team to sign him, but no team came calling. So Blackburn started substitute teaching for a middle school in Ohio. On 29 November 2011, he received the call he had been waiting for: the Giants were in dire need of an experienced linebacker due to injuries. Blackburn was back on the team.

What makes the story even more impressive is that Blackburn made what I believe to be the pivotal play of the next game the Giants played against the Patriots. While covering the Patriots' Rob Gronkowski, Blackburn managed to make a key interception that helped prevent their opponents from retaking the lead. Pretty impressive for a guy who had been cut from the team and was substitute teaching less than four months earlier.

So what is the takeaway from this that applies to our choices and actions in life?

Planning

This goes hand in hand with all professions, not just coaching or business. The Giants' coach, Tom Coughlin, outplanned and, more importantly, outcoached the Patriots' coach. For instance, not having a formal business plan to run a business or a plan to run your life is never advised. It will be met with misguided, unsynchronized activities and failed expectations irrespective of the size of the opportunity. If Coughlin had failed to plan the way he did and said, "I've beaten the Patriots in the past and I can do it again," this attitude would have been the Giants' undoing. Fortunately, Coughlin took nothing for granted and planned the game like a NFL coach is expected to do . . . and more.

Let Your Young Talent Shine

In any organization's ongoing success, continuity and sustainability of top-notch results are a necessity. The only way to make this happen is by setting up a pipeline of talent that keeps feeding new crops of skilled individuals as the older talent begins to fade with age and exposure. Call it succession planning or anything else that you want to, but this is the key to guaranteeing sustainable performance for any operating unit.

Now, back to Coughlin . . . instead of playing his starters all the time, Coughlin allowed his young, promising players to get playing time. This was beneficial in exposing these lads to the real world. What was outstanding in this process was the planned and methodical exposure of the young talent. They knew exactly how much time they would get under the lights to sharpen their skills and soak in the experience of playing at the highest level of the game. Compare this with the standard operating procedure of new talent being randomly thrown into a game due to injury substitutions or when the game is more of a stalemate in the last few minutes and a star player wants to bail out.

This same philosophy is usable in businesses and life. Give the next crop an opportunity to feel what the stage is like. Let's give them an opportunity to get real. Make them aware and give them the exposure in a predictable manner. Be critical of their shortcomings in a positive way and generally encourage them. Then watch them shape up. This is why, for example, internships are so important for students. They gain important experience that not only allows them to practice their skills but also let's them learn what skills they will need to add or improve upon before they have to play at the pro level.

Know Your Competition

We're all familiar with the saying, "Know your friends, but know your enemies better" (a variation on Sun Tzu). Coughlin spent hours mapping the rival Patriots team. He looked at his team and the Patriots for their strengths and weaknesses—essentially a SWOT analysis. He planned the game strategy that leveraged the Giants' strengths while covering and minimizing their weaknesses. He studied the Patriots' previous games and leaned heavily on attacking the weaknesses that the Patriots demonstrated.

Now you are thinking—is this not normal to expect this at the highest level of the game? My response is—no. Well, theoretically, yes.

Ask all coaches, and they will violently agree that sizing up the rival and playing to your own strengths is pretty much a given. Check their planning methodology and thoroughness of execution and you will be surprised. Why do you think that the top two or three spots in the Major Leagues rotate between a handful of teams? The rest are good enough to play in the league but never good enough to take the top spot.

Now think about a CEO or any other business leader. Is it any different for them? No.

Do all of them do this? No.

Do the ones who are consistently successful do this? Absolutely yes.

Leadership

I always marveled at the philosophy of "a CEO at every desk" in one of my workplaces. It is a brilliant representation of the fact that you do not have to be a CEO to make things happen. There are hierarchies and authority levels in organizations, and rightly so. However, nothing that deserves merit and needs to get done should be prevented from being done just because you do not have an executive tag against your name. Leadership and the desire or authority to do the right thing for the team or the organization flows right through the ranks in most successful outfits. If you are bubbling with ideas and actions that your hierarchy is not interested to hear, validate, or support, then most probably you are in the wrong place.

John Mara, the Giants' president, instilled a culture in which leadership and a desire to make the difference went down the ranks of the organization to coaches, captains, and the players. Mara's leadership brought in the right coaches, who then got the right players to perform at the right time, was integral for the team's success. CEO's and leaders at any level have to be confident, decisive, and willing to take a position, devise a plan, and execute despite the risks involved. These could be a strategic merger, breakthrough research, revenue execution, new product introduction, opening new markets.

Or, getting to the top of the Superbowl table through planning, execution and thoughtful reflection.

Plan, Execute, and Reflect

Our fast-paced world requires speedy execution. It is virtually impossible to create the perfect plan. The perennially changing circumstances and the limited time to execution will not permit that luxury. As has often been said, "No plan survives first contact with the enemy" (or the competition). Diligent planning is crucial, along with reflection on past practices, success, and especially failures. Do not give in though to what is commonly called "analysis paralysis." These are instances where individuals get so engrossed in the process of analysis that they lose track of the main plot. They forget that the analysis is a means to the end goal rather than the end goal itself. Put genuine effort into preparing the plan, then execute like a rock star! Very often, the quality of execution ends up being more crucial than the plan in determining the end result.

You are wondering why I keep mentioning the end result. Successful individuals and organizations approach an initiative with the end result in mind. In fact, in many instances, they determine the end result and then work their way backward. Conventional wisdom would suggest that you work from start to finish—this approach is incorrect.

The steps backward are carefully considered in terms of priority—in regard to their impact on the end result, and each step is then provided an apportioned amount of time and effort based on its priority—this will never be uniform. Working backward from the end goal ensures that resources are apportioned realistically and effectively. A professional sports team doesn't build its offensive and defensive squads simply by recruiting "good" players; it takes into account the context (other teams' abilities, the playing conditions, skill balance etc.) and the end goal (having a winning season). The definition of "good" must be informed within the context of the players already on the team and by the talent on the opposing teams.

Good planning leverages the knowledge, experience, perspective, and critique of as many team members as possible. It is a shame when collective teams fail to leverage the incredible know-how and experience that exists within them that can be inserted into the planning process with little or no additional cost! Organizations that implement feedback solicited from employees on organizational changes, product ideas, and customer service can use this input to design and implement plans that require fewer in-line adjustments later.

The best ideas don't always come from the top; they often come from the people with the most direct and recent experience of whatever part of the plan is being examined. For example, senior management isn't likely the best team to design a customer complaint response system; it's the people on the phone who deal with dissatisfied customers every day who have the best insights to offer on this. The other hidden benefit of soliciting ideas from the rank and file and involving them in the planning process is the feeling of inclusion among these individuals. Once they feel included, they are personally committed and ready to influence all their peers in making the plan successful. They are now serving as the force multiplier for the plan owner in the process of implementation.

Share and borrow best practices from around you. These ideas are free, and as long as we don't—for reasons of ego—insist on reinventing the wheel, it makes absolute sense to borrow these ideas, tweak them if needed, and implement them in our environment. The best way to leverage the experience of others is to emulate successful people and organizations. This allows us to avoid pitfalls that might not be obvious at the outset and to adopt strategies and practices that have proven value. Nations and organizations have modeled themselves successfully on previous successes. Why can't people?

Imagine that you are tasked to run a fundraiser for your child's school. You might decide to make and sell peanut butter cookies (your favorite), only to find that many of the students have nut allergies. This simple error could easily be avoided by conferring with someone who had previously been in charge of the fundraiser. A simple but devastating mistake was responsible for Chevrolet's failure to sell the "Nova" in Latin America. They built a reliable, affordable car, but in Spanish, "Nova" translates as "doesn't go." This fundamental marketing error could have easily been avoided if Chevrolet had sought outside inputs with representations from its major markets or language groups.

It is as important to solicit advice as it is to share it. Let's not be miserly in this department. As people communicate and share, the value of information grows much faster than that of the sum of hard-thinking individuals. Look at how Metcalf's Law spurred on the entire computer networking industry, an industry that now generates hundreds of billions of dollars every year. The same goes for Wikipedia, where the act of sharing started by a committed group of people has led to the creation of the largest general-purpose information repository in human history. According to Wikipedia's own listings, "At a rate of 600 words a minute, 16 hours a day, a person could read about 17,000,000 words in a month. In the month of July 2006 alone, Wikipedia grew by over 30,000,000 words. Reading the current incarnation at that rate would take over seven years, and by the time they were done, so much would have changed with the parts they had already read that they would have to start over again."

> Wikipedia is not only the most-used general reference tool in the world; according to a 2007 article on Search Engine Land (and also according to Wikipedia), it also is the sixth most-visited website in the world (*http://searchengineland.com/wikipedia-enters-top-ten-most-visited-sites-10536*). Early concerns that the accuracy of Wikipedia articles would be compromised by having been written by amateur volunteers rather than paid professionals have been answered: according to a 2005 article on CNET, Wikipedia is measurably more accurate than the *Encyclopedia Britannica*. (*http://news.cnet.com/2100-1038_3-5997332.html*).

Wikipedia articles are vast collaborative efforts in which the knowledge of many is combined and distilled into a product that is continually improved as new information and points of view arise. Additionally, the collaborative nature of Wikipedia has birthed several sister projects (Wikipedia Commons, Wikiquote, Wikibooks, Wikiversity etc.) that would not have been possible without the solicitation of many different ideas and perspectives. Sharing your advice and experiences generously also lays the groundwork for future collaboration, relationships, and favors.

At execution, every plan has its inherent risks and must adjust to real-market conditions. This has no negative bearing on the planner. It's the checks and balances that the planner subsequently puts in place that determines the quality and class of the planner and thus of the likelihood of success of the plan. Roles and responsibilities of groups and individual team members within the plan will also inevitably shift. This kind of flexibility is central to the plan. Sun Microsystems first conceptualized Java as an operating system for consumer appliances—however, Java morphed and ended up being almost the de facto programming language that powered the first generation of web-based applications and is relevant in that capacity even today.

Google is another example of this kind of necessary flexibility. Having been conceptualized and initially built as an accurate and very scalable search engine company, it has continuously reorganized its priorities as it has encountered new market possibilities. Google today is a key player in mobile operating systems (via Android) and a cloud-based provider of Infrastructure as a Service (Google Compute Engine) and Software as a Service (Google App Engine and Google Docs). The next frontier for them is even more revolutionary and inspired—Google Glass and self-driving cars.

Nothing teaches us better than our mistakes and failures, provided we seek them out, accept them, "fix" them, and ensure they are never repeated. We do all this while spreading our learning to those around us. Most of us have not figured out how to leverage our failures. We learn little from our successes. When we succeed, we drown in the euphoria and feel that our initial assumptions and plans were correct. We are quick to assume that they are the best—and perhaps the only way—to approach a new situation. When we fail, we are confronted with our mistaken assumptions and the holes in our assumptions and our general strategy. This is the point where we can learn the most. Failure shouldn't keep us from objectively examining where we went wrong and discovering what we could have done differently.

We see this every year in professional sport: a coach who has a losing season owns up and then urges the team to regroup. He changes the approach based on the lessons taught by failure and not only survives but even triumphs. Coaches who are not looking out to learn new lessons from either success or failure attempt to apply the same strategy year after year. They grossly ignore that the circumstances around them are constantly changing—these guys are eventually replaced.

I know it is hard for achievers to talk about failures, but failures help build knowledge-based organization that thrives and grows using its collective, acquired wisdom in the face of any adversity. As a society, we are programmed to seek out success as a signpost of capability and competence. Failure is consistently viewed as a stigma—the scum that needs to be quickly swept under the carpet. Cannot failure be categorized as an important addition to knowledge—one that inoculates an organization or individual from falling short in the same way the next time because of what he has learnt? Ask any successful man what he has learnt more from—his successes or his failures? I bet you I know the answer.

The consumer electronic group within Samsung learnt from not only their own mistakes but also from those of the previous consumer electronic giants Sony and Panasonic. They learnt and then rolled out an incredible line of products that dominate almost every category of the space. Another example close to my heart is Adam Scott, the Australian pro golfer. Scott came close to winning his first major title a number of times in the past years, at the British Open, at the Augusta Masters . . . but sadly, victory eluded him. This year, 2013, he was again on the top half of the leader board on the final day at Augusta. Despite his standing, Scott had many a failed putt, which, if successfully executed, could have put him on the lead to easily win the tournament. But on the eighteenth hole and again on the third hole of the playoff with Angel Cabrera, when it really mattered, Scott sank in the "pressure putts." As the ball disappeared into the hole, Adam Scott was crowned the winner at the 2013 Augusta Masters in the midst of its haloed fairways and its magnificent greens. All the learning from the losses of the past would have certainly played a part in getting Scott his first US Open win!

While there is nothing wrong (and much good) with failure, it is repeated failure that concerns me and is the real problem. It indicates that past failures have been a waste and lessons have not been learned. This could be either because the individual does not care or they do not have the skills to do what it takes. Consider some of the technology titans of the past decade—after dominating the microcomputer era, they have miserably failed in the smartphone, mobility, and cloud-computing spaces which define the "new normal" platforms. One has to wonder what they have not been able to learn and whether they will learn it in time or continually lose their revenue, market cap, and place in the sun to the new Turks who are storming in to take on the stage.

A similar rationale applies to individuals as well; adopting what is working for others with modifications that suit my style or embracing the learning opportunities that a failure presents can improve the everyday experience for anyone. My workplace is like a suction pump that just draws me in the moment I start my workday, so I know how difficult this is. We all have to balance our many demands and responsibilities at work, with our families and with our own health and quality of life. I have learnt to deal with these challenges through some great advice from friends, family and well-wishers. I remember the times when I was certain that there just weren't enough hours in the day to do all I had to do. In the end, I learned that it wasn't a lack of time that was the problem, it was my approach to the time that I had. Having failed to manage my time most efficiently, I turned to others for better ideas.

A solo morning walk, meditation, listening to music followed by personal journaling (a key skill where I record what I do and need to do) helps not only to reflect on the previous day, week, or month but also enables me to plan a micro-period like a day or a week, a major initiative, or a career action. Once I have reflected, learned, and then planned my actions, my personal GPS is set. I know exactly what to do and why I am doing what I am doing. I can then go ahead and run my day or week with confidence and get the most out of it.

I take time out in December and use part of the holiday season to reflect on the year gone by and plan for the year ahead. This plan involves my personal, family, financial, intellectual, professional, and philanthropic goals. Come January first, I am set to execute my plan. It's not just that this cycle of "plan, execute, reflect" is as applicable to my personal life as it is to my professional life; in fact, there is a synergistic effect. The more I apply this approach to my personal life, the more energy, time, and inspiration I garner to drive my professional life.

Step by Step: The Nails in the Coffin of the Financial System

I could not get to stop myself from writing a section in this book on how things unfolded for the global financial system. I thought that I would stay away from it, but then what's the point of writing about success without mentioning what to stay away from? So this segment was added almost as we were about to start the editing rounds.

In discussions over drinks, lunches, or dinners, my conversations with folks from different walks of life veer toward the topic of how a financial crisis of the dimension we have experienced in recent years happened. My answers vary based on who I am talking to and where. I also get their point of view. So here's my attempt to piece the disaster together. I studied economics but never got paid to be an economist. Nonetheless, let me try to construct a layman's model in simplified terms of what led to this doomsday for those of you who care to know.

Like any terminal illness, all this did not happen in a day, week, month, or even a year. Years of neglect, greed, and improper governance were the root of the crisis.

The financial world at the turn of the twenty-first century created radically different trends, with Asia generating massive surplus riding on the macroeconomic waves in China and India. The US, on the other hand, faced account deficits despite being preceded by a Clinton era where the president actually turned around a deficit-laden economy and balanced the budget before his term was over.

Despite the wobbly financial fundamentals in the United States, the Bush government's foreign policy was built around massive government spending, a significant portion of which was linked to the defense expenditure incurred in Afghanistan and Iraq.

Instead of Americans paying this bill, foreign borrowings (presumably the surplus from China) funded the spending while taxes were cut and interest rates were kept low at home to lessen the cost of the borrowings. A surplus of cheap money was built from several sources for general consumption, falling into the hands of people who did not know how to use it wisely. Stock, securities, and real estate flourished, and the equity that was generated through asset appreciation-related gains were reinvested in more of the same instruments and used for other forms of consumption, many of them needless (also called conspicuous consumption).

The evolution of the free market economy in the United States also radically changed innocuous financial instruments, which I believe, were built during the Clinton era to increase home ownership and labeled collateralized debt obligations (CDOs) on subprime properties. These CDOs are a form of security backed by a pool of bonds, insurance, and other assets. CDOs do not specialize in one type of debt but are often non-mortgage loans or bonds. These CDOs subsequently turned into vicious financial tornadoes. Add to that, the collapse of sub-prime mortgages, uncontrolled financial leverage practices that went high above the risk tolerance of the most established financial institutions. Now the proverbial camel's back was breaking in many places!

In parallel, the excessive import-related deficit of the Bush administration quickly eroded all the budget surplus benefits that the Clinton administration had accrued. The US dollar faced downward pressure, and suddenly, creditors, both domestic and foreign, had better options to route their funds.

The Federal Reserve had no choice whatsoever but to raise interest rates (despite a slowing economy) as the dollar fell and commodity prices rose, driving an inflationary climate.

As interest rates rose, some of the subprime mortgagees began to realize that the interest rate rise had suddenly turned their mortgage payments unaffordable. The snowball began small but grew rapidly and soon led to situations where lenders started revaluing the risk, which in turn led to de-leveraging of assets.

Large-scale divesture of risky assets followed in increasingly illiquid markets, while at the same time, a radical fall in asset valuations dramatically impacted the balance sheets of very prominent establishments. The establishments had no choice but to raise capital as the money market ran dry—paranoia ran high among investors.

Banks stopped trusting each other and interbank lending virtually stopped. Interest rate cuts do not help as the cash level in bank vaults continued to stay low (as the banks stopped lending to each other), affecting both the individual and the corporation alike.

The US administration heeded the internal advisory and stayed out of any direct involvement for too long. By the time Paulson, Bernanke, and their cronies got involved, it was too late. The bailout plan that was prescribed by presidential decree was mired with conflicting opinions of why the common taxpayer should bear the brunt of a trillion-dollar rescue package needed to fix the greed and misdeeds of a virtually unregulated banking sector.

The financial community internally and externally lost all confidence. Investment withdrawals and redemptions followed, causing the breakdown of financial systems worldwide and complete pandemonium.

While the US government's corrective policies have started to have an impact, the European Union's follow-up actions of injecting cash into their banking system and guaranteeing credit facilities have set bank collaboration going, freeing up the financial system and setting the world markets on an upswing.

There is still a long way to go before the tremors subside, but any buck in the trend is welcome. Borrowing the lessons of greed (in an earlier chapter), I hope the world will learn and end up being a better place going forward as we painfully navigate through the quagmire that is our own creation. In the end, we have to learn again and again that any currency is an agreement about the value of the things (houses, banks, the currency itself) it represents. Disasters like this are, at their root, an excess of faith in what we agree an asset is worth today against what we might believe it is worth tomorrow. What might be a "regret" in an individual capacity ("That sports car I bought is putting a dent in my budget") can translate into a "fiasco" on a larger market scale ("Those home loans we made aren't worth the paper they're printed on").

Even an intern can understand and learn from this!

Internships—A Step Above the Rest

Imagine this. You are in your senior year in a university and the realization that you will be interviewing and competing for employment is fast dawning. You have studied well, participated in group discussions and engaged with industry representatives who have visited your campus. Despite this, there are doubts. Most people at this stage, have problems in honestly accepting how ready they are to deal with the practical realities of their chosen profession, let alone excel in that space. They are not as ready and as sure as they ought to be.

If you are reading this (and smarting) and raring to tell me that you are different from the rest, and that I am being presumptive, then my apologies. You might have already done what I am about to suggest in this chapter. If so, then . . . great! If you agree with my prognosis but have not done the things I am talking about, then do not spend time mulling over why you have waited so long. Just get on with it.

As you go through the final years of your tertiary education, every break from classes is an opportunity to apply your knowledge in the real world, whatever field you study in or aim to pursue as a profession. Find a way to go out and gain that valuable experience that will set you apart from those who you will compete with when you start off as a job seeker.

Businesses are quite open in welcoming student interns and paying them fairly for a short engagement where both the student and the organization benefit. Obviously, the quality of the institution and the caliber of the student may have some bearing on the compensation.

The Krannert School of Business at Purdue University published their Internship placement statistics for the MBA Class of 2013. The results were impressive. Placements were in organizations like Bank of America, P&G, GE, Air Product, Dell, and Schlumberger, among others. The compensation seems exceedingly generous to me and not an appropriate sample of mean values across other universities in the United States and definitely not so in other parts of the world. Regardless, it demonstrates trends and the industry's commitment to reach out to in-program students, especially in postgraduate programs.

Now visualize this: you are the hiring manager, interviewing three fresh grad candidates from the same university for a position in your company. Candidate 1 has had multiple internships in a variety of functions in your industry segment with good endorsement from supervisors, Candidate 2 has had one internship with equally good endorsements, and Candidate 3 has had no internships at all but better curriculum grades than the other two. Now without even interviewing them and just looking at their resumes, it's clear that Candidate 1 has a definite advantage on paper.

Summer or other holiday internships are one of the best ways to gain this experience for a variety of reasons other than making a buck or two. It allows you to apply what you have learned in the classroom into the workplace. You will validate your classroom learning and research work, and you will be able to spot tweaks required to make the

Internship Placement Statistics—MBA Class of 2013
Krannert School of Business at Purdue University

(*http://www.krannert.purdue.edu/departments/gcs/about/statistics/resources/MBA_Internship_Stats.asp*)

Placement rates of those students seeking an internship or an assistantship

	Domestic	International	All
Secured an internship	98%	88%	93%
Secured an assistantship	0%	2%	1%
Total with summer work	98%	90%	94%

Functional Summary

Finance/Accounting	18%
Operations/Supply Chain	53%
Marketing/Sales	14%
General/Strategic Mgmt	4%
IT/MIS	4%
Consulting	4%
Other	3%

Geographic Summary

Midwest	47%
Northeast	8%
South	12%
West	3%
Southwest	10%
Mid-Atlantic	12%
International	8%

Industry Summary

Manufacturing	17%
Financial Services	5%
Technology	7%
Consumer Products	16%
Pharma/BioT/ Healthcare	18%
Other Services	16%
Petroleum/Energy	9%
Government/Non-Profit	3%
Consulting Services	9%

Average Compensation			
Monthly Base Salary			$5,202
Monthly Total Compensation*			$5,790
Average Salary—Functional Comparisons			
Functional Area			**Base Salary**
Finance/Accounting			$5,276
General/Strategic Mgmt			$3,567
Consulting			$6,171
Operations/Supply Chain			$5,338
Marketing/Sales			$5,452
Information Technology/MIS			$3,260
Internship Sources			
	Domestic	**International**	**All**
Krannert Professional Development Center	69%	67%	68%
Self-Directed Job Search	31%	33%	32%

learning in undergraduate or graduate school applicable in the real world with real people. A lot of the learning at work happens outside typical work settings. They happen during company outings, business off sites, or even in pubs over a jug of beer on a Friday evening. An intern gets automatically enrolled in all these forums to "soak in" and learn. I'm a strong believer of hiring and promoting from within, and interning is a great way to get your foot in the door and jump-start the path to professional success.

When companies hire fresh grads, their biggest concern is the new hires' time to productivity despite their educational smarts. Often, the transition from the academic, tuition-paying world to a salary-earning employment world is a frustrating one for both employees and the employer. Interning helps bridge some of these challenges and mitigates some of the risk by preparing you for what to expect when you go into the workplace.

Organizations and industry segments (finance, technology, manufacturing, legal) have their own cultures, how they go about the daily workday, dress, communicate and so on. The more experience you have adapting to company cultures within your target profession, the less your "culture shock" when you start. Internships give you a preview of what the "real feel" of your preferred professional function is versus your perception. Internship stints allow you to look up close and personal into the daily workings of your chosen profession. Come graduation, you are in a position to make an informed decision whether you really wish to pursue that profession or not.

So, it's never to early to look into internships. One, it will set you apart from your competition, two, it will provide you with realistic expectations of what is needed and expected at work, and three, it will help you understand your strengths and weaknesses better.

Internship is a vehicle that can get you into the first groove that leads towards your success.

Getting into the Groove: The Year Ahead

I wrote this chapter in January 2011, the beginning of a new decade and a brand new year. Technologically speaking, 2010 introduced a new generation of gadgets to satiate the needs of a tech-hungry, online community of a zillion GenY denizens—high-speed graphical image rendering, cool 3D TVs that will get cooler as 3D content starts to become more pervasive, smarter phones that help socialize, shop, game (and, of course, talk), and eBooks or electronic readers to read them on. There was the reemergence of the tablet as an independent device category, lighter in weight, more battery power, easy-to-use handwriting recognition software, and a host of other gizmos within, that will gradually and sadly move the paper-based content to Jurassic Park, save the trees, and make the planet "oh! so green"!

After spending most of the holidays figuring out what was in store for us in the New Year, I turned to writing my resolutions for the year on paper—I trust carbon more than silicon when it comes to tugging at my thoughts. This year, I want to keep my resolutions "simple and stupid"—the more I think of it, the more it makes sense. Complex and convoluted recommendations or strategies mostly emerge from simple basics. They are then layered with extras that do little other than to make the creator look knowledgeable, audience confused and implementation that much more difficult. As one of my heroes, Albert Einstein, said, "If you can't explain it to a six year old, you don't understand it yourself."

My first resolution is pretty elementary: to be a "listener." I am taking this on after preaching the virtues of listening to millions of people around the world over the last twenty-three years. Well, here is my thinking . . . we are in the midst of a civilizational paradigm shift—in a cusp between a past as we knew it and a very different future that we are entering with bated breath. The gap between these two realities has never been more radically wide in the history of mankind. The way our children, our families, our friends, the people at our workplace and our neighborhoods will emerge over the next years will be different from anything that we have seen in the past. Their evolution will be molded by their changing beliefs, the changing influence of the media (more ubiquitous and much more connected with the advent of multipath communication as driven by the Facebook, Twitter, Tumblr, and Instagram generation). There will be changes in perceptions of success and failure at home and work. So I am parking my twenty-three years of acquired knowledge and experience. Instead, I will follow nature's guidance in providing me with two ears and a mouth and listen twice more than I talk: simple as that.

I will listen and observe how the new technologies transform businesses, how the new generations of professionals coming out of our educational institutions will collaborate and grow workplace productivity with their new mindset, and how they will use social media platforms to brand themselves, their accomplishments, and, consequently, their organizations. That said, the fundamentals of the past that made people and businesses successful will not wither and die—they will need to be tweaked. I will certainly contribute in that department, but not before I have listened enough.

My second resolution is "zero conflict." Strive not to *reduce* conflict . . . *eliminate* conflict. Sounds tough, unrealistic, and impractical? Not if you can figure out what lies below a conflict. You have no control over anyone around you other than yourself. You can either focus on the things that you can control or focus on the things that you cannot control (and so possibly be controlled by them). The choice and the consequences are for you to face. We have the right to self-expression—to say what we feel about any subject. In doing so, we are most often expressing our view, not claiming that what we say is the absolute truth. We should also reciprocate by being prepared to listen to others' views on the matter. Not necessarily agree with what we hear, but in the least allow the other person to voice their thoughts and beliefs. Both these actions are well within our control, perfectly doable, and create cooperation, eliminate conflict, and very often provide new food for thought based on the perspective of the other person.

Opinions alone are not good enough in a situation—sometimes an individual (especially a leader) needs to take a position and make a statement. That's perfectly fine as long as the statements are backed by facts, past data, and logic, for all to understand. There will be contrarian views to be considered and, if it makes sense, be integrated with the original opinion to make it more solid and balanced. Once this is done, acceptability of the opinion generally increases, especially in group situations. Thus far, everything that has happened is within the opinion-owner's control and perfectly doable. But tread on the alternate path—force your opinion without sufficient supporting data, be closed to other people's views—and you start a chain reaction of other people's actions that you have zero control over. You start a downward spiral of negative emotions and choppy relationships. The choice, again, is absolutely yours.

With these two actions under way, I look at the world through a pair of refreshingly tinted glasses. I feel good. I also look forward to the super gadgets that are coming our way through the year and marvel at the progress of the human mind and the progress of our civilization—the sucker for technology in me is ever alive.

I will listen to what these new technologies and their early adopters have to say, and I will learn from them with an open mind and zero conflict.

I am all set to be smarter, stronger, and wiser.

Smarter, Stronger, Wiser . . . Now!

After the year-end holidays, most of us think longingly about the spring and summer break ahead. All the cheery fun is over, and December partying and merrymaking has sucked the life out of everyone, right? You can't seem to build up any momentum because it's cold and the days are short, so why do anything at all till spring comes knocking?

If you allow yourself to think like this, you are missing out on a huge opportunity to get smarter, stronger, and wiser. January is the time of the year to recharge and prepare for a new beginning in, well . . . January, not March. It is time to prepare your mind and body for the successes you are going to harness in the year.

Yes, you can't go down to the beach or play outdoor sports in the cold, but you can improve yourself so when the flowers and trees blossom; you can shine and stand out with them. So how do you get the most out of the winter months? Now, don't look back and wish you could have done things differently because all you are guaranteed is now.

- **Read . . . read . . . read.** Get your hands on books. Books, e-books, audio books . . . it does not matter as long as they are books. Your knowledge and ability to put that knowledge to practice in your chosen field and its adjacencies are your value.

Your financial and non-financial success depends on it. Success requires us to set knowledge goals every year and drive home the outcomes. As our knowledge grows, we grow.

Work Harder on Yourself than You Do Your Job. It sounds difficult. There are so many demands at work that you hardly are able to make time for yourself, family, and friends. Where is the time? I am sorry, but if success is desired, you have to *make* the time. Where there is a desire, there is a way. Make time to identify and improve every aspect of yourself, especially the weaknesses that are holding you back. Then see the difference. Your value will increase—even at the workplace.

- **Do Not Just Think—Write! Start a Personal Journal**

  Many of us want success, but we do not write down what we believe success is and how we plan to get there. People who put their values and goals on paper are able to visualize them and are more likely to keep working on them and achieve them. Never trust your mind to remember everything because it is more burdened and distracted than you think. Ideas and thoughts will slip unintentionally most of the time. Take notes, capture your ideas, thoughts, and action plans, and then read them regularly. New realizations will dawn when you read the notes well after the event.

- **Reflect before You Sleep**

One of my sports teachers taught me to replay every game piece by piece in my mind before sleeping at night after the game: analyze good shots, bad shots, right or wrong strategies, decisions and what could be done differently. The analysis would normally take about eight to ten minutes and help fix my mistakes while making the good actions more repeatable and consistent. Then it struck me—if I could do this for success in sports, then why not implement it for success in life? And so it began, and I started analyzing my day on similar metrics. The discipline has served my sporting, personal and professional development well.

Let's get our physical and mental gym gear out and start working the body, mind, and good habits. Let's do it now so that as the year progresses and summer arrives, we are in shape for the world to see. If you wait until May to start working out, you would have put the clock back, and the results will show only at the end of the year. All this while, the entire year, and the opportunity it presents, glides by you.

Plan for the end game early on. Start building your knowledge repository, stay focused on developing yourself, work your personal journal, and self-reflect every night.

Practice this simple formula on yourself and those you lead. Start treading the path towards the end game.

Will You Own the End Game of Leadership?

I have a friend who is treading a new path to professional and personal success through some interesting initiatives, challenging the conventions of "how things can be" rather than "how things are." We were chatting, and he gave me his belief on how he views the actions of a leader to evolve. He says that the leader is responsible for defining the vision. In doing so, he challenges conventions, thinks outside of the box, morphs past success methodologies, studies failures, assesses present circumstances, and most of all, knows how to dream.

Defining the vision is relatively easy, but what follows is difficult: structuring and articulating the vision, giving it shape and spelling it out in words that are understood by all involved who will bring the vision to reality. Every successful vision ever put into action has a common property: simplicity. If a vision starts off by being difficult to understand, the adoption, the planning, and the implementation that will follow will be difficult to deliver. The result, you guessed it right . . . difficult to attain.

Think of your favorite sports team. The coach delivers the vision, which in sports is uncommonly simply: to WIN. Convincing the team that they can win is a short step from convincing them that they *will* win. It doesn't need to be more complex than that, and I would argue that a more complex vision for a team can do more harm than good. Of course, the articulation, planning, and implementation will add detail, but the vision, to win, remains unadulterated.

Articulation of the vision requires empathy—seeking other people's perspectives, their views, their circumstances and their relevance to the vision. Irrespective of the skills and abilities of the leader, one does not know it all. Even if one does, one's thoughts and experiences represent one's "nuclear" perspective based on one's personality and environment.

I have seen good leaders consider the result of their contribution (and the efficacy of their vision) by the incremental impact they deliver to their team's results over the long-term. Examining and addressing the different variables that manifest a vision creates the impact. The scale of impact is created by broadening of the scope of the vision, enabling it to touch a large macrocosm, over time. In sports, the impact is delivered by assembling a team with diverse skills. A team that can counter rivals with a variety of playing styles and master different playing conditions. And, do all this while playing as one coherent unit. The skill is about translating win patterns against lesser opponents and intent study of the game patterns of the winning teams into strategies to take on and beat stronger teams and win tournaments.

Next comes implementation and execution, and this is where my friend laid out a different view that he subscribes to. He believes that very often leaders spend too little time in conceiving the vision and articulating it. They are way too keen on executing the vision, close off the campaign, roll out the scorecard, and start celebrating success. In the process, they garner short-term tactical results and fail to fully milk the impact and scale of the vision.

Instead, how would it be if the leader patiently carved the vision, articulated it expertly to his team, making it as simple as possible? He then empathizes with and openly solicits his people's feedback selectively but ensuring that as many conceivable arguments, counterarguments, and perspectives are covered. The leader then constructs the unique nuances that are identified through empathy and feedback into the fabric of the vision, making it optimal, powerful, and relevant.

Every member of his team now understands the vision, knows that it has been examined and tested robustly, believes in it, and supports it from their mental core. The leader then steps away and watches his team (led by the next tier leaders) drive the execution rather than leading the execution himself. He takes in the bigger picture, stays on top of the results, and makes modifications and tweaks where needed, again in consultation and with involvement of the people on the ground.

So why will the leader be confident that his team will pull this off? It is because he himself believes in the vision, he believes in the process of engagement and inspection through which the vision was crafted, feedback solicited and integrated, and he believes in his people. He believes that by trusting the implementation to them, the true impact and scale of the vision will be realized.

What about the people? They trust their leader's ability, his candor, fairness, credibility, and integrity. In the back of their minds, they know that there is an outside chance that the leader's and their own collective wisdom might prove incorrect and the desired results might fall through. These thoughts are far outweighed by the belief that the direction their leader has shown will sustainably deliver the desired results and represent their collective best interest. They execute in earnest, and most often, good results follow.

It is not surprising that good leaders attribute the success of a campaign to their teams while carrying the heat of failure on their able shoulders. The best leaders are, in a way, like the best sporting coaches. They prepare the team for success with the right vision, articulation of the vision and then its execution. When all goes well, the leader directs the adulations towards the team and basks in the reflected glory. When things do not go well, he is quick to shoulder the accountability, be open with where the team went wrong and involve the team to collaboratively chart the path to recovery.

It Is Not *All* about Work

Have you ever heard people say that they are too busy to work out, go to the movies, or just relax? Not to stereotype, but yes, heard this a lot among Americans and also among Singaporeans. Other nationalities might also feel the same way about their own. Some might describe these people as workaholics or those who 'bite off more than they can chew'. While work is important, life is not all about how hard or how much you work. One has to be able to detach from work and take in other things that life and our beautiful world has to offer. During a memorable vacation in the North and South islands of New Zealand, a celebrated chef chatted with me over a meal about life in New Zealand and Singapore. I remember him mentioning that in his country, people "worked to live"; he felt that in Singapore, people "lived to work." I thought he was right albeit there are valid reasons why Singaporeans are the way they are. However, those words have stuck with me as much as the memories of the gastronomical fare that he had laid out for me.

Whether it is reading books, taking time to meditate and reflect, observing the masterpieces in a museum, playing a sport, or taking in the sights of distant lands, time off is important. For those reluctant to schedule time away from the office, you should know that recreation teaches, energizes, gives new ideas, and allows us to perform at a higher level at work.

Starting a new hobby is one of the best ways to de-stress from work. Even taking fifteen minutes to do things that have nothing to do with work can refocus us. As long as we are enjoying time away from work, that is all that matters. The key is that our mind and body are in a state of gentle relaxation and having fun with something different and exciting. Even if the effort involved is substantial, it still relaxes the mind.

When it comes to traveling or vacationing in other countries, it is easier for young adults to travel. With fewer responsibilities and a paycheck to boot, they are capable to go and explore the world. Visiting a foreign land is both humbling and a great learning experience. You never know what you will gather while abroad . . . maybe your next big idea, a new hobby, a unique skill, new cuisine or a great friend or soul mate?

Unfortunately, Americans and Japanese are considered the workaholics of the world. Most US companies only offer a two-week vacation, and it is frowned upon to have those two weeks back to back—not to mention that they will probably be checking their e-mail while on vacation in fear of being left behind. Some countries have adopted laws that make mandatory paid time off that usually last for three to five weeks a year. So if you like your time off, perhaps choose to live in France or Sweden or Australia. Developed countries that still give you time to chill out!

Whether it's reading a book, relaxing with friends, starting a new hobby, or traveling some place new, remember that it is important to make time for yourself. Life can be harsh at times; but take pleasure in it, and recharge and pamper yourself where you can.

As you start treating yourself with care, respect and dignity, as you start appreciating the joys that life is giving you, as you start associating with elements that do not link to your day job alone, your self esteem will sky rocket. Affording this luxury requires a little bit of money and time but most of all it requires the right attitude. If you have the attitude . . . great! If not, let's start to build it immediately.

New Year—Harsh Starts

Well, the party is over. Everyone had a nice break with extended weekends over Christmas and the New Year. My own spin cycles significantly decelerated along with overindulgence in good food, merrymaking, and the company of friends and family. I did all that the textbook asked me to do over the holiday season . . . but now the party is over, so it's high time we all smelt our coffees and woke up!

We all mull, heave, and groan about how tough the previous year was, but let's not pretend that the years ahead will be a walk in the park. The American economy seems on a artificial high fed by low interest rates, exuberance in capital markets and the promise of shale oil. All of this can deflate quickly as the Fed tapers debt and the interest rates start to rise. Japan has been spurred by Abenomics, reversal from stagflation and a strengthening export position due to a weakening Yen. However, it faces political and defence challenges from China and South Korea every time the Prime Minister visits the Yasukuni shrine to pay homage to departed war heroes. Many of them, with questionable backgrounds in the eyes of these nations. Most of Europe continues to be a freaking mess. China and India have new leadership, inflation woes and slowing economies with India specifically seeing diversion in foreign direct investments that is murderously decapitating the currency. Despite low interest rates, capital formation is limited—job market pressures are mounting, and you will have to be really good to keep your job, leave alone grow in it.

I will share with you three insights that set you firmly for the year in anything that you plan to do. To some, these may sound cliché . . . don't fall for that, though. Most people slip on the floors that they know all too well. So much for clichés. So here we go:

Prioritization: Your work will seem like an unending maze of "to-do's," especially when you are back from time off. The best way to rewire purposefully without panic is to prioritize. I list all the "to-do's" and then line them up in the order of priority: absolutely-do, must-do, have to-do, and finally, do if I have the time. Get it? Stacking our priorities gives us a vision of all that needs to be done, kind of like the radar screen at an airport air traffic control tower. Some of those planes have to be landed immediately, and others can be asked to circle for a while. Once you have this list going, set a goal, a timeline to get each to-do done. Be absolutely committed to this goal.

If you were to peek at most people's priority list, you would see that the have-to-do or do-if-I-have-time have crept at the top of the list. Not that this is by design. Human psychology takes comfort in doing the easy stuff first and pushing the more difficult actions out as much as possible. This is fine as long as the "easy" stuff is also important. Otherwise, you are not getting the most out of the time you have.

Once each goal is attained, do what you love doing the most: Strike out the task. Done. You will start to feel really good as you plow through the list and see more than one "done."

Procrastination: Let's cut the literary gush . . . basically, I am asking you never to delay anything you plan to do and need to get done. Cut all the excuses that all of us are so good at crafting to justify our actions. This often is the difference between the successful and the also-ran. You will see folks prioritizing correctly but then never getting to complete or even commence the task—this is classic procrastination.

Build a solid system that prevents procrastination. A diary or calendar are tools that help remind you, the electronic versions even cajole you to get stuff done with frequent reminders. However, it finally boils down to us. For me, pain works better than pleasure in ensuring I do what I am supposed to do within the time I have set for myself. The pain of not keeping a promise I made to myself, my family, or my close friends is far more acute for than the momentary pleasure of delaying a difficult action. This works well for me. Find something for yourself. Keep the calendar handy, but do not forget the system.

This systematic approach is as applicable in your life outside of work as it is at the office. It applies equally well in every role that we play in life—at home and at work. Have you been delaying making home improvements that will make your house more comfortable and valuable? Have you stopped going to the gym (or never started) despite reminding yourself to do so every time you stand in front of a full-length mirror? Have you put off taking night classes for acquiring a unique skill that can help that pay raise? Put everything down on paper, create a system, and begin. Once you've started, things will start to fall into place.

Position: When was the last time you judged your suitability and interest in your current employment position? Many choose to be unaware that they are neither suitable nor happy in the roles that they are employed in. They get up every morning and trudge to work because they get a paycheck at the end of the month. There are others who know they are misfits in their profession, but don't do anything about it because it seems like a lot of work to better themselves or find something else that they could be better at. Others do not make changes because they are cocooned within a organizational machinery (people, products, skills, market leadership) that comforts them and camouflages their weaknesses.

Well, the coming years might well be the year of revelations for all the laggards, so if you are even vaguely in this category, make your moves now. Check your position—talk to friends and family that you trust, and talk to your boss if possible and determine your ranking versus your peers and areas of improvement. Another bit of advice: you will improve rapidly by fixing your areas of weakness rather than strengthening your strengths. Once you have a prioritized list, work on it with intent. If the list is too daunting and/or the odds are horribly stacked against you, then look at another role or even another vocation if you have age on your side.

The least I expect from you is that you will take action; choosing not to do so invites uncertainty, even chaos. Be fair to yourself, and do this before the invisible hand acts against you.

Let's go get that cup of coffee now.

Leading Inside Chaos and Disruption

Every new day presents opportunities that nudge us toward leadership.

If we already have leadership positions in colleges, universities, social settings, or organizations, then these opportunities nudge us to become better at them. Leading does not require you to have a team behind you. Leading starts with "us leading us" toward specific goals and accomplishing successful outcomes. The teams that we earn the right to lead, come afterwards.

While leaders should be looking for ways to improve themselves constantly, it is no mean feat to do so. The bar is set fairly high—insight and execution are both needed. I have taken a keen interest in the mindset and operating pattern of the successful leaders I have come across, especially within conducive situations of chaos and uncertainty. What I have extracted from them are five elements for you to consider that can help you go up at least a few notches as a leader going forward. I will then show you how two famous leaders succeeded and failed to take advantage of chaos and disruption in the world of technology.

1. Clarity in Thought and Communication

By clarity, I mean clarity as in thinking and communication. Good communication is integral to good execution in any organization: a sports team, a school, or any group of people working together socially toward a common objective. If a leader cannot communicate to his teammates what the goals are, what is expected of them, what the priorities are, then it is game over even before the band starts marching! The precursor to good communication is clarity in thinking—to be able to isolate the "important and urgent" from the clutter. Once the clutter is eliminated, the picture is clearly defined and set up to be communicated well.

2. Assessment of Process and Strategy

In the rapidly changing times that we live in, especially in the midst of uncertainty, the baseline and the goal posts are forever shifting. It is foolishness not to be mindful of these shifting sands and not consider what these changes mean to us. The assessment I am referring to involves assessing ourselves—what is it that we ourselves can do differently that will lend impact in the present time. Then let's assess the people we work with, the processes that we use with them, and the strategies that are employed. Assess and make changes where appropriate. Improvement does not have to wait for the company to make these changes—individuals and small workgroups can start the change and show the positive outcomes from the change. These little flares of transformation ultimately transform the organization. The people who light these flares are the real leaders.

Changes that follow a reassessment exercise are almost always met with resistance. Involving employees by making them a part of the assessment exercise makes the changes that follow a lot easier to implement. The employees start to feel that their opinion is valued—retention, morale, and productivity improvements naturally follow.

3. Manage by Walking Around (MBWA)

Instead of confining yourself within a cubicle or office, a great way to understand employees, customers, business partners and the business landscape is to walk around. Or take a cab ride, a plane or a train. Get in front of people and give them a chance to talk to you. You will get pin pointed insights regarding the chaos, the disruption and opportunities within. If you cannot meet people in person, talk to them on the phone, write to them. Reach out in all possible ways. Communicate what you and your organisation is focusing on during the troubled times and convey a shared vision of hope that is realistic. Solicit ways in which you and your organisation can help employees, customers and business partners. The floodgates of valuable feedback will open up. All of them will also remember your actions—this is meaningful when the good times roll in again.

Other than the new insights such walkabouts provide, this is also a great way to motivate employees. Feel responsible to pat one or more backs during your journey for a job well done and do a couple of high fives for some specific accomplishments. Recognition of people's efforts in public is a powerful motivator and most often works even better than cash bonus payouts.

I am a believer that individuals who aspire for positions of leadership should start to demonstrate behavior that associate them with the position before they actually get the position. I do not include ego and tantrums in the list of behaviors, though—I mean the real hard and soft skills. Uncertainty and chaos are wonderful opportunities for individuals to step up and do this.

4. Admit Failures

There is a terrible stigma about failure that makes people afraid to fail and afraid of admitting that they failed, especially when the going is not very good. This is a limiting factor that prevents long-term success. Failure is a real and undeniable part of everyone's life, especially within uncertainty. We are all human after all. Admitting this takes the tension away, eliminates the time wasted in unnecessary justification and sets the stage to learn from the failure. I, for one, have learned more from my failures than I have from my accomplishments. Being comfortable talking about your failures and what you learnt from them does a lot more in painting your professional portrait than if you were continually bragging on your accomplishments. As former United States Secretary of State, Colin Powell put it, "There are no secrets to success. It is the result of preparation, hard work, and learning from failure." No one is perfect, and no one expects you to be either.

5. Understand How People Work

Everyone has his or her own way of working. Some people need to be told that they are doing a good job, and others need to feel internally motivated. Certain employees may be able to perform their work better at home working in isolation, while other employees need that office atmosphere where they have the comfort of being surrounded by co-workers. You as a leader or a colleague need to know the many types of personalities that are within your span of influence and have an understanding how to make most of them tick. How do you motivate an individual if you don't know anything about them? That is where managing and leading by walking around comes into play. You get to know the people you work with and how to deal with them in physical and mental planes. This knowledge is invaluable.

Now for the story of the two leaders . . .

In the world of technology, two very successful men and their companies chose two different paths with regard to defining their destinies. There is Michael Dell, who immersed himself in Radio Shack and personal computers while in his teens, went to college at nineteen, turned his dorm room into part inventory hub, part lab, and part sales outlet of the company he named Dell Computers in 1984. By 1992, the company had gone public with a $30 million IPO. Soon after, Michael Dell was the youngest CEO of a Fortune 500 company. He was twenty-seven.

The center of Dell Computer's existence was a maniacal focus on the customer. The company executives managed by walking around, talking, and listening to customers. They eliminated the middleman and used the margin to build a dramatic customer experience, including building bespoke products *after* the customer had specified their requirement. This reduced their inventory-related cost and risks, provided better profits for shareholders, and provided for further spending that enhanced the customer experience. Thanks to Dell's strong umbilical link with their customers, they were able to spot two major trends or disruptions, one positive and one negative. They saw the positive rise of the power of the Internet, not just as an e-mail exchange platform but as a framework that would change the world starting with e-commerce. Dell moved their direct sales transactions with customers onto the e-commerce platforms that the Internet provided, saving hundreds of million dollars while their competitors were still using old brick-and-mortar manually driven sales models using layers of sales partners. Dell also saw the negative swell of the dot com bust early and was able to tighten the screws before the ship leaked. During the same time, well-entrenched companies' (e.g. Cisco) market capitalization were beaten and bruised once they declared unsold inventory, which had piled up in the expectation of inflated sales forecasts that never materialized. The bust hurt Dell but not as bad as it did the others. Jeffery Krames writes in his book *What the Best CEOs Know*, that the "Internet was tailor-made for Dell, enabling the firm to gauge demand very accurately." Even after the dot com bust, by 2002, Dell was generating $60-$70 million in sales, daily, over the Internet. Michael Dell had the vision of doing 100% of Dell sales over the Internet. While this might border an utopian vision, it definitely defines the virtues of communication, contact, and understanding how people work that I have described earlier. Dell has faltered in recent times as PC margins have dwindled to levels where even the direct business cannot hold up profitability. Dell's attempt to tap the profits from services, cloud applications, and mobility devices have also come up short. A perennial disruptor of the playing field, Michael Dell is trying to disrupt what he has built by taking the company private. If you are competent, disruption and chaos are your two good friends.

Now to our other story . . . Microsoft.

It is not uncommon for two friends to stand on Harvard Square, notice an article in a scientific magazine, determine that their time has arrived, drop out of campus, and go start a company. It is not commonplace at all that the company they form is relevant thirty-eight years later as I write this, owns a market cap of $264 billion, approximately $80 billion in annual revenue and employs 99,000 people. In the process, it catapults one of the lads, named William H. (aka Bill) Gates, to the stature of the richest man on the planet some years later, and subsequently, he becomes the largest philanthropist of the human race. The other lad, one Paul Gardner Allen, also earns the status of a fellow billionaire and goes on to build and fund technology companies, biological research, sporting teams, philanthropy, and finally is a collector of rare World War II aircraft. Anyway, in the early days of Microsoft, the culture was to crank high-quality code to make the whole computing experience fun and easy. Microsoft maintained close ties with the external developer community, their OEM partners (hardware vendors who bundled Microsoft's operating system), even their distribution and reseller partners. But they somehow seemed allergic to the end customer, whether they declared this publicly or not. After years of dramatic success they met with a severe pitfall—one that they are yet to completely recover from . . . the Internet. Even Gates did not see it coming. By the time they did, there were new names like Netscape, Yahoo!, Hotmail, and then Google, all of who would have had a hard time getting any airtime if Microsoft had been at the top of their game. What Microsoft lost because of likely customer coverage gaps, the company made up by accepting failure rather than defend their inactions. They started to seek feedback from all corners of the company leveraging their large base of intelligent human capital. Piece by piece they drew, what they believed in how people would work and collaborate within an internet enabled society. The architecture was built and the products started to roll out—fairly quickly given the size and complexity of the company. Then the fabled Microsoft marketing machine with multi million dollars of budgetary spend started to crank out the message. They executed, but it was not as well as they had executed in the desktop era. Look at Microsoft today—still a mighty organization but substantially marginalized in the domains of cloud computing, social networking, smart phones, and mobility devices as the newer entrants like Google, Facebook, Amazon, and LinkedIn stole the show.

You have seen the opportunities that chaos and disruption bring about to organizations and their leaders. Chaos and disruption also fires different forms of disruptive distractions at people employed within. Each of them may be different, but they have one common trait. They affect productivity. If you are supervising these people or intend to do so in the future, then it is as much your job as their own to keep people on the ball and fully engaged despite these negative onslaughts.

Left unchecked—disruptions can spill the valuable beans that you have accumulated over the years!

A Mixed Bag of Beans

I have always held immigrants in high regard, having been one myself. After leaving India for the unknown, foreign shores of Singapore in 1991, this regard comes naturally. Immigrants have the inherent ability to take risks, challenge the status quo, continually innovate, and naturally disrupt. These are not just virtues that they naturally have (well, some may), but they are forced to develop these traits to carve a place for themselves in the new society that they migrate to. The status quo in fact is their biggest foe. The land that accepts them usually benefits collectively—Singapore and its emergence as a first world destination is a fabulous proof point of this theory. National strategies in many instances have included acceptance or even solicitation of immigrants as a means for economic, social, and political evolution. On the contrary, nations that have been dogmatic in protecting their native population and defended a homogeneous society have mostly not been able to sustain development, innovation, and, consequently, economic progress. Not to mention having to contend with a rapidly ageing population as birth rates fall. Think of Japan here.

The United Nations report on World Population Policies (2005) listed UN member countries by immigrant population as a percentage of total population. The data clearly tells the story. The United States (12.3%), Germany (12.8%), New Zealand (15.48%), Australia

(19.9%), and on the higher scale, Hong Kong and Singapore at >40% are endorsements of the wonders that immigrants bring to the economic development of the country. The total immigrant population worldwide was estimated to be approximately 200 million.

I was recently speaking to a Swedish friend of mine about his motivation to move himself and his family from Sweden to Singapore. Turns out that this gentleman lived with his family of four in an affluent community just outside of Stockholm. Almost everyone in the community had blond hair and blue eyes. The husbands were mostly in executive positions within Swedish organizations in nearby Stockholm. The women were mostly housewives—stayed at home in the mornings and socialized, sipped beverages, or played tennis at the country club in the afternoons. The children spent the day within their private school routines with their blond-haired and blue-eyed friends and then settled in nicely with their well-trained nannies at home. In social gatherings and parties, the routine was similar—men chatted with men, the women with women—the discussion topics were the same, and everyone agreed violently with whatever everyone else said with the exception of a few radicals like this friend of mine. Seemed like a society matched together in heaven, the perfect harmony. Or is it?

Long story short, my Swedish friend and his family had enough of this harmony and unified perspectives and homogenized life. They figured out that the comforts of homogeneity would make a serious dent in understanding the contrarian cultures, lifestyles, beliefs, and perspectives that the rest of the world has to offer. They traveled East to Asia and arrived in Singapore. Just to set the record straight, I do not label Sweden as a regressive society or as one that is opposed to immigration. Neither is the social setting that I described my friend living within a macrocosm of the Swedish society. On the contrary, Sweden has long been a seat for growth and innovation. Swedish global brands endorse the country's contribution to human progress. My personal experiences in Sweden and with Swedes have been incredible in different ways. My Swedish friend's circumstances could have been played out in homogeneous pockets of many countries or cities worldwide.

So What Does a Heterogeneous Society Entail?

Well, first, it provides diversity. Different nationalities, language groups, and social, cultural, and political beliefs congregate. They are provided with equal opportunities to grow and evolve and create a melting pot of diversity that is unique. The diverse mix of people makes the society vibrant with their expertise, perspective, cultures, and beliefs. Individual contributions multiply in impact when cross-pollinated with another person's contribution, while still ensuring a unique identity.

Immigrant-friendly societies normally enjoy first-class governance, where the thoughts, ideas, and output of the people within the society can translate into productive actions, process, and products. These are then fairly meted out to the people while rewarding the creators through sound policies and guidelines.

The smart governance that usually runs these societies (built by people who may themselves have been, well, immigrants!) provide for freedom of speech and action. An efficient judiciary ensures (ideally) that every individual and his mental faculty is respected and regarded. Freedom is paramount as long as this does not conflict adversely with another person's freedom. And what about success? Well, every immigrant is the underdog—and the natural mindset of every underdog is to take a shot at success. It all depends on how much he desires it. Show me a cluster of immigrants, and I will show a cluster that has the highest probability for professional and financial growth in the next ten years.

How does this theory play out in organizations? An organization is best viewed as a microcosm of the nation. Actions and decisions that build or break nations work in similar ways to impact organizations as well. In the two large businesses that I was fortunate to build in my professional career, diversity, freedom, fairness, and strong, capable governance have all played critical roles in the outcome.

Every opportunity I get, I do my best to ensure that I board a first-class crew on the bus. An A-player will attract other A-players, and you end up with an A-team that is wired to deliver first-class results. Introduce one B or C player, and you start on a downward spiral that will attract other B-category and C-category elements, and the slide begins. If you are not yet a leader, associate with the A-players first—their attributes will rub off on you. B-players are easier to associate with but will not do you as much good.

As you go about assembling your A-team, keep an eye on the diversity. Most international business centers are naturally diverse today—Silicon Valley, New York, London, Frankfurt, Singapore, and Hong Kong epitomize this. Shanghai, Gurgaon, and Kuala Lumpur are not far behind. I have always believed in leveraging the diversity of Asia and the rest of the world rather than succumbing to it. Having a diverse team sets a group or an organization in the right groove to accomplish this.

Next, just like governments of the nations I have mentioned earlier, successful teams need the right framework to succeed—the goals and boundaries are needed. That done, take the onus to determine the way to get things done. Speak up and express your views—even if they are contrary to conventional thinking. Again, a diversified team will value-add and feed off each other. Use this leverage. Authority and accountability, however, will go hand in hand. One cannot be served without the other.

Finally, the value of good governance cannot be diluted. Good performers are demanding; they need and seek attention and want to be treated fairly. Many wear their egos on their sleeves. Leading a band of first-class performers is neither a walk in the park nor is it a popularity contest for any leader. At work it is impossible to keep everyone happy at all times. While a leader has to be fair and equitable, his actions are not viewed in a common and shared light by everyone. While leadership is not a popularity contest, fairness and integrity are the best ways to earn respect in the long run.

A diversified bag of top talent from different nations will serve any organization well. Be careful when you put them together in a room when their national teams are playing a soccer or cricket match. The spirit, pride, and passion that goads them to professional success will make them go for each other's jugulars in support of their respective teams with the same intensity that they demonstrate at work.

See 'Work Hard—Play Hard' in action here—it sure is a fun, high-energy environment to be in!

When Work Seems Too Much Like Play

Don't get me wrong: I've written about the need for passion in what you do. But I have also written about the omnipresent need to make every employee and student accountable in his or her place of work or study.

While social networks, the Internet, and new gadgets (that are on a dramatic rise) are powerful tools of personal and group productivity, the extent and form of usage can easily slip from a state of productivity to an absolute lack of it.

Once usage morphs into a distraction, even the most well-meaning employees and students get sucked into it at the expense of productivity. Creating policies that outline acceptable and unacceptable behaviors in regard to social media platforms, social networks, and over-the-top self-promotion through personal branding are needed more than ever before.

The Use of Social Technologies in the Workplace

The blurring lines of the adoption of social media and new technologies for work and play are creating complex situations related to productivity and compliance. Many companies are seeking answers in how to organize and implement policies to both leverage social technologies and mitigate the associated risks from their usage.

Policies regarding the use and the application of social technologies in the workplace are increasingly a discussion point. And with good reason: these issues affect and can positively (and/or negatively) influence the organization in a number of ways.

During the 2010 World Cup, worker productivity fell dramatically. In Britain alone, the forecast was that "over nine million employees . . . would skip work on an average of 3.5 days during the (World Cup) event." In the United States, prominent baseball, basketball, and American League football games bring their own malaise of distractions.

In the United States, one of the biggest drains to productivity, time, and company money is the NCAA Men's College Basketball Tournament, also known as March Madness. It was estimated that the first week of the tournament would cost companies around $1.8 billion. This is due to employees updating their in-office brackets, checking scores, and, more recently, watching live streams of the games during office hours.

Organizations often try to block sites by sealing them up behind firewalls. This approach is only half-witted, though. Office workers have access to everything that the Internet has to offer that does not use the office network—the cell phones and tablets that communicate through 4G/LTE mobile networks. Good-bye corporate networks and good-bye firewalls, there is now a simple workaround to a world of distraction! Clearly, setting guidelines that work with the natural flow of human behavior is more harmonious and ultimately a more rewarding approach for companies and employees.

Use cases and data appear to suggest that an increased opportunity to partake in social networks in a responsible, result-oriented manner actually benefits the organisation, rather than hurting it. There are always exceptions. While sharing company secrets, sensitive information or the like isn't desirable, social media can help build brand, consensus, and supports specific marketing initiatives at substantially lower cost than traditional approaches. So it is not the usage but the policy for usage that needs attention.

Organizations are as unique as the individuals in them. What this means is that each organization has its own needs, its own objectives, and its own situation. This uniqueness deserves consideration as the organizational structure, and the policies regarding the use of social technologies are instituted.

I would ask of you to support social technology initiatives in your organization or institution—be a player in these initiatives, contribute to it. As these platforms grow in prominence to determine professional success, you will be able to ride the wave if you can spot and catch the swell early. As a prominent Silicon Valley Venture Capitalist recently tweeted—"the population will soon be divided into two groups. Those who are good at working with intelligent machines, and those who can be replaced by them. The first group will prosper . . . the second group will get to play a lot of video games.

Use the new age tools to "move up" or misuse them and risk "moving out."

Moving Up and Moving Out

Wherever you happen to live and work, the workplace is evolving at light speed from where it was even a few years ago. The inevitable organizational, sectoral, and macroeconomic challenges face every organization on the planet. The underlying opportunities that these challenges present to us are dramatic, and many of us are morphing ourselves in many ways to address them. It's an exciting time to be around but also an intense period of introspection, planning, and execution, especially to help stay clear of the pitfalls that these opportunities will come accompanied with.

In times like these, the ability to travel and the willingness to listen and feel the pulse of people in your own field and adjacencies are crucial to remain on top of your game. My travels enable me to engage in situations, opportunities, and challenges that excite me tremendously regarding the possibilities while presenting opportunities for invaluable learning. Let me tell you about two interesting incidents . . .

Moving Out

Recently, I met a prominent Chief Information Officer (CIO) friend over lunch. After exchanging pleasantries, he enquired how we were dealing with the integration of a major acquisition we had done in 2009. He wanted to know what we had learned. He was in the same boat, dealing with an acquisition that closed earlier in the year. I was battle-tested by integrating two major acquisitions in the previous three years, so I went about explaining the blueprint, planning, integration, ownership, and the related metrics that could be externally shared. Halfway, he stopped me, and asked, "Tell me about the people." I was about to get there anyway, but he seemed impatient. I spoke about how we profiled the organization we acquired even before starting the integration based on our vision of the combined organization and how we matched people to the roles we envisioned and judged coverage, enablement, fair placement, and training needs as we went along. I spoke about dealing with redundancies, role overlaps, and elimination—these are never easy to face but have to be dealt with. We discussed communication, managing expectations, and managing operational execution through quantitative metrics—all extracts from business school curriculum (aka "MBA speak"), which we had followed very well.

He listened intently, nodded and then sat back. Narrowing his brows, he said, "How do you deal with people you think are good enough for the job but they themselves think they are not?" Now that is a hard one, but I have seen some of these in passing myself. I did not have a well-constructed response. So I paused uncomfortably.

The CIO sensed that I was waiting for him to speak. He started to speak softly, almost to himself: "I feel that success, brilliance, and results come out of basic mental conditioning within the individual. I find it hard to believe that any individual can consider himself a lousy performer with subnormal skills yet come up with brilliant results. So how do you rate a person highly when the person lacks self-esteem? One of you has a horribly incorrect assessment, and it most likely is you."

I kind of get that. There are individuals who thrive in startups or smaller companies and come with a glorious track record to boot. They enjoy the close-knit work environment, the informality, the loosely structured hierarchy, operational challenges and so on. Put them in a midsize or a large company environment, and they are overwhelmed. Worse, they feel like they have been straightjacketed. They like the infrastructure and the support system for a while, but then the excitement begins to wane, and both passion and creativity begin to sputter. The formalities, processes, and accountability wear them down and dilute their ability to duplicate the results of the past.

Disillusionment creeps in quickly as they struggle to cope and communicate through the formal layers. My CIO friend continued, "In my review sessions, I have encouraged supervisors to look out for this malaise because it is not readily visible. Once identified, they need to deal with it swiftly. It really does not matter how talented the employee is; they are not much value to the organization in this state. They leave their passion at the doorstep, and there is no desire to attain meaningful outcomes." If I were to add to what he said, I'd say these demoralized individuals very unconsciously taint every other impressionable person who happens to be around them.

I have seen these in the past and have had some amount of success in dealing with them, so here's my formula. Empathy and openness usually work best in addressing these situations. I will normally be candid about the situation with the employee or any individual for that matter in a non-work group situation. I will explain the negativity and lapses that their attitude and state of mind are bringing to the role, the team, and to themselves. I will then contrast this by painting the positive outcomes that the individual's separation from the group will bring to both the organization and the individual's future. The organization will be free to hire someone else who can do justice to the role, while the individual will be free to move to another suitable role that can potentially give him a higher probability to succeed.

This is very similar to couples whose marriages are going nowhere. A balanced, honest dialog between a supervisor and a subordinate, where both individuals commit to understand each other and take a collaborative decision regarding the future, is a brilliant outcome. Separation on a positive note often grows mutual trust and esteem among the individuals. It prevents the damage from worsening. I am personally proud of my relationship with people at work who we let go but who have continued to be my golf buddies though we no longer work together.

We've all seen this in sport. There are many players whose early promise sputters when they are picked up by a professional franchise, only to shine in later seasons after they have reprogrammed themselves into a new set of realities. Indian cricketer, commentator, politician, and now a reality-show judge Navjot Sidhu comes immediately to mind. Sidhu rose through the national ranks rapidly and wore the India national team colors at twenty but failed to make a mark. He confessed later that an article criticizing his dismal performance changed his cricketing career. Following his failure in 1983, a cricket columnist described him as "Sidhu: The Strokeless Wonder" in *The Indian Express*. The epiphany altered his career as he started to reprogram himself to perform and keep succeeding under critical glare. In the 1987 Cricket World Cup, he scored seventy-three against Australia. He then scored fifties in four of the five World Cup 1987 matches in which he batted. Following his brilliance in the 1987 World Cup, the journalist made amends via an article titled, "Sidhu: From Strokeless Wonder To A Palm-Grove Hitter," applauding his performance.

Sidhu's innings of 201 against West Indies in 1996-97 was memorable, as were the eight sixes in the 124 against Sri Lanka in 1993-94, and the four fifties in five innings against the Australians in 1997-98, with a brutal offensive on leg spin magician Shane Warne.

Moving Up

The "moving up" story is quite the opposite of the one on moving out. One of my close business associates is Terence Woo (not his real name), the divisional president of a prominent conglomerate in Southeast Asia. He is responsible for the group's telecom services subsidiary. Over five years, Terence built a robust business by assembling a top-quality leadership team who then went about hiring the best talent in the industry. By employing operational best practices and great people and by leveraging the strength and influence of the conglomerate, the telecom subsidiary has delivered remarkable growth very quickly. Jenny Mendoza (not her real name) was the marketing VP in the conglomerate's consumer division, a maverick who had made quite a name for herself by taking four out of the six consumer products of the division into the top two in brand equity and market share in their respective categories in the region. The telecom business was evolving and growing rapidly, consumerism was the call of the day, and it was no surprise that at one stage, Terence, the "master talent scout," was keen to have Jenny in his team to help build brand and share for the outfit. Jenny was also eager to take on this challenge and test her skills in a new space.

Great idea! Not the right thing to do without a proper think-through. The move would neither be right for the consumer division nor for the conglomerate and definitely not for the shareholders. While these moves are quite convenient for the individuals and benefits the receiving subsidiary's interests (in this case, the telecom division), it creates a hole in another part of the organization. Without doubt, actions like this show immaturity, poor judgment, even selfishness among those involved who, in most instances, do not understand the long-term ramifications of their actions.

Terence Woo impressed me by the way he dealt with the situation. Early in the cycle, he expressed his thoughts to the CEO of the consumer subsidiary (that employed Jenny), who happened to also sit in the board of the telecom subsidiary. The discussion was easy because the CEO from his position in the board was able to understand the opportunities that the telecom subsidiary had in front of it and how Jenny could add value to the future of the division. He also knew Jenny well and understood that once she made up her mind to go after something, she usually found a way to get it. Besides, there was hardly any reason to stifle a top-class professional like Jenny; competitors were ready to give an arm and a leg to have her on their side. Once the rationale was sealed, Terence asked Jenny to take the next six months to find the division a suitable backfill and train the person amply to eliminate any exposures during and after her transition into her new role. Her transition to the telecom division would not commence till she had accomplished this task. He also ensured that in the first three months of her new role, Jenny would check in with her backfill in the consumer division and his supervisor to ensure that the person was on top of things.

Terence explained to me how he helped Jenny understand her legacy. His offer to the consumer division CEO to minimize any risk from this move was no mere lip service. He did realize that it is never an easy feat to build four market-leading consumer brands. While it was all a team effort, Jenny provided the vision and the leadership that made this outcome happen. While she absolutely deserved the opportunity in the lucrative telecom unit, it would be a shame if her move to a well-earned bigger role destroyed her present legacy that she had worked so hard to build. Not only was the right person needed to fill her very able shoes, but the person would also be required to be prepared to take on the responsibility and integrated with the team while she was around to minimize or eliminate any risks.

This needed time, commitment, and freedom. Had Terence rushed the process, a potential disaster would very much have been on the cards. The maturity and patience that he demonstrated bode well for both the telecom and consumer divisions, who have since benefited tremendously from the induction of the two new marketing executives.

Moving people in the organization is fair. It keeps people motivated, helps them grow, and enables the organization to align the right resources to the right roles. In doing so, let's understand the bigger picture, set the right expectations, commit to a zero-risk transition, and the results are incredible. Do it poorly, rush it, or implement a poor transition, and it poses all sorts of continual business risks and even bad blood among those involved.

In a prominent school that I am familiar with, a talented and respected teacher was elevated to administration. He has since become a fine administrator and enjoys the same level of respect from students, colleagues, and parents that he did while in the classroom. However, his promotion was done without much thought to who would fill his position as a teacher and head of department. Sadly, his replacement does not have the same level of talent and experience, and the whole department is feeling the loss of a capable administrative leader. The opportunity for a win-win solution was passed by.

In most instances in life—how you win is more important than what you win.

Multinational Leaders Who "Win"

As business in international markets grows in size, relevance, and complexity, I see organizations struggling to choose the right profile of the person who is suited to be the leader of the geography. The early days of business development could well afford the "man from the mother ship" (the corporate headquarters), who was familiar to the executive team, was soaked into the business and culture of the company and was a source of comfort to all within. A chap who could be trusted to run the business by the larger powers who resided many thousands of miles and several time zones and cultural zones away. Those days are long gone.

So what does it take to develop and put in place—not one, but a string of successful regional leaders who can skillfully navigate this global organization through its different stages of evolution in a geography like Europe or Asia? Do not assume that the profile of the leader who sets up the first beachhead operation in the geography will be the same as the one who builds the team and the run-rate business or the one who drives tier two and tier three growth initiatives while building a strong, robust, and real organization. The skills, experience, mindset, personal brands, and individual competencies of these individuals are very different, and they normally thrive and live in very different worlds. It is very seldom that we do come across individuals who scale and transform through these levels, possess a unique mindset, rapidly change and evolve their personalities and capabilities, and end up building their destinies very differently. These are the folks who make it all the way to the corner office.

So let's get back to the DNA of this leader who can be entrusted to build a new business in a new geography. This leader needs to use the distances and diversities of the geography (think Asia, the Pacific, Europe, Middle East, Africa—all large far flung, very heterogeneous geographies) to his or her advantage rather than succumb to them. The leader of the geography takes in the big picture. Determines the unique moving parts, then leverages and uses them. The outcome is a robust business with competitive advantages and growing revenue, profitability, brand and share. The business continually delivers value to its customers and partners. A tall order, but doable.

All initiatives normally start and end with people. A background in leading different nationalities, linguistic skills, subscribing to different religions, and business practices does not necessarily help. So how does one get this diverse band together? Here's how. They start by building a powerful **Vision** for the geography (I am not talking about the corporate vision here) that stands for success, commitment, value, and integrity specifically for the geography alone. This, backed by a clear explanation of the "why" behind each statement that gets through to the people, is a great starting point.

Communication is key—leaders in these far-flung regions have to be extra-great communicators with a strong ability to sense the business pulse in the territory and the sentiments that prevail within the company at any point in time. They need to be able to keep their troops in the geography motivated and on message with corporate dictums. On the other hand, they need to be natural marketers of their geography and the opportunities and risks it presents to the corporation. Credible business acumen and a dependable vision of the future is what headquarters is seeking from the leader—he cannot let them down.

As the team grows, **Consistency** in quality becomes a severe challenge—people, practices, processes, and infrastructure. This cannot be addressed through intervention by the leader alone, as was the case when the organization was small. What is needed is an automated, scalable process of ensuring this quality—one that in a best-case scenario can be put on autopilot to a large extent. Every large and successful company has this in some form.

No leader should be worried about **hiring** people smarter than them. This is not easy in practice, and most supervisors succumb to the lure of ensuring intellectual and professional superiority over the subordinates. I understand and appreciate the paradox here. All things being equal, would not a smart capable team be expected to perform better than a mediocre one? Performance alone makes the leader's position strong. Next, a capable team needs less supervision and micromanagement than a mediocre one—this frees up the leader's bandwidth to focus on other important areas that support and strengthen the team and its performance externally and internally, especially in getting the attention and assistance from the operating functions in the HQ. I do not need to look far for a proof point. I was fortunate to lead a very capable and committed team whom I was able to retain despite very high attrition during the days of economic prosperity in Asia. This team, as it solidified, very capably led the day-to-day business and delivered predictable revenue and profit growth while ensuring customer and business partner satisfaction. The leadership team's ability to successfully do this enabled me to focus on customer needs, build the infrastructure in the geography that was needed to support our future business growth, and identify and execute on growth opportunities. It also enabled me to cover all stakeholders in the corporate headquarters to garner the confidence and support that was needed to ensure success to all my focus areas.

Next, the ability to **curate**. Assuming the leader has the right team in place, it is very easy to stifle top talent if they are not provided a supportive environment to thrive in and grow. Again, let me show you how I have personally benefited much by following a simple set of procedures with the talented teams that I have been fortunate to lead. I am a big believer in establishing a common understanding and agreement regarding:

- "Why we are doing what we are doing,"
- Setting agreed upon goals. These need to be practical but "stretched,"
- Determining and providing what is needed to get the job done,
- Setting the right expectation of what operating latitude is available to the individual (you cannot obviously give everything that you are asked for),
- Providing adequate authority and holding the individual hugely accountable for the results.

Let me reiterate—authority and accountability go hand in hand. One does not work without the other.

I am sure by now you are looking for the shopping list of the attributes of these successful leaders, whether you want to seek one out or plan to be one. Well, it's common sense really: seek out people who have a demonstrated track record of impressive and sequentially growing contribution to the organization's top and bottom line (this is a ticket to entry to the Hall of Fame), ability of growing faster than the competition, which means that the leader and his team have grown the business faster than the general market, and the ability to grow faster than the rest of the organization.

There are often "high tides" where all boats go up not necessarily because of the effort of one man or group of people. When an individual or a team demonstrates things that would not have happened if they did not drive it, then you know you have the icing on the cake. Let me give some examples. Entry into a new market or segment, game changer disruptive partnerships, creation of net new revenue stream. Add to this, people development programs that help build a winning team and a first class leaders' bench.

Do these and you will surely build your legacy where you are. You will look back with pride at the "tuned up" engines that you have left behind that will continue to propel the company forward when you choose to walk away.

Think Like a Champ—Tune Your Engines

I am an avid follower of the professional golf circuit in general and specifically the Masters Golf Tournament at the Augusta National Golf Club—the home of the legendary Bobby Jones who built the facility with Clifford Roberts in Augusta, Georgia. Alister MacKenzie designed the course in 1931, and the inaugural event was played in 1934. Alas, MacKenzie did not live to see the day—he died a year earlier.

In April, right in the middle of spring, hundreds flock to the pristine, scenic, and haloed fairways of this golf course, waiting for magic to happen and history to be made. Millions sit glued to their TV sets to watch the best golfers in the world rub shoulders and play to win one of golf's most prized grand slams. The final round of the 2011 Masters was as close as could be. With an hour from close, six players were within striking distance of winning the tournament. In a nerve-racking finish, South African Charl Schwartzel emerged winner, beating the Australians, Adam Scott and Jason Day. I felt happy for Charl as he donned the traditional green jacket that every Masters winner is ceremoniously cloaked with. Charl proudly wore the jacket fifty years after Gary Player, another South African who, in 1951, was the first non-American golfer to win the tournament.

The focus and resilience that Charl demonstrated in Augusta in the final round was a demonstration of ability, focus, and flawless execution like all previous champions. It was a class act . . . simply brilliant. But what was equally impressive was the fact that barely forty-eight hours after holding aloft the Masters trophy, which is a replica of the fabled clubhouse, and pocketing over a million dollars in prize money, Charl was 10,000 miles and twenty-two flying hours away in hot and sultry Kuala Lumpur in Malaysia, playing in the Maybank Malaysian Open tournament. Despite a radically different stage and a long-distance flight in between, Charl was striking the ball with the same focus, authority, and rhythm that he had displayed at Augusta. Although he was playing in very different conditions and in a different time zone two days earlier, it almost seemed like he had just walked over to a neighboring course and resumed his game from where he had left it over the weekend.

So what makes this happen?

Discipline . . . of both the body and the mind. The foundation of sporting champions is to self-program themselves to deliver consistent peak performance regardless of location, under any amount of pressure, in any weather condition, and in any circumstances. The minimal ticket to entry is fitness—to condition the body at a level of fitness where the mind stays alert to execute the physical reflexes and coordination that it is trained to do through hours and hours of intense practice that is hardwired into their brain and every sinew of their muscle tissue that pulls off those outstanding results. These champions understand that the first compensation of a tiring body is a drop in mental alertness, concentration, and focus. At the highest level of the game, this is always the difference between success and failure—a thin shot, a missed putt, a long serve, mishitting an easy volley into the net, or a misdirected header . . . you know what I mean. World class tennis pros, footballers, golfers, cricketers, and formula one drivers who crisscross cross the globe, participating in high-stakes events with millions in prize money demonstrate their physical and mental fitness every day as they go about wowing their audience despite their demanding schedules, intense competitive pressure, and the media glare.

I was in peak physical shape by the time I was out of college and into my work life. As I stepped into life within a multinational corporation, the lure of expense accounts and client entertainment was strong and the experience as exciting as you would expect for any rookie. It felt great that someone else was paying for the beers that I was drinking and the kebabs that I was chomping on to further business with my clients. All these excesses multiplied as my work took me into international travel. Now, I was on longer flights, across time zones, and often flying overnight, sleeping on the plane (the proverbial red-eye) and going straight to work the next day. Add to that greasy fast food working lunches, rich and elaborate gourmet dinners, and the alcohol that accompanied. All this into a gradually aging body with a decelerating metabolism that did not belong to a strapping eighteen-year-old anymore and you started to see the results. You do not feel it at first, or might not do so for a long while. Then it starts to creep in. Your biological constitution is no different from the sporting greats I mentioned earlier. The first realization of a tired body that is not 100% fit is in the lapses in energy, alertness, and focus. I suddenly started to feel it—in my thinking and in my natural responses. I thank my stars that I heeded these early nudges . . . there is no dearth of instances where seemingly healthy people have ignored these early signs, continued with the decadence, and succumbed to much larger health threats that impacted their careers and even their lives.

So let's do ourselves a big favor. Let's view ourselves as a competitive, professional sportsperson with a "winning" destiny to strive for. The physical and mental rigors that we are subjecting ourselves to in the modern-day workplace are no less than what top athletes do in their workplaces. So is it unnatural to groom us physically and mentally in the same way that these champions do? With the commercial boom of modern times, people are working across time zones, in punishing schedules, long workdays, taking red-eye flights, and spending countless hours within confined spaces, riveted to telephones and computer screens. There is almost zero exposure to fresh air and sunlight, which are minimal for the healthy functioning of the body. Given these grueling circumstances and the ever-growing expectations of better performance and higher returns, mental and physical discipline, there is no differentiator between professional sportspeople and career professionals. This is the ticket to entry for both categories who have even the slightest inclination to succeed, and all this starts with a fit and healthy body and an equally healthy mind.

This might sound like a tall order, but I have worked up a six-step routine that has worked great for me and is easy to implement. These steps address the key aspects of health and have worked predictably for me over the years. I am quite hopeful that they will work for you:

Step 1: Health and vigor starts with lots of ***oxygen*** at a cellular level. A properly oxygenated cell does not allow viral or bacterial infestation. Consequently, a well-oxygenated body is disease resistant. Make sure that you find time to breathe deeply. Simple breathing techniques and basic exercises help you accomplish this in fifteen to twenty minutes in the morning.

Step 2: Hydrate your body. Drink eight to ten glasses of ***water*** a day. No excuses. Somehow, find a way to do so. Besides maintaining balance of body fluids and keeping us in shape, water energizes the muscles, turns the skin radiant, and keeps our kidneys working at their best capacity in eliminating toxins from our body.

Step 3: Follow the ***80-20 diet***. If you follow even an average healthy diet 80% of the time, you can get away with excesses in the other 20% of instances. I am aware that when I travel or entertain, I am not in control of what I eat—besides, it is also impolite to be finicky about food when you are dining in a group in some cultures. I am mindful of what I eat in all other instances where I can control what I eat.

Step 4: Find forty minutes to ***work out***, four to five days a week. Contrary to some beliefs, you do not need to labor for hours, pant, and grunt your way to health and fitness (and hurt yourself in the process) unless you aspire to make that your profession and live off it. All I am talking about is cardio fitness, stamina, muscle tone, great circulation and a positive, adrenaline-fueled attitude. An hour of yoga or about thirty minutes of weight-training three times a week is time I can easily afford. This keeps me physically and mentally satiated. Talk to a physical instructor, and take your pick based on what will work for you, your body type, and most importantly, what you want to strive for.

Our body burns about 50% fat and 50% carbs at rest, though it tends to tip toward 60% carbs or so when exercising. The reality is that there is not a secret to weight loss, and there is no exercise that "burns fat": it's just calories in versus calories out. I am told that resistance training (weight lifting) burns the most calories and increases muscle mass (muscle, in turn, burns more calories even when you are at rest). Resistance training is also better at keeping the metabolism running high and burning calories for longer (hours) after the workout ends. The French apparently have a nice way of putting it—"eat a little less, exercise a little more." Once again, talk to your health advisor, and take your pick.

Step 5: Don't ignore the mind, the flip side of the physical fitness equation. History and religion both teach that calming the mind is the path to ***mental mastery***—a skill all champions in every field possess. They control the mind and allow only positive and empowering thoughts to enter in the midst of a situation. The untrained mind keeps its floodgates open and allows itself to be deluged by zillions of thoughts, most of which have little or no benefit and take up the mental airwaves at that time. Yoga and meditation are simple tools for mental mastery. It is easy to start small and progress to advanced levels based on your inclination and time—plenty of help is available in terms of virtual and live guidance in both these areas.

Step 6: ***Fun and companionship***. Time spent with friends and family is my final recipe for top physical and mental shape. Outside of a scheduled physical and mental exercise routine, find time to get together with friends and family. Do some nonwork-related activity together . . . a barbecue, a picnic, charitable activities, or karaoke perhaps (no matter how badly you sing). You will enjoy all that our nature has to offer; bond with your companions, and increase camaraderie, trust, and mutual respect while toning yourself physically and mentally on the side, all the while preparing yourself to reach for the sky.

Tune up and power your engine first . . . prepare the body and mind. You will reach for the sky naturally.

Reach for the Sky . . . There's a Carrot in the Right Corner

Telecom service providers are big buyers of networking technologies. The evolution of mobile devices (e.g. phones and tablets) into a ubiquitous platform for e-mail, instant messaging, games, social networking and access to rich media like music or video means that the payloads to and from these devices that run through the invisible pipes that connect to other similar devices are also changing. I have been fortunate to be in some of the organizations that have established technology leadership in intelligently directing electronic traffic through these network pipes. The networking industry is undergoing massive transformation through mind-boggling innovation over the past twenty years. In the beginning of 2011, I hired a sales leader to drive our service provider business. He joined us with capability, passion, and a commitment to succeed. As this leader settled in, I suggested that he organize a team boot camp, set some priorities, build team spirit, and go after this burgeoning marketplace.

He agreed and asked me if I could kick off the two-day session and speak briefly to his team to set the tone and the expectations from the boot camp. Unfortunately, I was on a business trip on the day but agreed to speak to the attendees via videoconference. Just before I headed out to the airport the previous day, I called the leader and his next-level managers for a quick chat on what they were planning to accomplish in the boot camp. They gave me a rundown, and the agenda was quite comprehensive. Then I asked the leader what near-term goal he had for his team to accomplish during the two-day session.

When a group of capable people get together on a mission, it is great to discuss priorities, target zones, strategy, resources and so on. But there needs to be a shared near-term goal that is practical, given the circumstances and the state of readiness. A goal motivates, drives, measures, and spurs performance. It also helps track the worth of all the work that went in. So my sales lead and I decided on a "big, hairy, audacious but practical goal" and rolled it out to the team as I kicked off the session. It was then clear to the team that everything that they would do over the two-day session was to drive that goal.

When you set goals, set them high. I was lucky to be trained on the art of goal setting early on in life. During my kiddy walks with my mother, I loved to aim stones at the clump of green mangoes that the trees bore during the summers. My mindset was naturally to go after the lowest hanging clump of fruits. Mostly, I would miss. One day, my mom stopped me just as I was about to launch my stone. She looked me in the eye and asked me to aim at a clump on a higher branch just above the lowest-hanging clump. I tried with earnestness. Well, my stone did not quite get to the clump that I had aimed for, but guess what: I caught the lower clump and down dropped the mangoes, to my utter delight. Great lesson learned. Stretch your goals. Make them bigger, go for them with earnestness, and you will get pretty darn close to them, even if you do not hit them. Or, better still—hit them!

If you watch high-handicap golfers during amateur weekends, you will often see golfers step up to the tee box, check the yardage (the distance of the flag pin from the tee box), take one look at the fairway ahead, and then hurriedly strike the ball. There is minimal consideration on where the ball needs to land, roll, and stop. Next, observe professional tour players on TV: not only is the pro golfer aware of the yardage he seeks, but he will actually deliberate and determine the exact location of the fairway where he wants the ball to land. This then sets the stage for his next shot that will carry him on to the green "in regulation" in search of a birdie putt to get to the hole. This is his goal. This fairway location he seeks will be decided based on what he wants his second shot to be, the slope of the fairway, the location of the green, the location of the flag, wind direction, hazards and so on. Once he determines his goal, he will decide what club he needs to get the distance and how he will shape his shot in order to get there.

Ben Hogan is a golfing legend. The story goes that he was once playing with a new caddy, and as he placed the ball in the tee box, he looked at his caddy for guidance. "Aim at the pine tree to the right of the fairway, Mr. Hogan," the caddy said. Ben Hogan asked, "I am looking at the right of the fairway. The left pine tree or the right pine tree?" The caddy then noticed that there were indeed two trees close to each other in the direction that he had pointed. This is the precision with which champions set goals. No wonder they arrive at incredible outcomes.

Goals and attainments are not an end to themselves—they are great feedback mechanisms. The untrained mind focuses little on setting goals and planning attainment but mulls longingly on the results, which are often unsatisfactory. On the contrary, champions focus on goal setting, then plan and execute the path to attainment with precision and finesse. They inspect results as feedback. They do not dwell on results for more than determining what they have learned and then make suitable adjustments. So what does it take to build great goals? Two fundamentals:

Make Goals Practical and Relevant—When goals do not match internal and external readiness, they are pointless. Internal readiness is the preparedness of the individual or the team in seeking out the goal to achieve. External readiness is the preparedness of the environment to absorb the efforts of the team and give them the result that they seek.

Make Goals Precise, Quantifiable, and Measurable—If they are not, then they do not provide feedback and cannot be subsequently acted upon. Quantification enables teams to stretch their goals. This lays the primary seed of experimentation, innovation, and growth.

So let's set our goals wisely . . . and let's not be shy to set them high!

Once we hit these stretched goals, there is enough reason to go out and party!

Interviews: Tricks to Gatecrash the Party

If you are fresh out of college and do not have top-class grades from a first-class institution of higher learning, you are part of the crowd that is queuing up to get into the "best parties" (aka best organizations). You get a huge advantage (really huge; and I am not kidding here) if you have strong academic credentials from a top institution because you make the hiring manager's job easy. But if you don't, it's not like the sky has fallen on your head! Here are some ways to improve your chances to hustle into the party.

Understand the Role and the Organization. Show Them What's Under the Hood. Ask Smart Questions.

You are showing up at the interview session to demonstrate your fit for the role and the organization, right? Do your homework. Make sure you have a good understanding of the role—organizations hiring fresh grads have specific functions on offer in their rosters—they also provide detailed information regarding the attributes and traits needed for the positions that they advertise for. I would also ask you to map your experience and accomplishments to every attribute and trait listed for the position or for as many as possible. Your examples should have quantifiable proof points as much as possible. Show the hiring manager what value and fit you bring to the role. Three examples are ideal, so have five ready. He will be satiated and tired by then. While at the university, you might not have exposure to real work environments, but there are societies, sororities and interest groups that you would have participated in. These participations often allow you to practice skills associated with careers that you aspire for. Sales, marketing, finance, operations. The trick is to spot these roles, involve yourself and test them out. Then there are the internship stints that I am a big believer of—all these add up to the experience you carry into an interview.

The 2008 movie, *21* is based on the true story about six MIT undergrads trained by a faculty member to master the art of card counting. They make millions from Las Vegas casinos before succumbing to the inevitable. There is a scene in which Jim Sturgess's Ben Campbell character interviews for the Robinson Scholarship at Harvard Med with a perfect portfolio of 4.0 GPA, an almost perfect 44 on the MCAT; he is the president of the American Legion Math League, holds a Teaching Assistant position recommendations from superstar professors and an early acceptance at Harvard Med. The person interviewing takes one bored glance at the document, which is similar to that of the seventy-six other equally qualified applicants, and tells Campbell that the Robinson is going to go to someone who "dazzles," someone who "jumps out of the page." To make the cut in life, play smart, use your strongest natural skills, and prepare to dazzle the interviewer. Commit to think and put up a plan. Differentiate yourself, especially if your study grades do not differentiate you—if your grades are good, then do some more! I assure you, it is easier than any of us make it out to be!

You are at the meeting to also test the organization and whether the role is fit for you, aren't you? Again, prepare a list of questions regarding the organization, its performance, brand, competitors, share and so forth. List them out and pop them when the interviewer gives you an opportunity to do so, which is normally the case. If not, politely ask him to give you an opportunity to do so. Your questions should be appropriate and well researched. Answers to these questions will let you know if the prospects of the position and culture of the organization are right for you, and they will highlight your preparedness.

Articulate Yourself—Have Facts and Figures Handy

You should sound as if you are 'suitable' to join the party. Just like I am asking you to research your prospective employer, analyze your own background—school, college, university, the sports teams that you were on—inside and out at all times. Your awareness of the history and details of your past institutions should be holistic and must transcend the specific department you came from. Your ability to articulate your background and your ability to show awareness and interest in the field where you want to build your professional future will be well accepted by the person reviewing you. It demonstrates your maturity regarding the overall business, which is an asset that every hiring manager and organization wants within his or her teams.

I am unimpressed when candidates are verbally keen to pursue a specific profession within a specific industry, yet are unaware of who the market leaders are, who the close competitors are, or even the basic financial and operation metrics based on which these organizations are rated. They are also unable, in many instances, to articulate the underlying fundamentals of these verticals and what makes organizations tick or sink. I cannot fathom their mindset or their ability if they do not feel the need to be aware of the basic benchmarks by which their chosen professional field and players are measured.

I have also heard of candidates assuming that for some strange reason believe a "profit and loss ownership" at the university irrespective of the size or scale is some kind of shortcut to professional success. Realistically, this is hardly the case—organizations expect fresh grads to learn and excel in their functions first before taking broader financial accountabilities. But here is our "young Turk" thumping his chest and proclaiming profit and loss (P&L) ownership in some insignificant or even silly scope. When the interviewer proceeds to ask them questions related to operating margins, internal rate of return (IRR), and so forth, important mileposts of their alleged financial journey, the candidate stammers, stutters, and tries to smart talk his or her way out of the situation while squashing their personal credibility. You know what that means: barring exceptions, the worst dressed and the tardiest have the least chance of entry while queuing to get into that hot party. It hardly matters where in the queue they stand.

Spice Up Conversations: Tell a Story

Here's another secret for you: most of the people who will interview you are bored and could do with a interesting but relevant story. Everyone loves a story, so regale them with an appropriate story that is relevant to the conversation, preferably involves you and highlights a key capability or achievement of yours. It could be about a deal that you cracked, a glacier you trekked to, or a herd of cannibals you got away from as long as it is linked to the context. It will provide the interviewer a reason to remember you for beside the resume.

Tell stories about yourself or others to exemplify a point that you are making. Sites like Virtual Tourist (virtualtourist.com) and Interesting Stories (interestingstories.net) either help you learn from other people's experiences or motivate and guide you to new experiences. Share these aptly in any social or professional settings, including interview chats, and I assure you that you will fuel your interviewer's curiosity away and stamp your uniqueness.

So whether in a nightclub party queue, in the crowded entrance of a popular restaurant, or in the interview room of a corporation, some people seemingly get the unfair advantage. In most instances, it is seemingly unfair only to the uninitiated. However, for the people who are getting the advantage, there is always a plan, an execution strategy, lots of preparation, and a predictable result. Make this work for you if you are not already doing so—be a Hunter.

Farmers and Hunters

Quite some time ago, when Nokia was a company with a lucrative brand and a strong customer base, my wife was a loyal user. I saw her migrate from one Nokia phone model to another when her subscription with the carriers came up for renewal. Nokia enabled her to make phone calls, check her calendar, take an occasional photograph, and send SMS messages conveniently. Life was good.

While my wife tinkered with the basic facilities on her Nokia, there was a worldwide revolution brewing in the field of social networking, e-publishing, music, video, and the mobile phone platforms that ran them. Along came 3.5-inch phone screens with 960 × 640 resolution, incredible graphics, 5 megapixel cameras, and access to a gazillion video, music, games, and published content, paid and free, from highly marketed repositories. Suddenly, the Nokia phone, despite all its familiarity, paled in comparison to this barrage of user-friendly offerings aimed at satisfying every user craving that rolled out from Nokia competitor warehouses. My wife chucked her years of Nokia loyalty and switched to using the Apple iPhone and the Samsung Galaxy tablet running on Google's Android engine. The incumbent "Farmer" has often been 'displaced' by the "Hunter". Hunters disrupt the conventional playing field through massive innovations in Product, Price, Place, Promotion—Philip Kotler's 4 Ps and his fifth—Purpose! Kotler is the eighty-three-year-old author of fifty books and the SC Johnson & Son Distinguished Professor of International Marketing at Northwestern University's Kellogg Graduate School of Management.

These disruptions cumulatively shift the customers' expectations along with the incumbent's leadership position.

So who is a Farmer and who is a Hunter? These terms emerge from the pages of sales manuals. Usually, sales organizations have two sources of revenue, both equally important. The first forms revenue streams from an existing customer base or an existing product group. This revenue is more predictable, more secure. Customer satisfaction and product quality ensure this form of revenue. This revenue is chased by a category of salespeople called "Farmers." They are strong on relationships and comfortable in executing proven strategies, selling upgrades, and servicing expectations.

The second form of revenue comes from winning new customers, new market segments, or even creating new market segments by disrupting the way things are conventionally done. This calls for a different profile of salespeople. They are the mavericks; the out-of-the-box thinkers and the out-of-the-box risk takers. They seek the thrill of fresh blood, new accounts. The "Hunters." It is easy to see the value of each form of revenue stream for continuity and success. Each of these revenue types require different strategies and a uniquely different sales force. The Farmer and the Hunter are not limited to the sales force. The principle extends to entire organizations and to every individual.

What does this narrative mean to the individual? Both the Farmer and the Hunter within you need to be in balance to drive your professional growth. As a Farmer, we stay aware of our capabilities, our innate faculties that set us apart from the rest and give us a head start.

Let's keep these skills razor sharp and sustain them. As the Hunter, we look out for new skills, information, and knowledge that will help us grow into new areas, broaden our span of influence, and differentiate us from the rest. All individuals and organizations progress and grow faster by building capabilities that help them operate in new segments and create new values rather than simply strengthening their existing capabilities. Champions in every sphere are the proverbial all-weather masters. They have developed skills and minimized most weaknesses in their profession while identifying and mastering a broad set of maneuvers that set them ahead of the pack. Roger Federer started as a grass court tennis maverick but then mastered all surfaces while retaining his natural supremacy on the grass en route to seventy-seven singles career titles, including seventeen grand slam men's singles crowns. That's the farmer and hunter in tandem helping professional and personal success, a solid strategy.

Keep the Farmer and the Hunter within you alive and kicking as you build your strategy for Professional Success.

Where Is *Your* Strategy Headed?

Strategy seems to be on everyone's mind these days . . . "Hey, you have to 'strategize' to build competitive advantage and drive organizational, team, or individual success." Is it not the ultimate differentiator against those who do *not* have a strategy? Remember Strategic Management at B-School—so we go, "Blah, blah, blah."

Seriously speaking, I value strategy for all the common virtues and have used it for attaining and performing in professional positions in many ways myself. That said, I often see strategy taking too much of prominence in time, focus, and mind-share where it begins to become a worry. Also remember that for all you may think, your competitors are strategizing too . . . against *you*.

I view strategy as one of the means to attain the end game rather than the end game itself—very often without you even realizing it. The end-game goals need to be definite—holistic goals like top-line, bottom-line, and share growth or specific goals like market share, productivity growth and so on. Simply put, a metric that delivers incremental value to the organization and provides it with a competitive advantage. Add to that a need for an accurate description of your current status—what is the point of figuring out where you need to go if you are not clear where you stand today?

Once that is done, the strategy needs to be socialized with all the functional groups that will drive the determined end game—sales, marketing, finance, operations, manufacturing—with commonly agreed sub-goals that will in sum drive the overall end game. Disjointed and often contradictory strategies and messaging between functional groups have a history of downing many an honest effort. Leadership, teamwork, and collaboration are keywords here.

Identifying Milestones and Defining the Path

In my career, I have practiced a Plan of Record (POR) Methodology for determining and executing strategy collaboration with multiple cross-functional teams. The POR glues the teams by documenting specific focus areas, specific action items related to these focus areas, designated primary owners, associated secondary owners (across cross functional teams), target completion dates, actual completion, and comments. Quantify these as much as possible and ensure they capture the *What*, *When*, *Where*, *Who*, and *How*? Watch out for the 'devil in the details', and you will stay on track.

While the POR guides our execution, let's not lie back just yet. Milestones along the way are crucial in determining whether the strategy is on track—quantitative milestones embedded in the POR are very useful in accomplishing this. If the variance between the forecast and actual is significant at consecutive milestones, it is very likely that we have a problem.

Socialize within the functional teams involved, and do not be afraid to open up the shell surrounding the strategy and relook at what you put inside. It is always better to take a step back and fix things rather than make the problem bigger than what it really is, not to mention the lost time. Your methodology and your performance against quantified preset goals will provide your team with confidence in driving toward the end game goals.

Assuming that you have set the goals right, you will be presented with the 'chances' to deliver incremental value and competitive advantage to your organization. Congratulations!

Life's Little Chances

Our world is severely shot with adrenaline. We are caught up in a haze of instant gratification and a "what's in it for me" syndrome. There are people, opportunities, and situations that give us the opportunity to benefit or grow personally, professionally, and otherwise. We appreciate these opportunities at times, assuming that we recognize them in the heat of the moment of our daily quest. Often, they are lost among life's other priorities.

We are even unaware of our own abilities that help us live the life that we do, build the relationships we have, and finance our lifestyle by the earning from these skills. All these gifts are not even afterthoughts in our list of daily considerations. Instead, we train our sights and thoughts at what others have and we do not. We spend incessant hours contemplating how cruel and unfair fate has been to us while showering incessant quantities of virtue on others who do not deserve them. Would you agree that all the elements that we have deserve more respect, more nurturing, and not be taken for granted? The downside is not pretty—you all know of people who disregard what they have, constantly clamor for what they do not have, and lead themselves to ugly and unfortunate realizations—often at a crossroads from where there is no return.

Let me take you back to the days of the Hollywood star, James Dean. By the time he was twenty-four, Dean had risen to iconic status with movie hits like *Rebel Without a Cause, East of Eden*, and *Giant*. His chiseled good looks and easygoing, nonchalant charm bordered on cockiness and earned him a huge fan following despite many of his indiscretions. He had it all, and he was at the top of his game. Then, on a fateful September evening in 1955, the new Porsche 550 Spyder that he was preparing for the weekend sports car races at Salinas crashed headlong with a 1950 Ford Custom coupe driven by a twenty-three-year-old California Polytechnic University student, Donald Turnupseed. The Spyder flipped up into the air and landed back on its wheels off in a gully. When James Dean was extricated from the Spyder's mangled cockpit, his left foot was crushed between the clutch and brake pedal. The velocity of the crash broke his neck and inflicted several internal and external injuries. He was dead by the time he was ambulanced an hour later to the Paso Robles War Memorial Hospital, twenty-eight miles away. A brilliant life extinguished and a solemn reminder of what fate can do at the flick of a switch. Dean was often quoted as being unaware of what had fuelled his meteoric rise, and it would not be impossible to assume that he didn't care. The rebel in him used his fame and fortune to live life in his own terms, constantly experimenting with life "without having his hands tied behind his back" (as he would say).

All this worked well till that fateful September evening and then time was up as the lights went out. I do not know how much James Dean as a person appreciated the faculties he naturally possessed. Certainly, there are others in the celebrity space that have visibly put in more effort in crafting their careers and refining their natural skills than Dean is perceived to have done. However, this is certainly a tale of how uncertain life is, even for people who seem to own the world.

Let me be a little more specific about what we should be grateful for and focus on making it better. I am not talking about the sublime consciousness of being able to breathe, see nature's beauty, and being able to smile. These realizations, while important, might just be opaque to most people, including myself. I am talking about things more basic, like appreciating the elements of life that materially fuel our existence—our families, friends, our relationships, health, skills, and capabilities. Being aware and responsible about these help keep us grounded and, more importantly, helps architect our success over time. There might be some who have been dealt a better deal by life in general (or might have worked hard to receive the deal that they have without our knowledge), but the cards that we ourselves have been dealt are better than what many others have—life is really quite fair, and if it is not, then let's get used to it or do something about it rather than moan and groan.

I often think about the little chances that life throws at us . . . a little rope, if you will. Then I think about how we normally respond to them or do not. You have to respect something to be able to judiciously respond to it, right? On the golf course, I once saw a high-handicap golfer hit a wayward slice that veered off the fairway, heading straight toward a water hazard. Along the way, it strikes a tree trunk and ricochets right back into the fairway. A little chance that fate threw in, or what? Instead of lapping it up and being responsible with the next shot, our golfer hits another irresponsible shot. On the other hand, Gary Player, arguably one of the greatest golfers of his era, enjoys his share of fate's little chances. Gary does not take these little gifts for granted. Instead, he says that the "harder he worked, the luckier he got"—he keeps persevering and no doubt will stay an icon in the annals of golf.

As a twelve-year-old, I got my first taste of these little chances that life or fate packages for us. More importantly, I learnt the way to deal with it. I was in middle school and had aced the intra school recitation competition, beating a very talented field chosen from a grueling internal evaluation. I was excited at the moment of victory, but the euphoria waned as time went by. By the time the competitions came around the following year, I was just another competitor competing for the honors. There was no particular desire to go after and reclaim what I had achieved the previous year. Since the field was substantially larger that year, a prequalification was staged. A new teacher had taken on the responsibility for the competition. He decided to grant no favors to the winner of the previous year's competition and had me join the prequalification with the rest of the boys. I did not even debate with him why that was not right—a winner in most competitive events in the world gets a free pass in the qualifiers in the subsequent year. But I was passive and did not voice my claim.

The pre-qualifier happened, and I missed the cut; slightly disappointed, I walked away. It was no big deal for me. On the day of the competition, I bumped into our headmaster in the auditorium. Seeing me in my civils without my school uniform on (all competitors had to wear the uniform), he was surprised. He was even more surprised when I told him that I had not made the cut in the pre-qualifiers. A quick conversation with the teacher in charge followed, and I was given the nod to change into my uniform and join the rest of the competitors. That was when a lot of anger and a lot of hurt enveloped me—all the feelings that I should have expressed when I was asked to pre-qualify not only welled within me but did so on an exponential power of ten. As I strode toward the competitors' section with my uniform on, my face flushed with anger; head hanging down, I sensed my path blocked. It was our headmaster. Smiling softly, he chided, "Stop seething and focus on winning. The others will not give you an easy ride."

That's when the nickel dropped: I had squandered my chance of winning the competition two years in a row, but here was a chance that life was throwing at me, and I was not preparing myself to grab it with both hands. Fortunately, I was the last to step on the podium. As the other competitors went up one after the other, I did not practice my reciting; instead, I steeled myself to give my best when I got up there. Fast forward ninety minutes, like one of those clichéd movie scripts, our headmaster announced, "The last competitor has won the competition—and won it the second year running." It was then that I started to drown in that incredible exhilarating experience. Tears welled in my eyes. A feeling of joy and attainment swept through me as the feeling of beating the odds and winning started to sink in. Every winner goes through this ecstasy. It is infectious. One of the reasons I love watching sports and champions is to experience that look of sheer joy after winning. It gives me a shot of adrenaline every time and propels me to do whatever I am doing . . . better.

Fast-forward another twenty-five years. I am in one of the administrative arms of my school, and guess what? I meet my middle school headmaster. We spend some time chatting in his spacious and tidy office. In between, he meticulously pours me a steaming hot, flavored infusion from a delicate teapot into equally delicate bone china cups. We reminisce about the times gone by. He asks me about life, family, work and how I am coming along. I make it a point to tell him about my memories about the recitation competition. I tell him about the lesson I learnt to take nothing for granted, to grab, appreciate, and leverage every chance that life throws at me, nurture it lovingly with the utmost respect, and perform the best I can to do justice to whatever it is.

He smiles first and then laughs heartily, leaving his laugh to ring in my mind as a reminder to leverage on, whenever I am faced with situations like this. For more on the subject of 'leverage' read on.

What Is Your Leverage?

I met with an old friend of mine at a social dinner. We began to reminisce about the past years, and before long, we got talking about the time when we started our careers. It was the very beginning of the personal computer revolution that swept the world, heralded desktop computers, and thrust computing into the mainstream. Bulky mainframe computers were pushed out further into the back offices and then subsequently into oblivion.

As young graduates, we were hired from among a herd of bright-eyed aspirants who were all bent on forging ahead in life and changing the world with technology. All personal computer brands held the same components, operating system, and functionality behind the marketing slogans and the beige chassis with a max of one degree of separation.

Differentiation to the discerning buyer was minimal to none—what mattered was the guy selling the box. There lay the difference—the salesman's skill. The better sales guy got the customer footprint. It was a hypercompetitive world, infested by alpha males with burning ambitions and dominating egos with low flash points. Life was never without an incident . . . not all of them pleasant. But what a wonderful ground upon which to learn, read human nature, and mentally self-program to win—like many of the sports champions I mention throughout this book! There was really no other point of existence.

The days I talk of were prior to large-scale automation—before the days of salaries being automatically credited to an employee's bank account and then withdrawn from an ATM machine. No . . . those days you would receive a physical salary slip in a sealed envelope. You would then go to a designated bank branch that had an arrangement with your company, make yourself a self-check or fill up a cash withdrawal form, queue up, and withdraw the cash. Very often, we would draw out our entire salary in one go. Two reasons: we did not want to repeat the hassle all over again for another withdrawal, and the size of our salary and the currency notes that made it up fit comfortably into the wallet anyway.

While we, the mere mortals, happily and patiently queued up to collect our wages, one of our colleagues would stride into the bank branch, go to one of the far-end teller counters, have a quick chat with the teller, and walk away with an envelope. No one really understood what was going on, but this colleague was never seen to queue up. The entire act was staged with such grace, style, and poise that it did not even occur to anyone to ask what was happening with him and why it was not happening with the rest of us. (This is another key lesson in life—ask questions if you cannot figure out! No one really cares if you are dumb or not). Even when ordinary people see 'out of the ordinary' events happening in front of their eyes, they watch in wonder but are mostly never inquisitive enough to find out how or why (either because they are plain lazy or simply embarrassed to ask), leave alone try and emulate them.

My friend then proceeded to enlighten me. This colleague of ours, to his credit, had apparently done a win-win deal with the manager of the bank branch. He had written a glowing endorsement on the efficiency and customer care demonstrated by the entire staff of the branch. The branch manager had used this glowing feedback as an endorsement of his own performance that must have served his career well. In return, our colleague was accorded with superior customer benefits that did not require him to ever queue up with other customers like us who did not have the leverage that "our man" possessed.

So we now come to what "leverage" really is.

Freedictionary.com defines leverage as "a positional advantage." In the financial context, leverage "serves to use credit or borrowed funds to improve one's speculative capacity and rate of return from an investment." Elsewhere, leverage "serves in acting effectively and influencing people with a tangible personal collateral."

Look around you and seek out all the successful people. You will notice that leverage is a key attribute all of them possess. Not leverage that is merely assumed. I am talking about leverage that can be "exercised", that provides a "differentiated and advantaged position" for the individual versus others. You are wondering what I mean by assumed leverage. Well, how often have you heard the phrase "I have a friend who can help you . . ." or "I know someone who will do this for me . . ." and so forth? I am not saying that you have only heard the phrase; on many occasions, I am certain that you can recall saying these words yourself . . . we all do this from time to time.

Now sit back and recall such instances where you spoke these words voluntarily or involuntarily. Then ask yourself, do you really believe that this friend of yours will go out of his or her way and do something for you? Is this a realistic expectation? If so, why? We all live our lives immersed in a zillion different demands and commitments—so do our friends and acquaintances. In the midst of all this, what will make someone prioritize me and do something that specifically benefits me? Be aware that in the twenty-four hours of the day, prioritizing an action means deprioritizing and trading off some other activity. In order for someone to do so, there needs to be a reason. And it is there that leverage comes into play.

But let us forget all that for a moment and get the focus of the discussion back on us. In most instances, we expect others to act in a certain way that benefits us without the slightest empathy about why they will do so. And there lies our *naiveté*.

Once my friend unraveled the cause of our colleague's mysterious benefits at the Bank, I started questioning myself regarding the probable circumstances that would lead to someone prioritizing me and my needs or requests over others'. I questioned why another individual would be committed in delivering a desirable and superior outcome for me as opposed to other demands in their life that they might need to service. As I start to find the reasons for all those actions, I begin to understand the meaning of what leverage really is. As I understand the meaning, I learn to acknowledge how to start collecting life's "frequent flyer miles," if you will. The more I accumulate, the greater my potential for success. Successful people have used these "air miles" to extend their staying power on the pedestal.

Now that we have traversed this far, let me help you with some common sources of leverage. Needless to say, you do not need to be a head of state or a CEO of a conglomerate or the scion of a powerful family to possess these. These frequent flyer miles can be carefully accumulated with intent, effort, and tact, without causing any harm to others.

So here is my list of five leverages that you may consider to arm yourself with. They are sequenced in the order of progressive degrees of complexity. But you have to start somewhere. As I write these, I feel that considering these early would have made my monthly journey to the bank to pick up my paycheck a lot quicker and simpler.

Knowledge and Competency

This is the one with the lowest barrier to entry. Any individual has the ability to build knowledge and competency in at least one domain of their choice. I have mentioned elsewhere in the book, and perhaps, you would have read and heard in countless instances. Find something that you really love, work hard on it, and get very good at it.

A subject-matter expertise in a specific discipline earns the respect of people involved with the discipline as they use the expertise of the "expert." As the competency gets more visible and prominent, the admiration, trust, and respect grow, further pulling the expert's leverage along—at least within his own community which benefits from his expertise.

In the incident at the bank, our colleague obviously took a keen interest in knowing how the reward system worked at the bank and benefited by using it to his advantage. The rest of us neither bothered to understand the game nor leverage it.

Past Favors

History is strewn with examples of characters that have helped others and have used the return of the favor at critical junctures. These remarkable insertions of leverage have, in many instances, defined the course of history.

A smart way to chart success is to quickly ascertain the people who will need to play key roles to make your success happen. The next step is to contribute to the success of these individuals and in making certain that they know what you did. That sets you up for a return of the favor and consequently to the buildup of this leverage.

Large Causes

I often visualize myself sitting in a deserted airport lounge and a prominent global personality walks in. We sit around for a while till boredom, and the uncomfortable silence or pure providence forces a conversation. What do I talk about that will fuel this individual's interest and possibly get me somewhere with this person? Unless I hit a personal interest spot on (which is quite unlikely), clay modeling or cooking paella or chasing a rainbow trout will not cut it. Prominent personalities follow large causes, get involved with them, influence them, make these causes and, themselves, prominent as a result.

Energy, education, poverty, human rights, and biotechnology are some examples. Adopting or attaching ourselves to a large cause often exposes us to individuals with influence. Our association with the cause creates an automatic leverage for us with these individuals as we ride the cause. This would have been hardly possible if we approached these same individuals in our ordinary individual capacities and professions. Now you will ask me, what if your profession has nothing to do with these larger causes? What if you are a doctor, an accountant, or a back office clerk in a manufacturing company? Well, that is your day job; it funds your living costs. Find a larger cause to attach yourself with, and serve that cause with your expertise—serve the medical, accounting, or clerical needs of a not-for-profit organization that serves poverty or education, for instance. Do it as a form of intellectual philanthropy, and see your exposure to leverage evolve within very powerful quarters.

Position

Leverage by position is similar to positional power. Prominent positions come with authority and influence to do certain things or get certain things done in a certain way. Many of these actions influence and impact others. While some of these actions might be "out of bounds" (that you read and view frequently in the media, like insider trading schemes), most are not. Once a position enables you to positively impact an individual without compromising your position, the act sets you up for a reciprocal favor. If this does not harm anyone else or does not compromise the position that you are in, there is no harm in exercising it.

Position power need not belong to people in formal positions of authority alone. In my journey, I have seen teachers, family elders who have served their family well, even lobbyists possessing incredible leverage with powerful people. None of these are necessarily in formal seats of power. I have seen friends leveraging the positional power and influence of their parents. While many of my other friends scoffed at this, I really did not have any problems with these fortunate ones—if you have it, use it! If you do not have it, no one is really prohibiting you from sourcing and building this positional leverage anyway.

Material Success

This is almost a given. Success creates leverage, which consequently begets more success. This is a rule that applies for every successful individual. We will need to make the cut first and become successful before being able to use this leverage.

As you step on the pedestal of incredible success that I wish for all of you, let's ensure that your feet are firmly planted on the gas pedal to building continual leverage using your position. Many falter as they cross the portals of success—they forget about the effort that got them there and start squandering their position by diluting the effort and desire to retain their position. Others are overcome by pride, ego, and vanity that starts to eat away the very foundations that they rode on to get to the top or are led to immature actions that rapidly lead to their downfall. As the saying goes, the higher the rise, the greater the fall.

Life is naturally tough for all of us. I do not, for a moment, want to take away any of the effort, grit, and determination that is needed from us and only us to be successful. Having said that, success is not about slogging all by yourself; it is also about using the ladders that life has discreetly placed for us by using some form of leverage that all of us possess. Now, do not tell me that you do not because I know in all likelihood you do, irrespective of what your current standing is. You will need to think creatively and take stock of your personal situation—very much like what my colleague probably did at the bank.

This combination is powerful. When done well, it creates larger leverages, larger influence, and more people working behind the scenes to ensure your progress . . . your success.

Seek, build, and ride the wave of leverage. An essential recipe for success.

Guts and Glory: The Success Recipe

Daniel Soh is a friend of mine for many years and has scaled the top echelons in the executive search business. I turned to him to write the foreword of this book, which he graciously agreed to do. Over the years, Daniel gave up the hopes of placing me within the burgeoning Asian technology sector as I was focused on building my existing business. As time went by, we switched our association from being a headhunter and client to being good friends and trusted advisers. The relationship has served both of us quite well. Daniel was once tasked to write an article for one of his internal publications, and he asked for my views on what it takes to build a successful organization.

Over the last ten years, Asia Pacific has grown in stature as a strategic and significant market for the organization I was running at that time. We rapidly grew revenue, share, people, footprint, and infrastructure. To respond to Daniel's question, I could not concoct a panacea that would deliver surefire results for every organization and for every leader (I wish I could!).

My formula for success is rather a blend of many small thoughts and practices coupled with incredible execution. After persistent probing from Daniel on what the driving factors for this transformation were, I put my mind to work. I gathered that the transformation rode on a set of common and consistent principles that most people are aware of but honestly lack the guts or even the desire to practice. No doubt "success" is a limited membership club.

People Smarts

We consistently hired and surrounded ourselves with smart and capable people. People smarts, coupled with 'shared goals and vision', 'authority and accountability' helped us accomplish incredible outcomes. Given that smart people enjoy the company of equally smart people and thrive in their midst, this move helped us build an energized organization that attracted, retained, and developed talent. Ask an average manager to knowingly hire someone better than himself. If he is honest, he will tell you how difficult this is. Want even better proof, ask this question to yourself. When I reflect on the smart people that I have been fortunate to work with, it almost seems that they were programmed for success anyway. I just happened to be able to weave them into my team and give them an environment to succeed. The team's success and mine followed. As Michelangelo once said, "I saw the angel in the marble and carved the stone until I set him free."

Walk the Innovation Talk

Talk is cheap. Showing the team that you mean it through your actions is key. We have succeeded in encouraging people to try out new things even if they make mistakes. Then we support and guide them when they are in the midst of these mistakes. These actions, however, have not veered us from our near or long-term end goals and commitments. Goals once set, are non negotiable (unless under exceptional circumstances) for A-Player companies. It is commonplace for average leadership and individuals to give "experimentation" as an excuse for unacceptable end results. These excuses stifle the spirit of experimentation and innovation within the organization. It is marvelous if good business governance is combined with innovation and experimentation when setting and meeting goals. This is no mean feat and requires judgment, maturity, and courageous patience.

Know the End Goal

"What are we trying to solve or attain here?" is a phrase that shows up in most of our meetings and brainstorming sessions. Every member of our team rapidly seeks the end goal in any activity they get involved in. They then work backward, involve the people with the right skills, table the right information, and collaboratively do what it takes to accomplish that end goal. We use a disciplined and effective operating procedure that drives accountability and productivity. We cut the fluff, which most office meetings get inadvertently drawn into. We keep meetings short, and laser-focused toward attainment of the end goal. And, we are mindful of not overrunning the meetings, which is really the hard part.

Diversity as an Advantage

Many global companies have been affected by the spread and diversity of the vast geographies they cover or aspire to cover. Interestingly enough, we succeeded in using the diversity of Asia Pacific, to our advantage. Learning and best practices from one country are implemented in other countries. Asia Pacific's mix of mature and fast-growing economies with diverse regulatory environments offer a variety of testing sites for products or business strategies. We leveraged competencies of demographic groups, which excel at certain functions within a multicultural team.

Fix the "Back-Office"

Revenue, market share, and profitability are scorecard metrics. They reflect business performance. I have never given them more attention than that. Let's focus instead on what drives these metrics. For many years, an economic boom swept the world. We, fortunately, did not have a demand-side problem. Any organization with a credible track record, strong offerings, and the qualities that I mention above became a viable supplier in their segment. All that jazz is rapidly changing. Today, we are being forced to play to melancholic tunes as economic growth stagnates, inflation runs rampant, and aggregate demand falters around the world. Governments of the United States, most of Europe, and parts of Asia work feverishly to restore sanity to their economic stagnation, budget deficits, and currency woes.

In the midst of this gloom, government and financial regulators try to jump-start the economy with infusions of money despite inflationary and currency devaluation risks. It is in every organization's interest to take advantage of this artificially generated demand and prepare for it. The variables that derail an organization's progress are the inability to fulfill demand often due to a lopsided back-office that cannot keep pace with the demand that the front end generates. This is where visible and invisible infrastructure comes into play. People development, legal support, operations, finance, supply chain, customer support, and logistics are back-office functions that need constant attention.

Based on what your position is, solicit or build each of these areas robustly with support for innovation, systems, process, and people skills such that they can naturally scale—couple this with a top-class front-end sales and marketing machinery and your organization is on its way to business success.

A back-office that is working well should not limit innovation. Should not prohibit disruption!

Innovation and Disruption Need Chaos and Darkness

I came across this memorable cinematic sequence in the 1949 Orson Welles's classic, *The Third Man.* The Harry Lime character steps onto the Viennese Ferris wheel and murmurs, "In Italy, for thirty years under the Borgias, there was warfare, terror, murder, and bloodshed, but they produced Michelangelo, Leonardo da Vinci, and the Renaissance. In Switzerland, there was brotherly love, 500 years of democracy and peace, and what did that produce? The cuckoo clock?"

With due reverence to my Swiss friends, I humbly acknowledge that the cuckoo clock is an understatement. The Swiss did take human precision in watchmaking to a whole new level, protected global wealth, produced the best chocolates, and gifted us with Roger Federer, arguably the greatest player who wielded a tennis racquet. That said, I appreciate Harry Lime's perspective. It does take dire, disruptive, and almost chaotic circumstances that give rise to the most incredible innovations. As the saying goes, "Necessity is a wonderful mother."

Bangladesh was ravaged by a widespread famine in 1974 shortly after their independence in 1971. In the midst of rising crop prices and national chaos, 450,000 people died. Dr. Muhammad Yunus, an economist with a doctoral degree from Vanderbilt University, was inspired in these circumstances to start a bank. He started by making a loan of US$27 (yes, that was all!) to a group of forty-two families to enable them to create small items for sale without being burdened by predatory lenders. 'Micro finance' was born! Yunus firmly believed that his innovative idea would drive capital formation in the lowest strata of the population and help uplift the society and the nation. The Grameen Bank ("Bank of the Villages") was the product of Professor Yunus's ideas and won him the Nobel Prize in 2006 and gave birth to the world of micro credit. By the end of 2008, Grameen Bank had disbursed $7.6 billion to the poor from 2100 branches and has dramatically revitalized the rural sector. Professor Yunus gained global stardom and was recognized with the US Congressional Gold medal for his disruptive contribution to finance and banking for social uplift in 2010.

Stability is a necessary evil. While it promotes a stable and predictable social climate and quality in life, it makes the society and behavior very mundane, and it makes the environment non-threatening. A peaceful, predictable environment—devoid of any urgency to change anything—is not conducive for disruption, innovation, or any large-scale progress. Where innovation does not thrive, creativity gets thrown out of the window, and you end up with brotherly love within a stable but non-innovative society.

I absolutely admired the turn of the millennium . . . the threat of Y2K paralyzing most mission-critical computer systems of the day (which, by the way, ended up being almost a hoax when the clock struck twelve at midnight on 1 January 2000), the lure of the telecom deregularization and the excitement and greed of the dot-com boom (that sputtered and stuttered a year later but then again came back strong). The perfect triumvirate, the perfect storm . . . the global surge of fear, uncertainty, and innovation led to one of the fastest surges of the human race both from a positive and a negative perspective. Technology evolved through that period between 1995 and 2000 like how the steam engine and railroads did in the 1840s, automobiles and radio did in the 1920s, and transistor electronics and space travel did in the 1950s and 1960s. All these boom times were fueled by an almost cataclysmic, almost chaotic transformation in technology and its adjacencies that dramatically disrupted and altered the political, social, and economic status quo and consequently the fabric of the society.

Through 1999 and early 2000, the US Federal Reserve increased interest rates six times to prevent the market from overheating. The dot-com bubble officially burst on Friday, 10 March 2000. The stock market crash of 2000-2002 caused the loss of $5 trillion in the market value of companies from March 2000 to October 2002. Similar to the Borgia's rule that spewed bloodshed and evil, the macroeconomic and financial chaos following 2001 led to shedding of a lot of red ink on corporate balance sheets. Greed and debauchery were the order of the day. Nortel Networks, producer of network equipment that powered the Internet, was permanently damaged by excesses in manufacturing, inventory and expenses, and other dot-com companies with many hundred-million-dollar valuations just months ago perished in the midst of excess spending, elaborate marketing, and little or no revenue.

Others, like Cisco Systems, who outsourced their manufacturing units, were able to bail out relatively well with huge inventory write-offs that dramatically pulled down their valuation, something they are still struggling to recover from, despite several corrective measures. Nortel declared bankruptcy in early 2009. The dot-com bloodshed and the catastrophic times that followed wiped out prominent players like Global Crossing, JDS Uniphase, and Covad Communications in the red ink of bankruptcy. Greed gobbled credible brands like WorldCom and Enron, who were found grappling with illegal accounting practices to inflate their annual profits. WorldCom's stock went swiftly into a downward spiral as the news spread, and they eventually filed the third largest bankruptcy in the history of US corporations. Many other executives were charged and convicted for misuse of shareholders' investments. Citicorp and Merrill Lynch were blasted for providing incorrect advisory.

However, in the midst of all this chaos, mayhem, and anarchy, a handful of organizations riding the dot-com bandwagon rose like the Phoenix from the ashes of other disaster struck corporations, stood tall and took on dominant positions in the technology landscape. Many of them hold that position even today. They were like the Leonardo da Vincis and the Michelangelos of the Borgia era. They are Amazon.com and LinkedIn and Facebook and Google. They were the poster children of sustainable and disruptive innovations. They epitomized cutting-edge innovation, business, and financial discipline, real world value creation, and strong management that did not just ride a fad. All of them are viable (some hugely profitable), relevant, and respected a decade later, generating billions of dollars in revenue, employing tens of thousands of employees and with a global footprint of customers and trainloads of shareholder wealth.

In the end, innovation is about delivering solutions to problems. There is risk in too much stability (political, national, or in a market). Without a certain environment where things are shaken up either by choice or design, there are fewer urgent problems for innovators to solve and thus less innovation. This applies not just to nations—it is equally true for organizations, social groups, or even for families. A dynamic world, organization, or market is more creative and productive than the static . . .

Its dynamism has led to the evolution of the "New Normal."

Heralding the New Normal

I am not calling out the Ryan Murphy/Ali Adler comedy creation for NBC where a happy and professionally successful gay couple in Los Angeles meet a single mother and waitress from Ohio and commission her as their gestational surrogate to deliver the baby they are missing in their lives.

The "new normal" that I am referring to is the much-used contemporary phrase that abstracts the future and envisions a world with endless possibilities. These possibilities and opportunities will need to be addressed by a new set of assumptions, rules, enablement, and capabilities.

Some years ago, Fareed Zakaria of *Time, Newsweek* and a columnist at *The Washington Post* authored a nonfiction bestseller, *The Post-American World: And the Rise of the Rest.* While underlining the global transformation over the years, Zakaria pinpoints three major tectonic shifts that have reset economics, politics, and culture in the modern history of the last 500 years. It started with the Western world in the fifteenth century, and then rapidly accelerated at the end of the eighteenth century. This period dramatically changed and revolutionized industry, commerce, legal systems, and trade unions and created the bastion for human progress in the following centuries—the epicenter firmly based in Western Europe.

The second shift was the rise of the United States, which rapidly wore the mantle of a super power similar to the Greeks and the Romans in the pre-Medieval ages. This shift was similar to the dominance of the empires of India, Egypt, and China in the history of the East. The United States and its policies and frameworks practically defined how trade, commerce, education, governance, industry, and technology was architected from the end of the nineteenth century to almost the end of the twentieth century.

The last ten years of this glorious American era saw the initiation of the third tectonic shift. This meant the rise of the countries outside the United States and Western Europe that Zakaria classifies as the "Rest," as documented in the book with stated figures from 2007-2008. You would suppose that the "Rest" means, well . . . Asia.

Not really. I myself opened up the CIA Fact Book for 2012 and checked the listing of the top twenty-five nations based on economic performance measured in terms of GDP growth ranging from 6.3% to 8.5%. The listing is very revealing, and the representation looks like this: two from South America, twelve from Africa, and twelve from Asia. The "Rest" represents all the developing zones of the world, not one specific cluster. There was no country that made the list from Europe and neither did the United States make the cut. In terms of current account balances for 2012, nineteen of the top thirty countries are from Asia, the Middle East, Africa, and Latin America. The United States was ranked 193 in the world. The change in this round is happening faster and with greater effect than the previous shifts.

The change in the stature and performance of nations because of changes in internal behavior including policy, governance, and pure drive is also replicated in businesses and organization in almost every industry vertical. In technology, shifts in leadership and dominance are equally dramatic if you were to consider the top ten technology companies at the turn of the century. This was the glorious era for the technology world fueled by three powerful drivers that I have mentioned elsewhere in the book—Y2K, telecom deregulation, and the advent of the dot com boom. *Fortboise.org* listed the following technology companies in the Top 50 in terms of market capitalization in December 1999: Microsoft, Cisco, Intel, Lucent, Nokia, IBM, AOL, Oracle, Nortel, Dell, Sun, HP, Ericsson, EMC, Yahoo, Motorola, and Qualcomm (at 51). Compare that with Fortune's list of technology companies that made it to the list of Top 50 in term of market capitalization in March 2012: Apple, Microsoft, IBM, Google, Oracle, Intel, Qualcomm, Cisco, Amazon, and EMC. A few interesting observations—

- The number of technology companies in the Top 50 had significantly reduced from 16 to 10.
- Apple, Google, and Amazon—three companies which were struggling and insignificant in 1999—have become the three prime movers and shakers of the technology world.
- Nokia, AOL, Nortel, HP, Dell, Yahoo, and Motorola are either well off the map or shadows of the tech giants that they used to be.
- Microsoft, Cisco, EMC, and IBM are commendably still on the list but have largely re-architecting their core business since 1999. This certainly applies more for EMC, Cisco and IBM.

This is the new normal, and it is touching the social, economic, and political aspects of our lives. Like all other paradigm shifts, this phase is heralding opportunities for nations, organizations, and individuals who are up for it. It also signals doom and gloom for people who are fossilized and are unwilling to change.

I have written a lot about organizations, but for the individual I can think of three trends that will largely symbolize the new normal, and that—if properly prepared for and taken advantage of—will benefit the individuals within them.

Skills That Organizations Need, Do Not Align with the Skills that Education Institutions Are Producing

"The Talent Shortage Survey" from Manpower, an international employment agency, estimated in 2010 that 31% of employers worldwide find it difficult to fill positions because of talent shortages in their markets. While seeking critical skills, the odds are more daunting. Towers Watson, an HR consultancy, says, "65% of global organizations and more than 80% of companies in fast-growth economies are struggling to fill the skill slots they need." This is a paradox when you take in the level of unemployment and growing ranks of college graduates.

This analysis is a good news-bad news situation for anyone aspiring to build a career over the next ten to fifteen years. The good news is that we are not faced with a demand-side employment problem despite the wild economic cycles that the entire developed world and even some of the developing world is in the throes of—at least not the ones with the right skills. The bad news is that a university degree alone will not necessarily get a graduate a job, let alone, guarantee them success. Every aspirant will have to skill-up with capabilities that are aligned with their chosen professions. While doing so, these individuals will have to discard old operational methodologies and adopt the new. Change, as the saying goes, is the only constant.

There is a reason why some of the corporate behemoths of 1999 did not make the list for 2012. In more instances than one, the prime reason is the unwillingness and inability to adapt and take advantage of the major tectonic shifts that were in play. The same applies to these individuals. The best way to stay on top of being relevant is to engage with organizations in the chosen profession during the academic years. Any excuse for involvement (trainee, intern, summer intern, you name it) will help, as I have stated in another chapter on 'Internship'. Being attached with new world organizations, soaking in the environment, the demands, and understanding, and getting used to standard operating procedures is invaluable. Obviously, the more such stints (more than one organization) one crams into a standard four-year undergraduate tenure, the better the readiness for the real deal when work life starts. The resume with a listing of these stints also glows brighter, especially if the organizations where you have interned are prominent leaders in their field.

Sacrificing the fun summer term breaks and doing some internship stints will be worth the while in the long run.

Talent Sourcing Is Increasingly Global as the Workforce becomes More Mobile

Ernst and Young have listed this trend as a significant demographic shift that is transforming the global workforce in their "Workforce Assessments" published in 2013. The talent congregation heat map has dramatically transformed over the years. It has followed the same pattern as Zakaria's tectonic shifts that I quoted at the beginning of this chapter. The migration of talented workforce to the epicentre of innovation and progress, accelerated in tectonic shifts two and three. As travel, especially air travel matured and became affordable—human mobility increased. People also started to get comfortable to live away from home. Cross-border migration has grown 42% in the last decade, from 150 million to 214 million, with most of the traffic directed towards the 34 OECD countries that were formed in 1961.

The dramatic global transformation of the stature of nations is also beginning to change traditional migration patterns. While old wealth countries continue to be the top choice for economic migrants, reverse migration is visible and evidenced in the findings of the World Economic Forum. Qualified skills from China, India, and Taiwan have been making their way back from the United States for a few years now as their homelands started to grow and prosper. While it is fair for capable talent from Europe and the United States to seek out their fortunes in the fertile pastures of Asia and Africa with immense possibilities, there are a couple of elements for the locals and the migrants to watch out for. The locals have to step out of the protective enclave that they are used to and prepare to compete with a global community for local jobs. Any government that resists the congregation of capable talent in their country will severely limit its ability to innovate, transform, and compete in the new normal. Enabling and supporting immigration and immigrants is a harbinger of economic progress, as I have discussed earlier. It is fortunate that most nations have now realized this and put it to practice, preventing the fate that Japan has suffered.

On the other hand, migrants need to realize that they are traveling to the chosen distant lands on their own desire for their own growth and progress. Barring a few exceptions, these individuals themselves stand to gain more than the lands that they travel to. Successful integration in these destinations becomes infinitesimally simple when these individuals are willing to learn the culture and practices of the lands they migrate into. When migrants integrate freely with the locals rather than clustering with their own kind. When they learn the local way of doing things and add value based on their own backgrounds. That's when magic starts to happen and everyone benefits. Individuals, teams, social groups and organizations. The concept of an 'expat' in an underdeveloped foreign land representing the mother ship, insulated from the local realities and cocooned within hardship allowances, country club memberships and other perks is disappearing very rapidly even within the largest multinational corporations. Today's migrant workforce will need to integrate and merge with the local surroundings and culture, while retaining their own individuality to drive the professional success they seek.

Women Will Be Larger Contributors to Solve the Skill Gap

Social, cultural, and domestic challenges have traditionally prevented women from coming to the workplace in most instances in the developing world. In the developed world, while some organizations have strived to build a gender balance by initiating a relatively favorable mix of women in the workforce, their roles have been mostly minimalistic and peripheral. This outcome has been due to women's desire to take up roles that do not compromise their domestic responsibilities while contributing to domestic spending in the face of rapidly escalating cost of living in most parts of the developing world. Men, often involuntarily, seek comfort in keeping the power bases among themselves with minimal feminine presence in the executive power suites.

Exceptions, like Indra Nooyi, who ran PepsiCo since 2001 as president and CFO and was subsequently promoted to chairman and CEO or Julia Gillard, the 27th prime minister of Australia and the leader of the Australian Labor Party (and also the first woman to hold either office) or Marissa Mayer, who was appointed president and CEO of Yahoo! in July 2012, are few and far between. Prior to this role, Mayer had joined Google in 1999 as employee number twenty and was the company's first female engineer. These incredibly accomplished women have already made an impact in their roles (and I am certain will do so across their careers) are great examples of capabilities within the fairer sex. There are many more out there who are equally capable and competent, if not more. There are enough trends to show that this category will be entrusted with bigger roles and responsibilities in the new normal.

Brainfitnessforlife.com offers some interesting assessments of a woman's brain versus a man's. This alone tells us about the attributes that the workplace is sorely missing out with a lesser and lopsided presence of women. This brain-topic has been viewed, argued, debunked, and reinstated from different perspectives around the world. What I state below is purely based on my assessment from what I have seen within organizations and teams that I have been in and my own judgment.

Men have been mostly categorized as left-brained—logical, analytical, and naturally adept at languages, numbers, critical thinking, and reasoning. Women's left brain-right brain balance gives them a unique blend of the attributes men have plus skills that make them suitable for expressive and creative pursuits. They demonstrate natural skills at expressing and reading emotions, creativity, and intuition.

While men are usually left-brained, women tend to be more balanced, demonstrating logical and creative functions in a balanced mix. They have relatively better communication and emotional intelligence than men, enabling them to work through issues better. In adverse situations, women will shun the fight or flight tactics that men often deploy and resort to a "tend and befriend" response, honed by their natural instincts of care, while having an understanding of the male's analysis of the situation. This ability to connect and attempt to collaborate even in a circumstance of confrontation, very common in the heat and intensity with which modern corporations operate, make the presence of women priceless.

It does not take a rocket scientist to figure out that the workplace is bound to benefit if we had more of these behavioral elements with larger induction of women in pivotal positions outside the human resources organization and the secretarial pool. This evolution, while imminent, will happen through a push and pull process. As lifestyles change and cultural and social shifts affect the developing world in the wake of economic and social progress, we look to women to push and take a larger responsibility in changing the workplace and the society. They will need to skill up, step up, and stake claim for bigger and more impactful roles wherever it makes sense. This is easier said than done—there is a status quo situation out there that spells male dominance. Women need to take inspiration from the several role models out there and make some definitive strikes. In parallel, the current establishments need to create a force field that pulls talented women to fill these positions. I am not talking about nominating a few heads to make a statistical proof point for equal opportunity—I am talking about instituting a culture of balanced gender participation in all walks of life so that every work group, department, and organization benefits from the virtue of this mix.

All this will start to construct structurally in some countries, within some industries perhaps, and will then gather momentum.

However, the writing is clearly on the wall.

Understanding the Flow of Cash

I held off sending the manuscript of this book for the final edit till I came back from a fortnight-long vacation in Scotland. I was pondering on the right closure—the final chapter, if you will. The idyllic and mysterious Scotland, the low-hanging gray clouds over the gentle ripples on the Lochs, the medieval stuccoed castles, the green-grey slopes of the majestic highlands that paint a bleak landscape, and the liberal shots of the finest single malt whiskies in the world pamper the mind to relax and think. And think I did . . .

That's when the nickel dropped. A book on success is incomplete without a key metric that it is measured by—money. Let me take a step back here. The *outcome* of success is personal—it is how *you* define it. The path to success is, however, consistent—a sustained repetition of certain behaviors and traits that deliver favorable outcomes till they become a habit. You will have to do this en route to any form of success that you choose to accomplish—success as defined by yourself or as defined by others.

An outcome of success for many of you is to achieve a consistent flow of cash, when you need it, in the quantum that you need it, for as long as you live. I am purposefully being generic here—I know that the readers of this book will have different forms of financial needs, which are all valid. Those who are thirsty for financial rewards to quench their egos, material desires, self-gratification, and vanity. Those who seek money to meet their personal needs comfortably and have some money left over to do the things they wish to do . . . travel, pursue a hobby, support a social or charitable cause. And, those who define success in other ways, whose financial needs are basic but still need money to be fulfilled. I will not spare a lot of thought to two other categories of people who do not care about money. They either have a lot of wealth thrust upon them through an inheritance or have already earned the money they need (good for them!), in which case, they probably do not need this chapter. Another category, who probably are broke, are critical of any effort to build wealth and have little or no knowledge or belief in how money works and is accumulated, which probably has led to their dismal financial position.

If you happen to be in the first three categories, then read on.

Success is a beautiful thing. Stellar school grades, graduating from a first-class university followed by a prized job that spells pride and envy for people around you (depending on who you speak to). All these are fantastic accomplishments. As you securely handle the grooves at your workplace, the recognition, promotions, and pay raises follow, life seems to get better than ever before. You start to feel that you have "arrived"! Yes, indeed . . . you have arrived professionally. Financially, I am not so sure. Even if your compensation is attractive. You see, an attractive compensation does not guarantee financial success. Income does not equate to wealth—income is the money that you earn; wealth is about what you do with that money.

Once you have the disposable income, it is natural that you want to fulfill all the things that you have always wanted to, not just for yourself but also your dear ones. The spending begins. Soon, a dear friend is upgraded to a fiancé or fiancée, and before you know it, you have a spouse. An apartment or a small townhouse becomes a necessity. Your cozy household now needs some furnishing, and by the way, how do you move around without a car? Children come soon after, and you want to lavish them with all that you craved and did not have when you were a child. School and tuition bills start to gradually pile up. I assume that your income keeps growing (I truly hope to God it does), but your expenses are probably growing faster. Now you are on a treadmill—running faster and faster just to stay in one place as the "expense treadmill" picks up speed. As the expenses continue to pile, you start to feel fear creeping inside you—you have built and gotten used to living in an expensive house of cards (i.e. your expensive lifestyle) that will collapse the moment you lose your job. You know how commonplace the odds of that happening are these days for no fault or shortcoming of yours! Depending on how much you have saved and how expensive your lifestyle is, varying degrees of despair and disillusionment follow. Self-esteem, relationships, and social standing all suffer. This does not sound like a nice situation to be in when you have diligently pursued success in life. In fact, I daresay it sounds ridiculously unjust and an unfair conclusion to your efforts.

The fix—I encourage you to master the flow of cash. Progressively make that a habit. Master the art of converting your income to wealth, step by step. And oh! Have fun while doing so. After all, we tend to perform well in activities that we enjoy doing.

It alarms me to see minimal financial literacy among educated, well-to-do professionals. Why do I say so? Well, let me be the lowest common denominator. Here I was, with a master's degree in Economics, an International MBA, and a successful and rewarding twenty-plus-year professional career. Add an attractive compensation package of base salary, commissions, bonus, stock options and restricted stock units, and a hefty expenditure column that the family and I had got used to fairly quickly. We were spending a lot of money but were fortunately investing, albeit in a fairly haphazard manner, on low-yield assets, with scant respect for cash flow. In other words, I was working very hard for the money that I was making, but most of that money was not working for me. I changed that with a conscious choice to take control of my financial destiny and work on it with the same diligence that helped me shape my professional career. As soon as effort is inserted, results begin to gradually show—and show it did!

In April 2011, ABC World News said that 89% of the 77 million people born between 1946 and 1964 are not convinced that they can live in comfort in their later years. 44% of these baby boomers express little or no faith that they have enough money to retire. 25% say that they will "never" be able to retire. So my assumption is correct. I am certain that most of us would like to stay active, mentally and physically, for as long as we live. But do not tell me that you are happy to do the nine-to-five grind every day to finance your living expenses for the rest of your life. If you are in agreement with me so far, spending the time to learn how money works and how cash actually flows and delivers financial success does not seem like a bad idea by any means. The knowledge you acquire, the practices that you then subscribe to, and the benefits you derive will form the icing on the personal and professional successes you will acquire and extend these pleasant experiences further.

Just so that you have some more context, Demand Media (*http://budgeting.thenest.com/average-person-saved-retirement-28301.html*) states that the average person in the United States with a retirement plan—particularly a 401(k)—has just a little more than $60,000 saved, according to the Employee Benefit Research Institute's May 2012

Retirement Confidence Survey. If this is the state in the United States, I shudder to think about the plight in nations with lesser means. This amount is hardly enough to sustain the rest of anyone's life, given the present-day living cost indices. Consider that the average retirement age is sixty-two and the average length of retirement of eighteen years. Bankrate.com provides a retirement calculator that helps you figure out how much you need to stash away to enjoy a set monthly income post retirement. Based on a 7.5% annual yield on investments with 2% annual inflation over twenty years, Bankrate's calculator determines that you need to have invested $205,243.23 for every $1,000 monthly income in retirement (i.e. $410,486.46 for $2,000 per month and $615,729.70 for $3,000). This is money on top of what you would collect from social security and pensions, which, unfortunately, will not be much.

Do not make the mistake of assuming that I am asking you to plan for your retirement here, which could be many years away. I am suggesting that you understand and build money habits just like the other habits I have described in this book. Plan to live a near-term future that provides independence, opportunities, and choice to do what you wish to do even during your prime years of employment. A future that you have aspired for and worked for can be within your reach many years prior to your retirement.

This book is not about financial education, and I am no financial advisor. I leave that responsibility to Benjamin Graham, Warren Buffet, David, and Tom Gardner (of *The Motley Fools*) or Robert Kiyosaki (of *Rich Dad Poor Dad* fame). They have spent a lifetime in building sound investing philosophies, practices, and teachings for those who want to be taught. I merely wish to nudge you toward beliefs and methodologies that will get you started on the path of understanding the Art of Money. I encourage you to learn from the works of the masters I have mentioned above and others whom you can find. Then, allocate the time and effort to build and implement a financial strategy that gives you independence, choice and security going forward. This strategy should be fuelled by your income from the hard work that you are putting in every day.

Eliminate the Fear of Finance and Investment—Educate Yourself

The basic tenet of personal and financial independence is about "money working for you" rather than "you working for the money." Well, I can hear some of you say, "I need to earn the money first before it can be put to work for me." Absolutely . . . but that is what this entire book strives to do: nudge you toward building little habits that will empower you to be good at what you do—assuming that you love what you do. Once you are good and successful at your work, financial rewards will follow. Now, what do you do with the money that you earn? Many have thought they will figure things out when their savings reach a certain critical mass. Unfortunately, they never did! The world is littered with capable individuals who went to the best schools, took up the best jobs, made truckloads of money, racked up huge expenses to fund their expensive lifestyles, and were never financially free. Their high income was diverted to fund their lives and expensive tastes if they were fortunate. If unlucky, they were struck by disillusionment and shock when they lost their jobs or the income stream sputtered in the face of various uncertainties that are rampant today.

It is not that these people lost the desire to live in comfort. It is painful for anyone to step down from the living standards they are used to. What failed these people was the fear of building, managing, and being accountable of their own finances. The lure of instant gratification and serving their present needs was overpowering. Add to that the biggest challenge of mankind—procrastination. Put these together and you have an undesirable end result, an equation of failure!

One reason to procrastinate, is the risk that finance and investment involves—the risk of losing money. This risk is no more or no less than crossing a busy street intersection or taking flight in an airplane. Yet we do not think twice before doing these activities. That said, your best foil to reduce the risk in any endeavor is to educate yourself.

The natural tendency will be to dodge the effort to educate yourself and seek out a financial advisor instead. The advisor won't just advise; they will tell you what to do, and you will most probably do it (whether you understand the Why? behind it or not) because that is what most of your friends and family do. So I ask you: were you told who you should date, what cuisine or restaurants to prefer, what clothes to wear, or what movies to watch? Mostly not, I presume. These are very personal choices, and you have learned over time what suits you the most. So why not do the same with your finances? Is it any less personal? Would an expert be more concerned about your financial well-being than yourself? As the saying goes, "Trust in God, for everything else, verify first." This could not be truer than when seeking advice on finance. It always makes sense to acknowledge opinion and advice, but do not immediately concede to the ideas of others. You cannot make your personal choices if you do not educate yourself though. So there you go! Education once again shows up as a stepping-stone to your financial success.

Financial education and the investments that will follow is not a walk in the park. They will take time and present ups and downs, success and failures. It is a journey that you will need to embark upon with your eyes wide open, just like any other skill we aim to master. So we choose a pace . . . and make ourselves generalists first. While specialization is a great virtue, you do not need to be a specialist to be financially successful. You see, financial markets are like game parlors with a floor full of game stations—there is always a season and a reason for every game. To create wealth consistently, we will need to learn as many of these games as possible. Learn them enough to seek out, verify, and validate the opportunities they present. There are enough specialists around who will be eager to assist us with the specifics, stay employed, and earn a good salary at the end of the month.

Understand Assets—Understand Liabilities

Whether you take a deeper interest in finance and investment or not is your choice, but I beg of you to understand and identify assets and liabilities in your life and treat them as such. This applies to relationships, work life, hobbies, and, in the things you choose to spend money on. Many of the elements that we have treated in this book—prioritization, focus, time management, leverage—lend a specific context when we are able to differentiate between the assets and liabilities. Simply put, I view assets as anything that provides me with a flow of positive outcomes and comfort over time, even if they are momentarily uncomfortable at the beginning. On the contrary, liabilities provide me with a flow of negative outcomes over time even if they are momentarily comfortable at the beginning.

There is plenty of confusion between these two categories. Educated and successful individuals often make their choices in life while misreading a liability as an asset and vice versa. It should be very clear to you that the more items you pack into the asset column, the better you construct your personal, professional, and financial destiny over the years. Your assets include and are not limited to your self-esteem, relationships, health, education, skills, and your financial portfolio. In the specific context of the financial portfolio, assets are investment categories that provide positive outcomes over time by either growing in value or by providing a stream of cash, or doing both. Good-quality, interest-paying bonds, dividend-bearing blue chip stocks and rented-out real estate are examples of financial assets—these make your money work for you by providing you with a cash flow. Extensive consumerism, that is, an expensive house with fancy trappings that you live in (if you rent it out—then it does'nt count!), an expensive car, consumer goods that are beyond necessities and depreciative in value are all examples of liabilities. We need some of this "comfort spend"—after all, what is it that we work hard for, without being able to reward ourselves for all the effort that got us here? So go for it, even though some of the spending may well be purely liabilities. However, let's spend after we understand what assets are, what they do for us. Let us also clearly understand that there are constant tradeoffs in our lives as we trade assets for liabilities. Every dollar spent on the liabilities column takes a dollar out of what could be used in building our asset column. Lets ensure that we understand the consequences of these actions.

Understand Cash Flow—Inflow and Outflow

At the risk of sounding like a financial pundit that I am not, let me restate the primary virtue of financial education and investing. It is to build a collection of assets that do one of two things: increase in value, aka asset value appreciation; or provide an ongoing stream of cash, aka cash flow. If you were to buy an apartment, a company stock or bond, or even a share of a small business, and the value of these assets went up over time, you enjoy "asset appreciation." Along the way, these holdings might give you payouts in the form of rental income, dividends, interest, or as net profits from your business—this is "cash flow." While both elements are essential for financial freedom, asset appreciation happens when you have actually divested the asset and booked the profits. That is why the house we live in is not an asset—even if it goes up in value, we do not divest it and book profits, unless we are prepared to downsize and move to a lesser home or upgrade by trading the property for a larger one. While asset appreciation expands your asset pool, it is cash flow that those assets generate that really sets you on the path to financial freedom.

Valuation (or de-valuation) and cash flow also comes into play for liabilities—albeit, the outcome is negative. High-end consumer electronic products, an expensive car for your own use or expensive designer wear are categorized as liabilities because they reduce in value (i.e. depreciate) the moment they ship from the retail outlets. The costs of maintaining and running these trappings construct the negative cash flow, which reduces the financial base that you have built. Vacations, retail therapy and fine dining are all desirable life style fixtures, but like all good things in life, they come at a cost. It is a negative cash flow. I love them all. I like to pay for them not through my base income or by diluting my assets or my financial reserves, but by using some of the passive cash flow that my assets generate.

Build Your Financial SWAT Team

Everything that you add in the asset column becomes your Financial SWAT Team. The sole goal of this SWAT team is to generate positive cash flow for you. This flow of cash may be spent in part to fulfill your desires. Go ahead and buy some liabilities if you wish to. However, do spend some of the cash flow on adding more soldiers to your Financial SWAT Team in the form of more assets. Once the army is assembled, they are never disbanded for any undisciplined (spur-of-the-moment) spending to buy liabilities. They might just be transformed into a different asset class to play a different game in the "gaming parlor" of the financial market for a reason. There will always be risks in investing, just as in anything else. This cannot be entirely mitigated despite all the education and preparation. There will be setbacks, and every successful investor is prepared for this. The SWAT Team that you have built might momentarily stall or suffer a setback, but with a disciplined approach over time, it will continue to grow. At the expense of sounding clichéd and banal, let me reiterate that to achieve success, we have to be willing to push the dimensions of the figurative box that we cage ourselves within.

Start early. Albert Einstein said, "Compound interest is the eighth wonder of the world. He who understands it, earns it . . . he who doesn't . . . pays it." The earlier you start investing, the quicker the assets you assemble starts to generate cash for you. The faster you turn this cash around to buy more assets, the quicker the expanded asset column generates the next level of cash flow. You can see where this compounding leads. It is a self-fulfilling prophecy, really!

Make Money Matters an Enjoyable Habit, Not a Chore

Every element of life introduces wealth creation opportunities. You are not confined emotionally or otherwise to a specific investable sector. Inquisitiveness in what you can do with your money is the best excuse to learn and open new frontiers and keep connecting dots in life. This is what makes it so much fun and rewarding—this is not just an ugly pursuit of wealth accumulation at any cost.

I have harped on the virtues of doing what you love endlessly. This is no different. Financial education and discovering the joys of passively growing the money you are earning might not be too exciting for some of you. Engineering a path to financial and personal freedom instead of a nine-to-five routine for a salary might sound like too much work. If so, then stop! No need to do any of this. Carry on with your life till you are ready. There is a quote attributed to Buddha: "When the student is ready, the teacher appears." When you are ready for financial and personal freedom, open this book again and read this chapter!

Check your readiness. Do you feel the need to adequately crown your past effort and outcomes with the rewarding future that you deserve?

A pragmatic measure of financial success is not necessarily wealth created and flaunted in the form of swanky apartments, sexy convertibles, expensive vacations and lifestyles that enslave you to your immediate employment. Financial success is about being able to progressively structure your accumulated earnings in a manner that gives you the freedom to make choices at any stage of life—to make choices in seeking out larger opportunities or fulfilling lifelong desires, without compromising your lifestyle. You can accomplish this, by riding on the cash flow bandwagon from your accumulated assets.

If this sounds like where you want to be, then start today. The sooner you start, the quicker you will get there. Do some research on the web or visit a bookstore and start your journey of financial education. This is a field with vast possibilities, so take that step forward to a financially secured and rewarding future that crowns your professional success . . .

Enough said.

Afterword

I began by suggesting that success is often grossly exaggerated to a point where it becomes a myth. The idea that grand visions and grand leaps combined with outstanding intellect, charisma, and epic hard work will lead to success makes for a great narrative. However, it fails to honestly treat the reality of what success can be and how most people can achieve it.

Success isn't a moment of brilliance—of greatness, as Ayn Rand might have said. It is a collection of sustainable habits that over time lifts us out of our mediocrity (that we are unfortunately programmed for) and allows us to raise ourselves to new heights. When we are mediocre, it is rarely our intelligence, our creativity, or our hard work that limits us. It's that we have decided and reconciled ourselves to not develop consistent, repeatable habits (that have been exemplified in this book) in our everyday life in whatever we do. Mediocrity is about our refusal to enchain these characteristics that we are very familiar with and empower a synergistic effect.

Having a brilliant plan is wonderful, but I would rather ask for a mediocre plan with superior execution rather than a perfect plan with mediocre implementation. What I have aspired to as I wrote this book is to encourage an enquiring mind to 'mine' meaning and substance of time tested approaches, to handle challenges and situations that we are continually presented with. All that is needed is awareness and inquisitiveness of what we are exposed to everyday—while watching, reading or while engaging.

In closing, here is an excerpt from the graduation commencement speech I delivered at SIM University in Singapore as I addressed the Graduating Class of 2012. I suppose many of you have left the university behind like me but have remained lifelong learners. I hope that my perspectives directed at those who are at the doorstep of their professional lives will also be relevant to you.

Excerpts from Deb Dutta's Commencement Speech for the Graduating Class of 2012 at SIM University in Singapore . . .

". . . Where do we go from here?" There is a big exciting world out there waiting for you! Woody Allen, the filmmaker and actor, says in his movie *Side Effects* that "the future holds great opportunities. It also has pitfalls. The trick will be to avoid the pitfalls, seize the opportunities, and get back home by six o'clock." You deserve success and quality of life both and not one at the expense of the other! The world out there is competitive and demanding and operates at light speed through fiber optic cables. Our world is always connected and always visible—your good and not-so-good actions will be magnified, thanks to the technology trappings that we have all gotten used to—cell phones and social networks. Someone somewhere is always watching you, so be self-aware. If this is a stressful thought, I am totally with you. It is okay to be mildly stressed as long as you stay aware of this reality.

My intent is to share ground rules that will potentially enable success in your journey going forward. Fortunately, the baseline rules have not changed much since the day I landed in Singapore in August 1991. That day I wore the wide-eyed visors of a twenty-something who had never ventured to a foreign land, leave alone succeeded there . . .

It is hard to provide you the formulae to navigate through your professional career's Formula 1 track in such a short space. So let me touch upon four techniques that have served me well and that should work well for you.

First . . . Keep the Thirst for Knowledge Alive

Benjamin Franklin believed that an investment in knowledge always pays the best interest. You have already committed to acquiring knowledge by enrolling in and completing formal coursework and working in your chosen field. Remind yourself that you are not on a fad-dieting program—you are on a lifelong commitment to healthy eating. Else, the knowledge premium you began with will wear off pretty quickly. The data in your memory will erode over time. Even if your retention is good, old concepts will get rapidly replaced by the new.

"Keep learning . . . stay foolish" has become cliché . . . but it is a meaningful cliché! Knowledge will de-risk your endeavors in an unpredictable and uncertain world. Knowledge will give meaningful returns to the time you invest, accelerate results, and protect you from professional pitfalls.

Second . . . Get Addicted to Building Value

What do successful leaders do with knowledge? If knowledge alone could guarantee leadership success, then librarians and research scientists would run the world's corporations.

The virtue of every successful corporation on this planet and the leaders within them or even people who have become corporations in themselves is their ability to create value. Value comes in many forms: let me give you some examples—Lady Gaga . . . Lady Gaga has sold twenty-three million albums and sixty-four million singles worldwide. She has won five *Grammy Awards* and thirteen *MTV Video Music Awards*, grossing more than $25 million in income in 2011. That is value . . . not just the money (which is substantial), but more so the underlying force she created that sold those albums and got her an incredible fan following around the world!

New technology companies like Dropbox have built software platforms that lets people store and carry their work and personal data, collaborate with friends and coworkers . . . all in the cloud. Users can access their information from most computers and mobile devices. One billion files (including this speech) are saved in Dropbox every forty-eight hours by over 50 million users from 250 million devices—that is value!

The Make-A-Wish Foundation's mission to enrich the lives of children with life-threatening medical conditions by granting their wishes and making them come true since 1980 has created value. This happens due to the combined resolve of 25,000 volunteers and thousands of sponsors in forty-seven countries who have facilitated over 100,000 wishes.

Value emerges from challenging conventions even if your assumptions are incorrect simply because you are giving birth to an idea, an alternate approach! Steve Jobs quipped in an interview in the mid-'90s just prior to his second coming at Apple that existing conventions and rules are made by mortals with capabilities and deficiencies like you and me. If mortals made these rules, then why cannot other mortals change them and make them better? This powerful thought alone can change your life!

Put your knowledge to work, pick an area that interests you, and create your value wherever you go. At work, in the community, among friends—I promise that there are so many opportunities that you will be spoilt for choice! If this sounds confusing, here is a mental cue that I use . . . every day, look out for something worthwhile that would not happen if you did not do anything about it, and then do it!

Third . . . Know What to Do with Time

Time is your most valuable asset; it is available to you in equal fairness, irrespective of your financial worth, unlike other assets. You have the same amount of time that a billionaire has. Henry Luce, who founded *TIME* Magazine, once said that he "owns TIME but has only twenty-four hours of it and no more . . . every day."

So does it not make sense to master how best to use it?

According to Wikipedia, Vilfredo Pareto lived in Italy from 1848 to 1923. An *engineer* by training, he was also a sociologist, economist, political scientist, and *philosopher.* In an illustrious career, his greatest gift to the generations that followed was a principle that 80% of the land in Italy was owned by 20% of the population. What made the principle referenceable even today and the reason I am mentioning it is its broad applicability.

80% of profits come from 20% of your customers. 80% of company sales come from 20% of products, and most likely 80% of the future professional results will come from 20% of the activities that you do. The discipline to seek out the 20% activities, however challenging they might be, and abandoning human nature and its tendency to try to go after the easier 80% activities that dilute our "time asset" is what knowing what to do with time is all about. Invest your time well, and sow the seeds for becoming an accomplished investor. And remember, as Woody Allen said, you have to get home by six o'clock!

I have observed many successful people, and they are laser-focused on filling up their calendars with the 20% of activities that will deliver them the 80% results. The moment we slacken, the other 80% that delivers 20% of even lesser results has a notorious habit of sneaking in and grabbing our time.

Fourth . . . Self-Branding and Communication

No man is an island—success at work and play is hard to attain all by oneself. Knowledge and value are wonderful differentiators as long as they can be communicated simply, interestingly, and confidently. Your audience today is very different from that of ten years ago. The world is overloaded with information, distractions are plenty, and attention spans are dramatically short.

Brand yourself like organizations do—your capabilities, accomplishments, and differentiation from others must shine through crisply and honestly. Practice your pitch every day and share it with anyone who cares to listen—pitch yourself like Coca Cola, Apple, Nike, and Samsung pitch their brand . . . every day! Use every vehicle that the connected world and its social networking platforms provide to say who you are and what you are good at. Nothing happens overnight, but slowly and progressively, you will see your brand build—your career will be constructed on this platform; so do not be shy in building it! This is not vanity . . . this is the reality!

In parting, let me tell you this . . . after you have finished reading this book, and you go about your life starting tomorrow, years from now, you will kick yourself for the unfulfilled desires that you did not go after when you had the time and the opportunity. What you have achieved will hardly console you when set against the things you never attempted.

So rev your engine up, know the rules, but take your chances and sail vertically away from the safe harbor like Christopher Columbus did. Set out to find success where others might not even be looking. Dream. Search. Venture. Grow.

Thank you and best of luck!

Index

A

A-team 118, 122, 248
accountability 15, 53-4, 76, 90, 124-5, 152, 183, 229, 249, 263, 300-1
Arreguín-Toft, Ivan 158, 162
Asia 13, 15, 55, 147, 150, 210, 246, 248, 260-2, 309, 313
Asia-Pacific 299, 301
assets 211-13, 277, 324-8, 333
attainment 34-9, 125, 189, 273, 301
Augusta 207, 265-6
authenticity 76-7
authority 54, 152, 183, 200, 249, 263, 266, 297, 300

B

banks 212-13, 294-5, 298, 305
Bobiles, Manuel 146, 149-50
Buffet, Warren 27, 130, 133, 152, 321
business 14, 18, 30, 34, 38, 41, 43, 46, 49-51, 80-1, 157, 198-9, 215-17, 260-3, 325-6

C

careers 48, 74, 78, 143, 147, 153, 156, 178, 256, 267, 276, 284, 287, 291, 293
cash 130, 292, 317, 319-21, 323, 325-7
cash flow 317, 319-21, 323, 325-7
CDOs (collateralized debt obligations) 28, 211
channel partners 164-7
clients 13, 49-50, 86, 267, 299
collaboration 29, 56, 98, 100-1, 122, 124-5, 132, 155, 169, 205, 284
communication 57, 93, 115, 127, 132, 147, 151, 157, 161-2, 171-2, 237, 242, 261, 334
compensation 54, 71, 92, 119, 141-3, 215, 318
competence 106-7, 188-9, 207
competency 60, 89-91, 107, 153, 183, 186-8, 295, 302
competition 199, 202, 218, 263, 289-90
competitors 118, 127, 131, 143, 159, 171, 241, 258, 276, 283, 289-90
conglomerate 146, 257, 294

Costa Rica 67-9, 71-2
Coughlin, Tom 198-9
customers 48, 50-1, 55, 67, 71, 76-7, 86-7, 108, 131-2, 163-7, 169-70, 239, 241, 261-2, 281

D

David (biblical character) 158-62
Dean, James 286-7
Dell (company) 215, 241-2, 310
Dell, Michael 241-2
differentiation 41, 118-19, 133, 160, 178, 291, 334
diversity 247-8, 261, 301

E

education, financial 321, 323, 325, 327-8
effort 12, 19, 23-5, 33-9, 41, 44, 49, 51, 57, 156-7, 182, 202, 298, 318-20, 322-3
EMC (company) 310
employees, 21, 37, 54, 57-8, 70-1, 74, 119-21, 124, 127-8, 140-4, 146-52, 203, 238-40, 250-1, 255
employer 141, 217, 311
employment 140-1, 145, 214, 321
expenses 28-9, 38, 47, 250, 306, 319, 322, 327, 330
experimentation 38, 108, 195, 274, 301

F

failures 50, 101, 118, 123, 176, 195, 202, 206-8, 220, 226, 229, 240, 243, 256, 323
feedback 56, 62-3, 82, 88, 92-3, 97, 148, 203, 228, 239, 243, 273-4
financial SWAT team 326-7
Four Seasons 69-70, 72

G

Giants 197-200, 287
goal setting 94, 148, 272-3
goals 17, 22, 24, 59-60, 81-2, 91, 95-7, 106, 117-19, 124-5, 202-3, 234, 237-8, 272-4, 300-1
Goliath (biblical character) 158-61
Google 73, 119, 133, 206, 243, 310, 315
government 27, 29, 172, 248, 302, 313
Gulf of Papagayo 69, 72

H

hiring manager 121-2, 141, 143, 151, 215, 275, 277
honesty 52, 67, 75, 77, 171
humility 76-7, 170

I

IBM (company) 310
implementation 83, 90, 92-3, 148, 186, 203, 219, 226-8
improvements 24, 139, 193, 236, 238
innovation 13, 23, 26, 28-9, 133, 163-4, 170, 191-6, 245, 247, 274, 301, 303-7, 312
interest rates 211-12
Internet 40, 241-3, 250-1, 306
internships 199, 214-18, 312

interviewer 276-9
investment 33, 134, 196, 293, 307, 321-4, 331

K

Krannert School of Business 215-16

L

leaders 14, 52-5, 57-60, 90, 92-3, 118, 123-7, 157, 181-3, 226-8, 237-8, 240-1, 248-9, 260-3, 271-2
leadership 51-2, 54-7, 60, 92, 100, 123-5, 127-8, 131-3, 151, 165-6, 180-1, 200, 226-7, 229, 237
liabilities 324-7
loyalty 73, 124, 150-3

M

manager 52-5, 80, 95, 111, 117, 272, 292
Mandela, Nelson 175, 179-81, 183
Manila 145-6, 148
MBA Challenge 55-7, 61
mediocrity 20-1, 107, 121, 192, 329
Mexico 112, 115
Microsoft 100, 102, 242-3, 310
money 26, 48-50, 84-5, 120, 130, 137, 140, 183, 232, 302, 317-18, 320-2, 324, 327-8, 332

N

networking 40-1, 43, 45

O

Oakland A's 90-1
outcomes 17, 23-4, 52, 60, 65, 82, 114, 132, 157, 182, 188, 194-6, 224, 248, 255

P

partners 55, 73, 117, 165-6, 261
Patriots 197-9
paycheck 140, 142, 231, 235, 295
personal branding 73, 75, 77, 79, 177, 179, 250
Pienaar, Francois (film character) 180-1, 183
POR (Plan of Record) 284
power, positional 53, 121, 297
preparedness 24, 106, 157, 274, 277
profession 49, 142, 148, 190, 198, 214, 218, 235, 269, 277, 282, 296, 311-12
profits 41, 164-5, 242, 326, 333

Q

quality 20, 43, 52, 69, 71, 104, 106-7, 118, 147, 151-2, 160, 163, 175, 177, 262

R

rejection 50, 83, 86, 88
revenue 55, 81, 96, 102, 133, 149, 164-5, 169, 195, 208, 262, 281, 299, 302, 306-7
rivals 160, 162, 200

S

salary 292, 320, 324, 328
sales 50, 141, 164-7, 242, 272, 276, 281, 284, 303, 305
security 123, 135, 211, 322
servant leader 57-8
shareholders 97, 130-1, 241, 257, 307
SIM University 330
Singapore 56, 61, 68, 98-103, 135-6, 145, 150, 172, 230, 245-6, 248, 331
skills 11, 31, 47-8, 54, 57, 59, 88-90, 107-8, 118, 141-3, 187-8, 199, 227, 311, 315-16
social networks 40, 56, 73, 76, 250-1, 330
status quo 193, 245
strategy 80-3, 97, 115, 125, 131, 158-9, 162, 204, 206, 219, 224, 227, 238, 272, 281-4
success 12-15, 18-22, 47-52, 54, 122-4, 126-8, 150-4, 204-8, 222-5, 246-8, 254-6, 261-4, 296-300, 316-18, 326-30
Sweden 231, 246-7

T

tactics 80-3
team 24, 53-5, 58-9, 89-93, 96, 118-19, 125-7, 180-3, 197-200, 203, 226-9, 237-8, 262-4, 271-2, 274
team members 33, 53, 60, 157, 183, 203
technology 17, 27, 46, 104, 161, 164-6, 192, 216, 218, 222, 237, 241, 291, 306, 309-10

U

United States 24, 116, 182, 197, 211, 215, 245, 251, 302, 309, 313, 320-1

V

value, shareholder 38, 119, 195
vision 51, 53, 88-94, 105, 181-4, 226-9, 234, 242, 254, 258, 261-2, 300
visualization 26, 105, 185-7, 189-90

W

Wikipedia 104, 204-5, 333
Woo, Terence 257-9
workforce 124, 147, 312, 314
workplace 21, 37-8, 73-4, 77, 106, 110, 118, 147-8, 176-7, 200, 208, 215, 217, 250-1, 314-16
World Cup 251, 256
WYSIWYG 104-5, 107, 109

Y

Yahoo! 119, 133, 243, 310

About the Author

Deb Dutta is a technology business builder, investor, educator, and a keen student of human nature. A business executive with strategic vision and laser-focused execution, Deb has led the evolution of three major technology waves—data and network security, data center networking, and software-defined networking. In doing so, he has built successful businesses with sequential revenue growth, infrastructure, and high-performance multinational teams. His contributions in organization transformation, M&A, and disruptive go-to-market partnerships have generated impressive revenue streams from nineteen countries.

Deb is an executive at Juniper Networks, a leading global networking company. He serves in the board of D&M Corporation, an education, investment, and advisory company. He is a columnist for several prominent publications and an advisor to SIM University in Singapore. He is also a member of the Singapore Institute of Directors.

Besides being an avid sportsperson and a natural competitor, Deb holds an MBA in International Business (University of South Australia), a Master's degree in Economics (University of Calcutta) and a General Management Certificate (Indian Institute of Management, Calcutta).

He lives in Singapore with his wife Mousumi and daughters Airashi and Aria.

Lightning Source UK Ltd.
Milton Keynes UK
UKOW03f0100250414

230574UK00003B/69/P